P9-EED-935

European History in Perspective
General Editor: Jeremy Black

Benjamin Arnold *Medieval Germany*
Ronald Asch The *Thirty Years' War*
Nigel Aston *The French Revolution, 1789–1804*
Nicholas Atkin *The Fifth French Republic*
Christopher Bartlett *Peace, War and the European Powers, 1814–1914*
Robert Bireley *The Refashioning of Catholicism, 1450–1700*
Donna Bohanan *Crown and Nobility in Early Modern France*
Arden Bucholz *Moltke and the German Wars, 1864–1871*
Patricia Clavin *The Great Depression, 1929–1939*
Paula Sutter Fichtner *The Habsburg Monarchy, 1490–1848*
Mark R. Forster *Catholic Germany from the Reformation to the Enlightenment*
Mark Galeotti *Gorbachev and his Revolution*
David Gates *Warfare in the Nineteenth Century*
Alexander Grab *Napoleon and the Transformation of Europe*
Nicholas Henshall *The Zenith of European Monarchy and its Elites*
Martin P. Johnson *The Dreyfus Affair*
Tim Kirk *Nazi Germany*
Ronald Kowalski *European Communism*
Paul Douglas Lockhart *Sweden in the Seventeenth Century*
Kevin McDermott *Stalin*
Graeme Murdock *Beyond Calvin*
Peter Musgrave *The Early Modern European Economy*
J. L. Price *The Dutch Republic in the Seventeenth Century*
A. W. Purdue *The Second World War (2nd edn)*
Christopher Read *The Making and Breaking of the Soviet System*
Francisco J. Romero-Salvado *Twentieth-Century Spain*
Matthew S. Seligmann and Roderick R. McLean
Germany from Reich to Republic, 1871–1918
David A. Shafer *The Paris Commune*
Graeme Small *Late Medieval France*
David Sturdy *Louis XIV*
David J. Sturdy *Richelieu and Mazarin*
Hunt Tooley *The Western Front*
Peter Waldron *The End of Imperial Russia, 1855–1917*
Peter Waldron *Governing Tsarist Russia*
Peter G. Wallace *The Long European Reformation*
James D. White *Lenin*
Patrick Williams *Philip II*
Peter H. Wilson *From Reich to Revolution*

European History in Perspective
Series Standing Order
ISBN 0–333–71694–9 hardcover
ISBN 0–333–69336–1 paperback
(outside North America only)

You can receive future titles in this series as they are published by placing a
standing order. Please contact your bookseller or, in the case of difficulty, write to
us at the address below with your name and address, the title of the series and the
ISBN quoted above.

Customer Services Department, Palgrave Ltd
Houndmills, Basingstoke, Hampshire RG21 6XS, England

THE REFASHIONING OF CATHOLICISM, 1450–1700

A REASSESSMENT OF THE COUNTER REFORMATION

Robert Bireley

The Catholic University of America Press
Washington, D.C.

MACMILLAN PRESS LTD
Houndmills, Basingstoke, Hampshire RG21 6XS
and London
Companies and representatives throughout the world

Published in North America 1999 by
THE CATHOLIC UNIVERSITY OF AMERICA PRESS
620 Michigan Ave., N.E.
Washington, D.C. 20064

Library of Congress Cataloging-in-Publication Data
Bireley, Robert.
The refashioning of Catholicism, 1450–1700 : a reassessment of the
counter Reformation / Robert Bireley.
p.   cm.
Includes bibliographical references and index.
ISBN–13: 978–0–8132–0950–0 (alk. paper)
ISBN–10: 0–8132–0950–1 (alk. paper)
ISBN–13: 978–0–8132–0951–7 (pbk. : alk.paper)
ISBN–10: 0–8132–0951–X (pbk. : alk. paper)
1. Catholic Church—History—Modern period, 1500–   2. Catholic
Church—History.   3. Counter-Reformation.   I. Title.
BX1304.B57   1999
282'.09'03—dc21   99–19230
                                                              CIP

Logging, pulping and manufacturing processes are expected to
conform to the environmental regulations of the country of origin.
This book is printed on paper suitable for recycling and made from
fully managed and sustained forest sources.

13 12 11 10 9 8 7 6 5
16 15 14 13 12 11

Printed in China

CONTENTS

PREFACE

In this book I have attempted a synthetic treatment of early modern Catholicism, that is, Catholicism from roughly 1450 to 1700. My reassessment aims to show how over this period Catholicism actively refashioned itself in response to the profound changes of the long sixteenth century and how it was in turn reshaped by these changes. So I find in the Catholicism of the period another instance of Christianity's continual and necessary accommodation to contemporary society and culture. My book proposes that the best way for us to understand early modern Catholicism is precisely in terms of this response to the changing world of which it was part. In our own day Christianity is undergoing a more profound reshaping.

I have written this book as an introduction to early modern Catholicism for advanced undergraduates and the general public, and as an attempt at a new interpretation for colleagues and scholars that takes into account recent scholarship and that goes beyond the usual terms 'Catholic Reform' and 'Counter Reformation'. Brevity has been in order, and I have necessarily been selective in the material that I have treated. Lack of space, and competence, has compelled me to pass over in large measure some areas of which the reader might legitimately have expected a more complete discussion, for example, English Catholicism, the French Religious Wars, and the arts. Yet I trust to have achieved a scope broad enough for a genuine synthesis. Because of their interest as well as their importance, personalities play a major part in the narrative. Given the choice of annotating extensively or expanding the text, I have opted for the latter. A Select Bibliography at the end will, I hope, at least partially compensate for the lack of notes.

I owe a debt of gratitude to many folks who have assisted me in the preparation of this book, but to three in particular. John W. O'Malley, SJ, of the Weston School of Theology in Cambridge, Massachusetts, carefully read the whole manuscript and furnished me with invaluable assistance.

My graduate research assistant in the spring of 1998, Elisabeth Fraterrigo, also read the complete manuscript and with her keen journalistic eye much improved the writing. Susan Schroeder, Professor of Latin American History at Loyola University, who carefully read Chapter 7, saved me from many errors and helped with the style. I am also grateful to the anonymous reader for Macmillan for his helpful suggestions. Many years ago I learned from two of my mentors, Professor Francis Paul Prucha, SJ, of Marquette University, and Professor Dieter Albrecht of the University of Regensburg, that there is no such thing as a perfect book. The shortcomings of this one are my responsibility.

The Jesuit Community at Loyola University has provided me with moral and financial support, and for this I am grateful, especially to the then Rector, Father Lawrence Reuter, SJ. The director of the Interlibrary Loan at Loyola's Cudahy Library, Lorna Newman, and her staff have with their usual remarkable efficiency obtained many books for my use. Jeremy Black, editor of the series 'European History in Perspective', invited me to undertake this book. Jonathan Reeve, the History Commissioning Editor at Macmillan, has been most helpful. They both merit my gratitude.

ROBERT BIRELEY, SJ

Loyola University Chicago

1
INTRODUCTION

[handwritten margin notes: undergone, outstrips., aggiornamento = updating.]

Throughout its history Christianity has accommodated and adapted to contemporary culture and society in order to reach people effectively and to have an impact on its world. In this sense it has undergone periodic refashioning. Surely, this is the case in the twentieth century which outstrips previous eras in the pace and depth of cultural and social change and in the degree of challenge to the church. It was precisely this refashioning to which the charismatic Pope John XXIII summoned Catholics when he convoked the Second Vatican Council in 1962. For this process he employed the term *'aggiornamento'* or updating. But over the centuries the nature and degree of accommodation has frequently generated dispute and division within the church. One present-day example is the reaction of Catholics to the changing role of women, arguably the most profound social change of the twentieth century. *[handwritten: 20th.]*

Yet the call to change, and conflict over its nature, has characterized the church from early New Testament times when what was initially a Jewish sect began to welcome Gentiles into its community, without requiring them to submit to the Jewish Law. Indeed the Acts of the Apostles and several letters of Paul deal at length with the struggle over this movement towards a universal church. Subsequently, and in particular after the Edict of Milan in 313, Christianity faced the issue of its relationship to the surrounding pagan Graeco-Roman culture. How was Jerusalem to relate to Athens? During the early Middle Ages the church confronted the barbarian invaders from the north. Much of early medieval history is the story of assimilation by the church and the Christian transformation of features of barbarian society, for example, of the mounted warrior into the 'Christian knight'. The expansion of

1

[handwritten: Edict of Milan in 313]

Europe into Asia and America in the sixteenth century required that the church adapt to both advanced and primitive societies as it sought to make known the message of the Gospel in the lands across the seas; indeed, this is part of the story of this book.

Early modern Catholicism, this book argues, was essentially the response of the Catholic Church to the changing world of the long sixteenth century, that is, from 1450 to 1650. Precisely this is what a new look at the church of the traditional Counter Reformation period reveals. The church's response or its refashioning was both active and passive in character. Just as the church reshaped itself in light of the evolving culture and society, so did this changing culture and society help refashion the church. Catholics were both agents and subjects of change. To use the terms '*aggiornamento*' or 'updating', or even the concept, for the active part of this process is anachronistic. Both Catholics and Protestants normally thought of reform and renewal rather as a return to the spirit of the Gospel and the primitive church as they understood them. Yet, in fact, they both were interpreting Christianity for the changing times. In this sense we can speak of competing attempts to renew Christianity in the sixteenth century. Hence we should expect to find reflected in early modern Catholicism, and Protestantism, sixteenth-century attitudes and values. Prominent among these were two which we will encounter recurringly throughout this book: the desire especially of lay people for a spirituality that made more Christian sense of life lived amidst worldly or secular pursuits, and increasingly in light of the upheavals of the century, the pursuit of order, religious, political, social, and intellectual.

But who made up the Catholic Church that undertook this implicit accommodation? It extended well beyond popes and bishops, to include clergy and members of religious orders, lay people, women as well as men. Charismatic figures rose up from the ranks to assume leadership, personalities such as Ignatius Loyola, Angela Merici, Francis de Sales, and Jane Frances de Chantal. Kings and princes such as Philip II of Spain and Elector Maximilian of Bavaria took active parts, often considering religion too important to be left to the clergy, to modify a statement attributed to Philip II. Lay confraternities participated actively, and as recent local studies have shown, the ordinary Catholic faithful often had a say in decision-making at the parish level. So the concept of church here is diffuse. With so many people involved, there were many views, and conflicts, over directions to be taken, and that too is a part of our story. Catholicism was hardly monolithic.

The term 'Counter Reformation' was long used to characterize Catholicism during the balance of the early modern period. But recent scholarship has tended to see 'Counter Reformation' as well as its often suggested alternatives 'Catholic Reformation' or 'Catholic Reform' as inadequate, and to search for a proper substitute which would do justice to all features of the Catholicism of the period. A recently suggested alternative is simply 'Early Modern Catholicism' because it suggests developments within the Catholic Church not only in relationship to the Protestant Reformation; as an umbrella term it places these developments more clearly in the context of the other wide-reaching changes of the sixteenth century.

The phrase 'Counter Reformation' came into general use in the nineteenth century with the assistance of the great German Protestant historian Leopold von Ranke whose *History of the Popes* began to appear in 1834. The term interpreted the movements within the Catholic Church as essentially a reaction to Protestantism, and it connoted repressive measures such as the Inquisition and the Index and suggested the political action and military force which helped instigate the religious wars. Frequently associated with this position was the judgement that the Catholic Church was progressively deteriorating throughout the Middle Ages, becoming increasingly decadent until eventually something had to happen to save Christianity. Hence the Protestant Reformation. This was a one-sided interpretation.

First effectively to employ the term 'Catholic Reformation' was another German historian, also a Protestant, Wilhelm Maurenbecher. Having travelled to Spain to undertake research into the origins of the Counter Reformation, he discovered significant reform efforts there antedating 1517 and so realized that one could not speak merely of a Counter Reformation. He entitled his volume, which appeared in 1880, *A History of the Catholic Reformation*. Important for propagating the term then was the Catholic Ludwig von Pastor, who employed it in the title of several volumes of his monumental *History of the Popes from the Close of the Middle Ages*, which was published between 1886 and 1933. Pastor had in mind Catholic initiatives before 1517 in Italy rather than in Spain, and he also stood under the influence of his mentor, Johannes Janssen, who had painted a rosy picture of German religious and cultural life on the eve of the Reformation in his multi-volume *History of the German People since the Close of the Middle Ages*, which appeared between 1876 and 1894. Implied was that these Catholic efforts at reform would eventually have remedied the undoubted abuses within the church without provoking the division of Western Christendom, for which the Protestants consequently stood responsible. This too was a one-sided version of events.

Certainly, there were those who took a middle position in the intervening years, but it fell to another German historian, Hubert Jedin, in an essay *Catholic Reform or Counter Reformation*, published in 1946 immediately following the Second World War, to work out a compromise that has gradually been accepted by the majority of scholars Catholic and Protestant. According to Jedin, there were indeed reform movements within the Catholic Church antedating the outbreak of the Lutheran Reformation in 1517. These he likened to streams or rivulets, which only the shock of the Protestant Reformation sufficed to merge into a river encompassing the whole Catholic Church. This happened once they were taken up by the papacy and then led to the Council of Trent, which opened at the end of 1545 and concluded only in 1563. So for Jedin the council and the renewed papacy that stood behind it were the driving forces behind both the Catholic Reform – Jedin preferred this term to 'Catholic Reformation' because of the special Protestant connotation 'Reformation' had in German, and one might add in English too – and the Counter Reformation. Neither term could be set aside. Both Catholic Reform and Counter Reformation characterized Catholicism until the end of the seventeenth century, with the Reform serving as it were as the soul of the combined movement, the Counter Reformation as the body.

Apart from its intrinsic merit, there were reasons for the widespread acceptance of Jedin's compromise. Certainly one was the Ecumenical Movement, a movement among the Christian churches which aimed at the return to unity of all those who believed in Christ. The Reformation period had bequeathed a legacy of suspicion and hostility to Protestants and Catholics which, despite occasional ecumenical spirits, persisted well into the twentieth century. Increasing contact with non-Christian cultures, growing secularism, and outright hostility to Christianity gradually persuaded Christians of differing coloration that they needed to stand together if they were to make the Christian message heard and to have an impact on the world. Two experiences in particular stood out. One was the increasing awareness of Protestant missionaries in Asia and in Africa that divisions among Christians not only alienated the folks they were attempting to evangelize but were often unintelligible to them. So from the Edinburgh Conference of 1910 there emerged the Protestant World Council of Churches.

The Nazi experience then convinced many German Christians of their need to come together in the face of hostile and hateful forces. So a new spirit of reconciliation among Christians came to life in postwar Germany, at the time along with France the leading country for theological and historical scholarship. Historians as well as theologians participated in a new readiness to admit responsibility for shortcomings and to set aside prejudices and long-held myths. The Catholic Church formally joined the Ecumenical Movement at the Second Vatican Council.

Secondly, there was the general acceptance of the position coming out of the nineteenth century that historical scholarship ought to pursue historical truth objectively, to the extent this was possible. History ought not be partisan, sectarian, or apologetic. Many scholars have entered the field of Reformation studies, especially since the 1960s, imbued with this ideal and with no confessional axe to grind.

Yet, as John W. O'Malley has pointed out, broad acceptance of Jedin's position has not generated agreement on a single term to denote the Catholicism of the period. Such a term is important because terms imply interpretation. 'Catholic Reform' and 'Counter Reformation' remain most popular, each with its own connotation, but 'Catholic Restoration' has also been proposed. O'Malley, while recognizing the validity of both 'Catholic Reform' and 'Counter Reformation' to designate many developments within Catholicism, objects to the use of either or both to characterize the whole period, for three reasons. First, they underline the relationship to the Protestant Reformation. Yet there were many aspects of sixteenth-century Catholicism that had little if anything to do with the Reformation, such as missionary endeavours across the seas, new religious orders devoted to the service of the poor or sick or to education, and the revival of the thought of Thomas Aquinas. Secondly, 'Reform' implies that the church in the early sixteenth century was more in need of reform than at other times, a fact that has been increasingly called into question if not refuted by recent research especially regarding areas other than Germany. There certainly was no progressive decline across the church. Thirdly, in the sixteenth century the term 'reform', according to O'Malley, had a technical, canonical meaning dating from the High Middle Ages and designating the enforcement of church law in areas such as the residence, preaching, and celibacy of pastors and bishops, and other issues addressed by the Council of Trent. O'Malley contends that the early Jesuits, clearly a force within the sixteenth-century church, were not out to reform the church in any traditional sense of the term, unless by reform one means either personal religious conversion or, more broadly, any significant change. Their goal was to christianize the faithful or to 'help souls', in the words of Ignatius Loyola. For this reason O'Malley argues for 'Early Modern Catholicism' as a comprehensive term to help capture the realities not contained in the others, essential as they are. In so doing he follows the French historian Jean Delumeau, who entitled his 1971 volume *Catholicism between Luther and Voltaire*, which had as its companion a volume on the Protestant Reformation that has remained untranslated.

Both Delumeau and the English historian John Bossy, profiting from our increasing historical distance from the religious changes of the sixteenth century, represent a new comparative approach to the study of the Reformation period. They focus on the similarities between Protestant and Catholic movements and point up rather the differences between medieval and early modern forms of Christianity, whether Catholic or Protestant. Delumeau argues that rural areas in Europe – where his focus is France – remained virtually pagan until the early modern period when they were first systematically evangelized by Catholic and Protestant preachers. This evangelization, however, often effectively supported by governmental authority, comprised a large dosage of fear that has left its mark on Christianity until the present day. In addition, for Delumeau, the period of religious reform dates from the fourteenth century. Increasingly, other scholars have followed him inasmuch as they have seen both Protestant and Catholic reform movements deriving from the culture and religious yearnings of the late Middle Ages. Bossy, for his part, inclines to romanticize the Middle Ages and to see early modern Christianity's individualism and loss of a sense for symbolic expression in both Protestant and Catholic forms as a definite decline.

More important for this comparative approach is the theory of confessionalization first proposed by the German historian Ernst Walter Zeeden in 1958 and subsequently elaborated by Wolfgang Reinhard and Heinz Schilling. Whereas Delumeau and Bossy concentrate more on the practice of religion, Zeeden and his followers look principally to the organization and formation of the churches or, to use the German expression, the different 'confessions'.[1] The theory of confessionalization, then, exhibits the parallels between the evolution of the confessions, and, furthermore, locates in their development a decisive step in Western modernization. Reinhard in a famous 1983 article designated seven such parallel features in the formation of confessional identity: the elaboration of clear theological positions, such as the Lutheran *Confession of Augsburg* (1530); their promulgation and implementation through institutional forms such as synods, visitations, and nunciatures; their internalization, especially through schools and seminaries; the use of the means of communication, especially the printing press, to propagandize, and of censorship to hinder the propaganda of others; disciplinary measures, such as the visitation of parishes and excommunication; control of the nature of and access to rites; and the development of a peculiar confessional language.

Advocates of this theory also consider the establishment of the confessions to be a major factor in the growth of the modern state in that the confessions fostered unity of subjects or citizens, instilled in them a sense of discipline and of loyalty to authority, and often made it possible for the ruler to make use of church resources for his purposes. More recently, Heinz Schilling and R. Po-Chia Hsia, the foremost interpreter of this theory in the English-speaking world, have distinguished between confessionalism, that is, the formation of the confessions themselves, and confessionalization, that is, the role played by the confessions in society, and especially their part in the emergence of the state. So one can speak of the confessionalization of society or of the state. Reinhard has underlined the contribution of the confessions to the coming of the modern world through their advancement of individualism, rationalization, social discipline, bureaucracy, and, especially in the case of Catholicism, a move beyond European ethnocentrism.

Finally, the approach taken by those employing the terms confessionalism or confessionalization is to look at the development of the churches over the long haul, that is, from the late 1520s, when the first steps were taken in the formation of Protestant confessions, until the late seventeenth or early eighteenth centuries when the new confessions had solidified their structures and achieved a decisive impact on society and culture. Thus, from this perspective, the Reformation period in Germany does not end with the Peace of Augsburg and the legalization of Lutheranism in 1555, or even with the Peace of Westphalia in 1648 with the further legalization of Calvinism and the fixing of confessional boundaries after the Thirty Years War. Rather it endures until the early eighteenth century, where there is no clear political or religious marker.

One flaw in the argument recently proposed by some historians that the Reformation failed is that they do not take the story far enough. The longer extension of the period corresponds to Delumeau's chronology and breaks with the traditional German position, which ended the Counter Reformation or Catholic Reform with the Peace of Westphalia. Indeed, confessionalization theory works especially well in conceptualizing the complicated and multifarious developments in early modern Germany, divided as it was into a multiplicity of virtually independent territories. But it places a disproportionate emphasis on organization and on the social discipline of the population and fails to appreciate adequately the properly religious elements of the period.

My own approach, or reassessment, attempts to incorporate many of the above considerations as well as elements of recent social history, and it draws clearly on the insights of H. Outram Evennett in his *The Spirit of the Counter-Reformation* of 1968. It considers the emerging confessions or churches of the sixteenth century – the Lutheran, the Anglican, the Reformed or Calvinist, the Anabaptist, and the Catholic – to be competing Christian responses to the challenges posed by the changing society and culture of early modern Europe. This book is about Catholicism's refashioning as it moved into the modern era. But there will be opportunity to draw attention to comparable developments within Protestant churches as we go along. From another perspective, it asks how the Catholicism of 1700 was different from its medieval antecedent.

As to the terminological issue, my preference is for 'Early Modern Catholicism' to designate this period in Catholicism's history because as an overarching term it comprehends the fullness of Catholicism's response to the changes of the long sixteenth century. 'Catholic Reform' and 'Counter Reformation' indicate significant parts of this response but not the whole, and they associate early modern Catholicism too closely with the Protestant Reformation. In this book, however, I will make use of all three terms depending upon the context. Here early modern Catholicism spans the years from roughly 1450 to shortly past 1700 when the changes of the long sixteenth century have been assimilated. Occasionally, however, following recent scholarship, in order to pick up long-term developments, I will have to make forays further back into the Middle Ages and forward into the eighteenth century.

Altogether there were five principal changes which marked the transition from medieval to early modern times. Some were more sudden than others, some had roots deep in the Middle Ages but reached a significant stage in the first three decades of the sixteenth century. The first was the growth of the state; that is, the consolidation and centralization of political authority over a particular geographical area, or the establishment of sovereignty, a term coined appropriately by Jean Bodin in 1576 to designate this emerging reality. To be sure, the modern state's origins reached back into the High Middle Ages and the state would continue to evolve into the nineteenth century. But the first half of the sixteenth century constituted a major phase in its growth with the three long-reigning monarchs: Francis I of France (1515–47), Henry VIII of England (1509–47), and Charles V of Spain (1516–56), who built on his inheritance from his maternal grandparents, Ferdinand of Aragon and Isabella of Castile, whose marriage in 1469 brought all of the Iberian Peninsula except Portugal eventually under their rule. In Italy and in Germany this consolidation led into smaller, territorial states rather than national monarchies and in Germany under the umbrella of the Holy Roman Empire. Indeed, as the century began it was not clear which would obtain the predominance of power, the territorial states or the Empire, and the Reformation itself significantly contributed to the victory of the territorial states. Characteristic of this consolidation was the gradual assumption of the principal functions of government by king, prince, or other central authority: the preservation of order and defence, the administration of justice, and the collection of taxes. This process frequently brought prince or king into conflict, first with representative institutions, which were his rivals for the control of government and were usually dominated by the nobility, and, secondly with the church, which was the only Western institution to have survived the barbarian invasions and had been the focal point of European unity during the High Middle Ages.

Conflict between church and government long antedated the Reformation, and secular authority was increasingly obtaining the upper hand. There were three principal areas of conflict. First there was the question of ecclesiastical appointments. Inasmuch as rulers increasingly considered themselves responsible for religion in their realms and inasmuch as major ecclesiastics often played important political roles, should not the government also have a hand in their appointment? By 1500 many governments in town as well as state had acquired the right to name pastors and preachers as well as bishops and abbots. The second area of conflict was legal jurisdiction. In case of conflict, which law was to prevail: the older, universal canon law of the church or the law of the new state? Were clerics to remain to a large degree exempt or outside the reach of the law of the state? Closely attached to this issue, then, was the third area of conflict, taxation. On the one hand, could the papacy continue to draw money to Rome – this capacity had been greatly reduced by the fifteenth century – and could governments tax church property or the clergy, which had largely been exempt from such taxation because of its contribution to the common good? If so, under what circumstances and with whose permission?

Associated with the rise of the state was a decline among the European elite of a consciousness of a united Christendom, which had peaked in the twelfth or thirteenth century at the time of the Crusades. Since then both pope and Holy Roman Emperor had suffered in their power and in their moral authority, to a good degree because of the destructive rivalry between the two of them. Contributing to this loss as well was the long residence of the popes in Avignon (1309–77), when they were thought to be under excessive French influence, and then the Great Western Schism (1378–1417) when two and then three popes claimed the papal office. By the mid-fifteenth century popes were coming to see themselves more as rulers of an Italian state. Yet consciousness of European solidarity persisted in men such as Erasmus and Thomas More, and in Charles V, Holy Roman Emperor as well as King of Spain, who considered the defence of Europe from Moslem encroachments in Central Europe, and especially in the Mediterranean, to be one of his main responsibilities.

A second change, or perhaps congeries of changes, was social and economic. By 1490 a demographic resurgence had set in after the disaster of the Black Death (1347–50), and the sixteenth century was a period of population growth, tailing off towards the end of the century particularly in southern Europe. Rough estimates indicate that the European population swelled from 55 million in 1450 to 100 million in 1650, with, of course, vast regional variations. Growth was prominent in the cities, though the great majority of folks continued to live in rural villages. The population of Antwerp, then the commercial and financial centre of Europe, jumped from 37,000 in 1500 to 100,000 in 1560, and that of Rome grew from 55,000 in 1550 to over 100,000 by 1600. Accompanying the demographic increase was economic expansion – more goods were needed to satisfy a rising population – in agriculture, commerce, and industry, a development that was fostered by the new contacts with the lands across the sea but was due more to the growth of internal European trade. Indeed, in the sixteenth century Europe moved rapidly in the direction of a capitalist economy. One feature of the period was the movement by 1700 of economic leadership from Italy to the northern states, the Dutch Republic, England, and France.

Economic expansion did not benefit everyone. Certainly it contributed to the relative social mobility of the sixteenth century and to the expanding urban middle class that was the principal lay carrier of both Catholic Reform and Protestant Reformation. But it was accompanied by an increasing discrepancy between rich and poor, especially in the cities. In 1526 the Spanish humanist Luis Vives, residing in Antwerp, published the first systematic treatise on poor relief, *On the Subvention of the Poor*, and throughout the century vagrancy and poverty, particularly in urban areas, attracted the concern of governments and churches. Throughout Western Europe peasants were relatively well off at the start of the sixteenth century, despite the great Peasants Revolt in Germany in 1524–5, but their lot generally declined between 1500 and 1700, and France in particular suffered a wave of peasant rebellions in the seventeenth century.

The expansion of Europe into Asia, America, and to a much lesser extent Africa, and the gradual formation of the European colonial empires, first the Portuguese and Spanish, and only after the turn of the century the nascent Dutch, English, and French, was the third major change that characterized the sixteenth century. From the fifteenth to the seventeenth centuries the foundations were laid for the European domination of the world that would endure into the twentieth. The motives for this expansion can still be summarized, it seems, in the old slogan 'God, Gold, and Glory', though not necessarily in that order; that is, the renewed missionary impulse of Christianity; the capitalist urge for new sources of profit and wealth, which often corresponded with the mercantilist thinking of the growing states; and the desire for adventure, glory, and achievement which is associated with the Renaissance. So Europeans came into their first extensive contact with the advanced cultures of India, China, and Japan in the East and of the Aztecs and Incas in America, as well as with many primitive cultures on both sides of the world. The Portuguese rapidly established their network of fortified trading posts first along the west coast of Africa, then along the coasts of the Indian Ocean and in the East Indies; they reached China by 1512 and Japan by 1542, where they were kept at arm's length by both, so that missionaries were compelled to enter without the benefit, or perhaps curse, of Portuguese protection. To the west the Spanish government gradually wrested control over its American territories from the conquistadores and set up its colonial governmental structure by mid-century, with headquarters in Mexico City and Lima. These territories across the sea posed an enormous new challenge to Catholic efforts at evangelization.

The series of intellectual and cultural currents which we have come to call the Renaissance marked the fourth change from the Middle Ages to early modern times. These first took root in Italy in the fourteenth century, where Petrarch (1304–74) stands out as the first major Renaissance figure, but they did not extend beyond the Alps in a meaningful fashion until the late fifteenth and early sixteenth centuries. Over a century ago Jacob Burckhardt encapsulated the spirit of the Renaissance in the words 'the discovery of the world and of man', a phrase which is still valid today if properly understood, and not taken as it was by Burckhardt as a return to paganism nor as a completely new development. 'Discovery of man' points not to a new sense of the value of human beings, which had always characterized Christian thought at least at its best, but to a new individualism, that is, to a new self-consciousness and recognition of the unique character of the individual human personality and to its potential for achievement often in the pursuit of glory. This implied optimism about man's possibilities for development, an attitude which was encouraged by the Florentine intellectual virtuoso Giovanni Pico della Mirandola in his *Oration on the Dignity of Man* in 1496. The artist was no longer the anonymous craftsman and guild member but an individual who signed his work, who imitated God the Creator in his production, and who in some cases rose to the status of celebrity, like Michelangelo, who consorted and contested with popes. Both the portrait and the self-portrait, increasingly popular in the Renaissance, sought to capture the individual and to draw attention to the individual's inner life as Petrarch had.

As for the 'discovery of the world', this indicates a new appreciation of the world about us, as seen, for example, in landscape painting or interest in human anatomy, and more generally, a vibrant interest in secular topics. During the Renaissance there was an explosion of knowledge often associated with the revival of Greece and Rome and with the new contacts overseas. Mathematics, astronomy, history, geography, law, political thought, and philosophy all greatly expanded during the Renaissance. But a word of caution is necessary here. As historian Jack Hexter pointed out many years ago, interest in secular topics did not mean a turn away from religion, as if there were only so much intellectual energy and energy which was devoted to secular matters was necessarily denied to religion. Rather the result of 'the discovery of the world and of man' was the desire and the demand for a style of religion or a spirituality that took more account of individuality and of life in the world around us.

Humanism was the main intellectual current of the Renaissance. By this was not meant an attachment to human values as it usually does today, when nearly everyone considers himself a 'humanist'. The term had a much more specific meaning. It designated first enthusiastic and scholarly study of the ancient classics, Latin first and then Greek, which presupposed knowledge of those languages. The medievals, of course, had known the ancient authors, but the Renaissance was different in a number of ways from the so-called Carolingian Renaissance or the revival of Aristotle in the twelfth century. Many more people were involved both as professionals and amateurs. So the movement had a much larger social base both in the towns among the prospering upper middle class and at the courts; it was not a matter only of clerics, though they too took part. Many more manuscripts from the ancient world were now available, recovered by diligent searches in the monasteries where they had been preserved. More significantly, from their understanding of the ancient world and its difference from their own, humanists came to a new historical consciousness, that is, the realization that there were different eras or epochs in history, such as the ancient and the modern, which was their own, and these epochs had to be understood on their own terms. There was discontinuity in history, and it had to be acknowledged. Moreover, men of the Renaissance often assumed values of the ancient world. Humanism encouraged devotion to the common good and participation or service in government in both cities and in princely states. Florentine citizens had themselves sculpted in Roman togas. Generally, humanism contributed to the optimism about human nature that characterized much Renaissance thinking.

Humanism also designated an educational and cultural programme harkening back to the ancient world and emphasizing what we call today the humanities. It looked more to the general formation of the individual than the preparation of teachers, lawyers, and theologians as had much of medieval higher education, and it was particularly attractive to the expanding urban middle class. For its principal goals it took eloquence in speech and in writing and the formation of character, two goals which had been united in ancient rhetorical education. They prepared an elite for participation in government and in the life of the community. The curriculum emphasized grammar, logic or dialectic, and rhetoric, which were all associated with the use of language, plus history, literature, and moral philosophy. Latin was the language employed, not the medieval Latin which humanists disdained as barbaric but the classical style especially of Cicero. For the humanists style equalled content in importance.

The Renaissance return to the ancients stimulated anew many areas of study, and it helps to explain the contemporary expansion of knowledge. The recovery of works of Plato invigorated philosophical thought. Galen's writings gave new stimulus to the study of medicine, and Renaissance legal scholars laboured to understand and to apply the ancient law of the Romans. Interest in the literature of Greece and Rome eventually led to renewed interest in the early Christian sources, the Scriptures and the early Fathers of the Church, and this generated the study of Hebrew as well as Latin and Greek. As humanism crossed the Alps it became increasingly identified with the cause of religious reform. Many humanists, led by the Prince of Humanists, Erasmus of Rotterdam, urged a return to a more biblical form of Christianity as the basis for its renewal.

The first author to live off his writings, Erasmus was able to disseminate his work effectively because of the 'media revolution' brought about by the invention of the printing press during the Renaissance. For a long time far-sighted entrepreneurs had been aware of the expanding market for reading material, especially in the towns. Johann Gutenberg, a goldsmith of Mainz, made the final technological breakthroughs that produced the printing press. About 1455 there came from his press at Mainz the first printed book, the Gutenberg Bible. The printing press's impact on the communication of religious knowledge and ideas was enormous and swift. By 1500 there functioned nearly 60 presses in Germany and perhaps as many as 150 in Italy. Luther proved himself to be a master of the new media, and both Protestants and Catholics were to exploit it effectively.

Another change associated with the Renaissance was the Scientific Revolution which stretched from the publication of Copernicus's *On the Revolution of the Heavenly Spheres* in 1543 to the appearance of Newton's *Mathematical Principles of Natural Philosophy* in 1687. This profound shift in the Western world view, from the *cosmos* of the Greeks embellished by Ptolemy and the medievals to a mechanistic vision of the universe, was crucial to the period, especially after the late sixteenth century when three competing paradigms fought for predominance, a struggle which provided the background for the Galileo Affair. The extent to which Copernicus and, more generally, the new science was indebted to the recovery of elements of ancient science and mathematics remains controversial.

The fifth change, of course, was the Reformation. The church was the dominant institution in European life in 1500, as it had been for centuries. Its influence penetrated virtually every aspect of life. The cycle of liturgical feasts determined life's rhythm for the town-dweller as well as the peasant. Folks moved from Advent in late autumn to Christmas and the Christmas season, from Lent to Easter and the Easter season in the late winter and spring, and then through Ordinary Time back to Advent. The year was punctuated with fasts and feasts, such as the Feast of St John the Baptist on 24 June, usually marking the onset of summer. Processions and religious dramas enlivened the feasts at the same time as they instructed the people. The church met men and women at the principal points in their lives with baptism, matrimony, extreme unction, and funeral. The social as well as the religious centre of the community was the village church, and Sunday Mass was a regular weekly event. Education had once been a near-monopoly of the church from the village school to the university, but this changed in the late Middle Ages as some cities started to assume responsibility for schooling. Most early education in Italy was in the hands of municipal government or independent masters by 1300, whereas in England a close association between church and school seems to have been the rule. By the late fifteenth century both town governments and the lay social and religious brotherhoods, known as confraternities, assumed a major role in the care of the sick and poor in many urban areas of Europe.

The state of the church on the eve of the events of 1517 belies easy generalizations. Overall, recent research has tended to evaluate it more positively and to underline its vitality. The situation in Spain was different from that in Germany, the situation in England different from that in France. The papacy reached a low point in its history under Alexander VI (1492–1503). Papal moral authority and political influence had declined since the High Middle Ages. During the Great Western Schism there revived the doctrine of conciliarism; that is, that an ecumenical council representative of the whole body of the church was superior to the pope, and it remained a threat to the papacy long after its condemnation by Pope Pius II in 1460. Rulers, especially the French kings, used the threat of a council to extract concessions from the papacy. Louis XII called a council for Pisa in 1511 in an attempt to counter Pope Julius II's policy towards France in Italy, but the pope outmanouevred him. Pope Leo X, then, in the Concordat of Bologna of 1516, yielded to Francis I the predominant voice in nearly all the major ecclesiastical appointments in the realm in exchange, in part, for the king's disavowal of conciliarism. Starting with Nicholas V (1447–55), the popes concentrated increasingly on their role as rulers of an Italian state and were themselves elected from aristocratic Italian families. Like other contemporary rulers they sought to consolidate their position against turbulent nobles, and as it became more difficult to draw funds from Europe, they worked to increase revenues from the Papal States themselves. A windfall was the discovery at Tolfa in 1460 of alum, a chemical used in the production of dyes hitherto obtainable only from the Middle East. In addition, the Renaissance popes used the patronage of artists and humanists to enhance the prestige of the papacy.

In 1494 the French invaded Italy, thus setting off the Italian Wars that continued on and off until 1559 and served as a background to the Reformation. Principal protagonists were the French under the Valois kings and the Spaniards, under Habsburg rulers after 1515, who fought for control of wealthy Italy, 'the cockpit of Europe'. The principal goal of Alexander VI in this situation was to bequeath a state out of the papal dominions to his son Cesare, the hero of Machiavelli's *Prince*. His successor, Julius II (1503–12), the 'warrior pope', took the lead in attempting to drive the foreigners out of Italy, and he drew Michelangelo and Raphael to service at the Vatican. Neither he nor his successor, the first Medici pope, Leo X (1513–21), was completely closed to reform, as we shall see. Despite the words attributed to him after his election, 'Now that God has given us the papacy, let us enjoy it', Leo was a moral man and an astute patron of the arts, but hardly the religious leader to encounter the challenge of Luther. Nor was his cousin, Clement VII (1523–34), who was pope at the time of the break with Henry VIII, an improvement. His political vacillations greatly harmed the papal position in Italy, leading to the infamous Sack of Rome in 1527. Fear of a council that would criticize him and the papacy seems to have haunted him.

Certainly there were abuses among the clergy, but these were hardly the whole story. Two prominent abuses were associated with the benefice system. A benefice was an ecclesiastical office with revenues attached; some benefices carried with them pastoral responsibilities, others did not. In the case of pastors or bishops, the revenue was meant to support the benefice-holder as well as to maintain the church and perhaps a school, and to supply assistance for the poor. One abuse was absenteeism or lack of residence on the part of pastors of parishes and bishops. Absentee pastors, perhaps bored with village life, hired a replacement and went to live in a nearby city off the revenues of the parish. Only 20 per cent of the pastors in the diocese of Geneva were resident on the eve of the Reformation when nearly half of the pastors in the French diocese of Grenoble lived in their parishes. Pluralism meant the accumulation of benefices in the hands of an individual. Obviously, a bishop could not be resident in several bishoprics at the same time. Many upper clergy held benefices by government appointment, and kings or princes often used church offices as a form of patronage. Nearly two-thirds of the French bishops on the eve of the Reformation were governmental councillors, and most English bishops were involved in the royal administration. Cardinal Thomas Wolsey, lord chancellor of England from 1515 to 1529, was a notorious pluralist and only entered his Archbishopric of York at the end of his life. Many bishops justified their absence by pointing out that they were not masters in their own houses because the papacy made it easy for members of their flock to appeal over their heads to Rome and granted excessive exemptions from their authority to members of religious orders, especially the friars.

The educational level of the clergy varied greatly, though the number who attended the university, without necessarily receiving degrees, was increasing. In some areas there existed an unbeneficed clerical 'proletariat'. A problem was the lack of a systematic programme for the education and formation of the diocesan clergy. Many village parish priests lived in concubinage. Numbers are hard to come by. Perhaps as many as 50 per cent did so in some dioceses. In many cases these were quasi-marriages, which the faithful do not seem to have strongly resented as long as the priest performed his pastoral duties conscientiously. On the eve of the Reformation some leading ecclesiastics favoured allowing marriage to parish priests.

Yet in the course of the fifteenth century there was a renewed emphasis on preaching, especially in the towns, and the friars played the leading role. Of France in this period one recent historian has written that 'there had never been so much preaching and with such success'. The Dominican Vincent Ferrer and the Franciscans Bernardine of Siena and John Capistrano enjoyed European reputations as preachers. Towns, and even villages, endowed posts for preachers. For their annual Lenten sermons Florence and other towns competed for famous preachers, who were usually expected to entertain as well as to instruct and inspire.

But the announcement of the Gospel was not limited to the spoken word. Despite some initial ambivalence, Catholics well utilized the new printing press. Religious books dominated the market. Bibles appeared in the major European vernaculars, apart from English, this because of the association of Bible-reading with the Lollard heresy by English bishops. Fourteen versions of the Old and New Testaments had been published in German previous to the appearance of Luther's masterpiece. Direct helps for prayer were a major genre, such as missals, psalters, and books of hours, and then there were devotional best sellers such as the *Golden Legend*, a book of lives of the saints and brief reflections on the Christian feasts by Jacopo da Voragine, which dated from the thirteenth century, and especially the *Imitation of Christ*, by Thomas à Kempis, which began to circulate in 1418. For the illiterate there were images and statuary in the churches and chapels, and with the coming of printing ordinary folks could afford religious pictures in their homes. Albrecht Dürer was the first artist to exploit this market systematically.

How to characterize popular piety on the eve of the Reformation? One undoubted feature was a tender devotion to the person of Jesus, especially in his passion and death, which was often represented in very realistic terms. This spirituality was newly propagated by the 'modern devotion', which took root in the Netherlands in the late fourteenth century and spread to Germany and eventually to much of Europe. It was an individual piety that emphasized the believer's relationship with Christ but said little about the church or the common liturgy. It encouraged regular meditation on Christ's life and passion, and it was practical rather than speculative in its orientation. As Thomas à Kempis wrote in his classic *Imitation of Christ*, it was better to feel compunction than to be able to define it. Source of the devotion was above all the New Testament, but it also drew upon the individual experience of its practitioners. Appealing as it did to those who desired a more personal form of religion, it was to have a widespread influence across Europe. Of the saints, the Virgin Mary was greatly venerated, under a number of titles, but especially in the late Middle Ages as Mother of Jesus in the Holy Family. New devotion to St Joseph and St Anna, the mother of Mary, may indicate a growing attention to the nuclear family.

Two other features of late medieval piety were fear and externalism, but the degree to which they were at hand is highly controversial. Some authors, and especially Jean Delumeau, have contended that fear of death, judgement, the end of the world, and Satan, permeated late medieval religion, provoking anxiety about salvation and an agitated spirit. Clearly there were strong eschatalogical strains at the time, along with a new awareness of the devil, both of which remained elements of Luther's piety. Yet a recent survey of French preaching before and after the Reformation finds little evidence of this fear and agitation, but rather a firm confidence in the mercy of God. Studies of confessional practice point in both directions.

Externalism designates the pursuit of salvation by the performance of works alone, particularly works of devotion such as pilgrimages or processions, rather than by genuine conversion of heart. Erasmus and Luther both pilloried this attitude, which often generated a certain pious materialism, so that folks piled up large numbers of Masses to be said for themselves or for their deceased dear ones. Sometimes practices appeared to be superstitious, if by superstition we mean attempting to manipulate God; that is, expecting an automatic return for the saying of a particular prayer or the performance of a particular pious act, a *quid pro quo* negotiation with the divine rather than a humble supplication along with the implicit condition that God's will be done. Relics sometimes were nearly the same as charms. But who is to determine in specific cases whether a practice was externalist or superstitious? That is often difficult. Indulgences were hawked and otherwise abused, to be sure, but they also encouraged a sense of community between the living and the dead, and enabled the former to aid those who had gone before them in the faith.

A final feature of late medieval piety seems to have been a desire for a more profound religious experience and practice on the part of a significant number of laity. The way to holiness and sanctity, or to the full Christian life, they wanted to be open to them as well as to clergy or members of religious orders. It has been argued that a major source of the Reformation was the dichotomy that had widened between theology and spirituality or the practice of religion after the rise of Scholasticism in the High Middle Ages. One reason for the popularity of a return to the Scriptures was that a more biblical theology promised to narrow this gap once again, and to provide a form of Christianity closer to the human experience of those living in the world. Evidence seems to show that the laity were increasingly participating in church activities, whether by donation and foundation or personal commitment of time and effort.

Late medieval Europe, especially the cities, was dotted with confraternities. These were social and religious brotherhoods under lay leadership that were often associated with occupational groups and that usually extended well beyond individual urban parishes. Indeed, they frequently rivalled parishes for the allegiance of the people. They practised a special form of piety, Marian, for example, or flagellant, that is, highlighting the use of penitential flagellation, and they otherwise served the social and religious needs of their members by providing, for example, care in illness and hard times, processions and banquets on feast days, prayers and funeral benefits at the time of death. Their numbers mounted in the course of the fifteenth century. Rouen in France, a city of roughly 40,000, counted 131 confraternities towards the end of the century. Developments particularly in Italy, which suffered the social consequences of wars from 1494 until after the middle of the next century, pointed towards a form of confraternal piety that in its charitable activity reached well beyond the members themselves to disadvantaged groups in society. This was found most prominently, perhaps, along with the desire for a more intense religious life, in the Oratory of Divine Love founded in 1497 in Genoa by the layman Ettore Vernazza, who was under the influence of the mystic Catherine of Genoa. Initially limited to 36 lay and four clerical members, its professed goal was growth in charity for God and the neighbour, and it combined regular religious exercises with care for the sick in a hospital for incurables, usually syphilitics. Groups in imitation of it were subsequently founded in other Italian cities, including Bologna, Naples, and (before 1515) Rome, from which were to come leaders of the later Catholic Reform such as Cajetan da Thiene and Gian Pietro Carafa, the founders of the Theatines. Another group in peril were girls and young women. At Brescia in 1512 a house was established under the patronage of Countess Laura Gambara for those who had been victimized during the sack of the city, and it stimulated other social initiatives including a hospital for incurables. So confraternities and the institutions they supported anticipated the expansion of social and charitable work fostered by the activist piety of the sixteenth century.

A new style of religious life in community traced its origins back to Gerard Groote, the son of a cloth merchant and patrician of Deventer in the Netherlands, born in 1340. After a long course of university studies and a brief teaching stint at the University of Cologne, Groote underwent a profound religious conversion in 1370, but after testing life in a Carthusian monastery he determined that he wanted to live his Christian life in service in the world. He was ordained a deacon in 1381, then after preaching vigorously against abuses in the church, such as externalism and the concubinage of priests, he was silenced by church authorities and died in 1384.

Groote founded several communities of laymen and laywomen, who purposely took no religious vows, but lived in community devoting their lives to prayer and work, initially the copying and binding of manuscripts or the weaving of cloth. They held property in common, and practised celibacy and virginity. These were to become the Brothers and Sisters of the Common Life, and it was among them that the modern devotion first flourished. Soon the Brothers began to conduct dormitories for students and then municipal schools where they introduced a humanist curriculum. Whatever his reservations about their methods, Erasmus, their most prominent pupil, represented a merging of the modern devotion with the new humanism. Enrolment at their school at Deventer in the Netherlands surpassed 2000 in the late fifteenth century. The Brothers' influence reached out from the Netherlands to northeastern France and to north Germany and the Rhineland. There were 26 houses in Germany by 1500.

During much of the fifteenth century there echoed throughout the church a call for 'reform in head and members', and there were many attempts at it prior to the Reformation. A recent French history of christianity entitles the volume for the period from 1450 to 1530 *De la Réforme à la Réformation* – from reform to Reformation – thus associating the early, stormy years of the Reformation with the late medieval call for reform rather than with the coming formation of the new confessions. Reform was a goal of the Council of Constance, which ended the Great Western Schism in 1417, and this projected reform comprised inculcation in the clergy of a sense of vocation and the allocation of greater autonomy to bishops. Pius II (1458–64) had Cardinal Nicholas of Cusa draw up a reform programme that anticipated many of the later reforms at Trent, but it remained a dead letter. Julius II, under political pressure, convoked the Council of the Lateran in 1512, and it continued under Leo X into 1517. Eventually reform decrees were issued as papal bulls. They restricted exemptions, bolstered episcopal authority, and regulated preaching, but they ignored the ills of non-residence and pluralism, and Leo X had neither the will nor the character to implement them. But the desire for reform was there among leading ecclesiastics.

Movements to introduce reform into the major religious orders were frequent in the fifteenth century. In some instances they led to the formation of Observant branches – that is, to groups intent on returning to the observance of the primitive rule of the founder. Often, as in the case of the Franciscans, the most prominent order at the time, this generated conflicts with the Conventuals, and in the Franciscan case Leo X established the two groups as separate orders in 1517. The great Florentine preacher Girolamo Savonarola played a key role in the reform of the Italian Dominicans. In the older monastic orders the tendency was to group monasteries into reformed congregations. This was the case with the German Benedictine Congregation of Bursfeld. The modern devotion had a particular impact on the reform of many Augustinian houses in Germany. All these efforts, which stretched throughout the century, met with varying degrees of success, but they testify to a desire if not always to a will for reform.

A further stream, to use Jedin's term, of religious renewal, if not church reform in the strict sense, were the humanists, who were influential among the elite and literate. Here Erasmus, of course, was the dominating figure, but there were many others such as Thomas More and John Colet in England, Lefèvre d'Étaples in France, and Johannes Reuchlin in Germany. The 'philosophy of Christ' advocated by Erasmus combined three elements: a personal devotion to Christ, a return to the original Christian sources, especially the New Testament but also the early Christian Fathers, and social responsibility along with advocacy for peace. On the eve of the Reformation, from 1515 to 1518, Erasmus published three of his major works: his edition of the Greek New Testament; his *Complaint of Peace*, a plea to the rulers of Europe for harmony; and a re-edition of his *Handbook of the Christian Soldier*, first published in 1503. Erasmus was at the pinnacle of his fame in 1517.

Reform efforts in Spain, where the crusading spirit was still very much alive, came from the top under Ferdinand and Isabella, who both recognized the importance of a vigorous Catholicism for promoting the unity of their kingdoms. The Council of Seville in 1478 determined that king and bishops together should undertake reform. The council issued a number of decrees touching upon the residence of bishops and exemptions for religious orders, but it is difficult to determine their impact. Isabella did see to the appointment of competent bishops such as Hernando Talavera, the first bishop of reconquered Granada, who initiated a pastoral programme to rebuild the church there and to attract the Arab population. More significant was Cardinal Ximénes de Cisneros, Archbishop of Toledo from 1495 to 1517, another royal appointee and a former Franciscan, who imposed on the order in Spain the rule of the Observants. Cisneros founded the University of

Alcalà for the education of clerics, and he prescribed for it a humanist programme of education. Under his sponsorship Spanish scholars published the *Complutensian Polyglot Bible*, with the original texts in Hebrew and Greek alongside the Latin Vulgate. At his initiative the *Imitation of Christ* and other works of the modern devotion were translated into Spanish.

The year 1478 also saw the establishment of an institution that has thrown a long shadow over Spanish Catholicism, the Inquisition. During the early Middle Ages the Muslims had controlled most of the Iberian Peninsula. Medieval Spanish society comprised Muslim and Jewish elements and had been, to a degree, a pluralist society. In the thirteenth century Jews numbered perhaps about 100,000, or 2 per cent of the population. Popular Antisemitism had surfaced increasingly in Spain throughout the fourteenth century, peaking in widespread riots against Jews in 1391. Many Jews received baptism under great duress, others freely. This resulted in the formation of a new class called *Conversos* or New Christians. Throughout the fifteenth century the genuineness of their conversion was frequently called into question, often by those Old Christians who resented their rapid social and economic advance. The original purpose of the Inquisition was to root out alleged heresy, especially reversion to Jewish practices, among the *Conversos*. Though it was founded by papal authority, it always remained under the effective control of the Spanish crown. Ferdinand, and perhaps Isabella, also seem to have created the Inquisition as the only institution that would function throughout their Iberian lands and so serve to help consolidate their power. Thus the Inquisition belongs in the context of state-building too.

The long Reconquest of the Iberian Peninsula from the Muslims ended with the taking of Granada by the Catholic monarchs Ferdinand and Isabella in 1492. That same year the remaining Jews were expelled from Spain. The principal reason for their expulsion was to remove a group that served as a temptation to the *Conversos* to return to their Jewish practices. Perhaps half of the 80,000 Spanish Jews converted rather than abandon their homeland, thus increasing the number of *Conversos*. After the completion of the Reconquest, an analogous situation existed in southern Spain for the *Moriscos* or Muslims who had become Christians usually under compulsion. The period until about 1530 saw the Inquisition proceed at its most brutal as it prosecuted heresy among the *Conversos* and then the *Moriscos*. According to the most reliable estimate, it executed during this time about 2000

Conversos. In addition, many more thousands faced ruin as a result of the confiscations normally levelled as a punishment for heresy, and had to don regularly the hated *sanbenito*, a penitential garment.

Subsequently, the institution moderated and regularized its methods as it turned its primary attention to other perceived threats to Spanish society. According to figures cited by Henry Kamen, of all the cases that came before 19 Inquisition tribunals from 1540 to 1700, roughly 2 per cent, or about three per year, ended in an actual execution. This was, according to Kamen, 'certainly a lower rate [of execution] than in any provincial court of justice in Spain or anywhere else in Europe' at the time. Still, the *Conversos* and *Moriscos* continued to receive the most severe treatment.

By the accession of Pope Paul III in 1534 the Catholic Church had experienced devastating blows, and found itself confronting a perilous situation. The Reformation in Germany had passed through its heroic phase, and after the tragic end of the Peasants War in 1525 Protestant authorities soon began to turn to the reorganization of the church in the many German cities and states that had gone over to the Reformation. Confessionalism was under way. That same year, 1534, Henry VIII and the English Church severed their bonds with Rome. The young John Calvin was forced to flee Paris after a Protestant demonstration, but he only made his first appearance in Geneva two years later in 1536. There he determined to remain in order to assist in the establishment of a Reformed church, but Calvinism had scarcely been born. Matters were confused. It was unclear in some areas who was or was not a Catholic, let alone what constituted a Catholic. Only gradually would lines be clearly drawn. As late as the 1580s in one case in Germany the same individual functioned as both Catholic parish priest and Protestant pastor.

Indeed, the Catholic Church faced challenges.

2

THE NEW RELIGIOUS ORDERS

Monks, nuns, and friars faced growing criticism in the late Middle Ages and encountered even greater strictures from the Reformers. Yet religious orders were to remain a distinctive feature of the Catholic Church. Indeed, early modern Catholicism experienced not only a revival but a creative adaptation of religious life to the new demands of the sixteenth century. This renewal consisted chiefly in two developments: first, an intensified commitment of religious, that is, members of religious orders or congregations, women as well as men, to new types of pastoral activity as well as to traditional ministries; secondly, in the creation of styles and forms of religious life that facilitated this commitment allowing religious more activity beyond convent walls. There was an effort to find a new synthesis of the contemplative and the active life in the world. As John W. O'Malley has written, 'Although surely not without its debit side, ministry in the Catholic Church in the 16th and 17th centuries was perhaps the most innovative and exciting in history.' There took place not 'simply a "reform of morals", but a reform of pastoral practice and an immense expansion of its scope'. New religious orders and congregations played the major part in this development, which was little related directly to Trent and Tridentine reforms. As preachers, confessors, missionaries, writers, hospitalers and 'social workers', catechists and schoolmasters, members of these orders and congregations served as active agents of Catholic confessionalism, or better, christianization.[1] Among Protestants there was no parallel.

The most significant and easily the most numerous of the many orders and congregations that made their appearance after 1500 were the Capuchins, the Jesuits, and of the women's congregations, the Ursulines.[2] Most groups owed their origins to charismatic figures such

25

as Ignatius Loyola or Angela Merici, founders of the Jesuits and Ursulines respectively, a fact which underscores the role of the individual in the Catholic Reform and in the historical process generally. Most communities made their initial appearance in Southern Europe, especially Italy, with little attention at the start to the Reformation in the north. In the seventeenth century more initiatives germinated in France. The Jesuits, and later the Capuchins, were committed to evangelization in the lands across the seas as well as in Europe, and nearly all the male orders focused on the age-old activity of preaching, giving it new forms like the popular missions that became great happenings in the European Catholic world of the seventeenth century. Both men and women religious attempted to care for the sick and dying and to respond to the increasing problems of poverty, vagrancy, prostitution, and abandoned children that accompanied the social change of the sixteenth century.

But above all, the new orders and congregations turned to education: catechetical instruction, seminaries for clergy, and especially elementary and secondary schools. The conduct of schools by religious orders or congregations was not a completely new phenomenon; the Brothers of the Common Life, for example, undertook this work in the fifteenth century. What was new was the scope of the commitment to education. This new direction emerged from the widespread conviction that preaching, no matter how effective, was not sufficient for the formation of the Christian people which the Catholic Reform envisioned. Protestants found this to be true also, and they too turned to education. Systematic religious instruction was necessary, as the Council of Trent affirmed, and this meant schools. Neither the Jesuits nor the Ursulines were founded with a view to education in any formal sense, but both soon came to control extensive networks of colleges. The member of a new religious order, female as well as male, was frequently a schoolmaster or schoolmistress.

These new orders and congregations were often characterized by distinctive spiritualities or ways of living the Christian life, such as the Franciscan or the Jesuit spirituality. Along with older orders such as the Benedictines and the Dominicans, they provided the faithful with a pluralism of ways in which to practise their Catholicism. This variety of spiritualities played to different temperaments and social groups. Different religious institutes maintained houses and churches not only in the major European cities and towns but in Latin American cities too, such as Guadalajara, Mexico. There by the late seventeenth century the Dominicans, Franciscans, Augustinians, Carmelites, Mercedarians, Oratorians (of Philip Neri) and Jesuits all had houses, and the Hospitalers of St John of God and the Bethlehemites, an order first founded in Guatemala City as a confraternity in 1663, had hospitals. In addition, there were four convents of nuns: two Dominican, one Discalced Carmelite, and one of the Recollects of St Augustine, a reform group of Augustinians. Many orders sponsored confraternities for lay folks which communicated their ethos. In a special category were the third orders of the older religious families, which had initially been created to enable lay men and women to live in the spirit of the order. Most of these tertiaries, as members of third orders were called, were women; some lived in community, others did not. Many third orders evolved to become proper congregations of religious themselves, both active and contemplative.

Indeed, focus on the new orders should not lead us to neglect developments within the older traditions, which, as we have seen, experienced reform movements in the later Middle Ages. The older male orders were much more numerous than the new ones. Despite heavy losses in the north of Europe, the Dominicans more than doubled their numbers to 30,000 between 1500 and 1700, the Franciscan Conventuals numbered 25,000 in 1775, up from 20,000 in 1517, and the Observant Franciscans reached 77,000 in 1775, a number which includes their offshoots, the Discalced Franciscans (7000) or Alcantarans after the Spaniard Peter of Alcántara, the Recollects (11,000), and the Reformed Franciscans (19,000). Movements of reform intensified within the older orders. Perhaps the most well known of the sixteenth century was that inspired by the Carmelites Teresa of Avila and John of the Cross, which began in the 1560s in Spain and resulted in 1593 in the formation of the Discalced Carmelites, a new order of stricter observance for men and women. These two figures, literary giants as well as mystics, greatly enriched the church's heritage of spirituality with their writings on prayer. Teresa, whom some consider the outstanding woman of the century, founded at least 15 new Discalced communities in the last 20 years of her life. The older monastic orders of Benedictines and Cistercians also underwent change – in some cases, especially in France, back to a stricter monastic observance, and in others, sometimes under Jesuit influence, to a greater pastoral commitment. The Council of Trent encouraged the trend already evident in the fifteenth century towards the formation of groups of monasteries into federations.

The new importance of religious orders for pastoral work was partly due to inadequate formation of secular clergy in the late Middle Ages and their virtual disappearance in some areas during the Reformation; there was a need for 'reformed priests', and some new groups, especially the clerks regular and societies of common life, saw themselves as providing these. The new orders had an impact on church structures, particularly on the position of the papacy and on the relationship between seculars, or clergy who were directly subject to a diocesan bishop, and regulars, or clergy who were members of religious orders, and among regulars themselves.

The Capuchins aimed to revive the primitive Franciscan spirit in the early modern age, and they came to represent anew the combination of poverty and austerity with an effective ministry of evangelization characteristic of the Franciscans. The movement began with the desire of the young Italian Observant Franciscan Matteo da Bascio, for a more genuine Franciscan life. From the small group which assembled about him, and which received initial papal approval in 1528, the Capuchins grew to nearly 30,000 during their 'golden age' in the seventeenth century. Early Capuchins showed an inclination to the hermitages of the first Franciscans, but the hermitages soon yielded to convents, and the initial renunciation of exemption from episcopal authority, which was found in the Constitutions approved by Paul III in 1536, disappeared in the Constitutions of 1554. The legislation of Trent compelled the Capuchins, who were sometimes suspicious of academic studies, to undergo a suitable theological education. The order faced early difficulties with the defection to the Protestants in 1539 of one of its leading preachers and newly elected vicar-general, Bernardino Ochino. But Pope Paul III maintained his support as did the influential Roman, Vittoria Colonna, who gave invaluable assistance to the early Capuchins. Paul III had restricted the group to Italy, where by 1574 it counted 3500 members in 18 provinces with 300 convents and had attained a distinct identity as a new member of the Franciscan family. That year the Capuchins were allowed to expand beyond the Alps, and they established a house in Paris. Soon they were to become a major influence in France, then in Spain, Germany, and eventually throughout Catholic Europe, not to mention in the Middle East and in the Congo, where they opened missions.

The Capuchins were known above all for their simple preaching of the Gospel and for their popular missions both among Catholics and in areas to be reclaimed for Catholicism, especially among the Huguenots in France. Their service to the sick and especially to the plague-stricken was legendary, as in the plague of 1630–1 which ravaged north Italy, and this earned them the respect and love of the people. The Capuchins' strict practice of poverty forestalled the establishment of large institutions such as the Jesuits were to found, and the Capuchin often functioned most effectively in circumstances where the 'personal equation' predominated. One thinks of Fra Cristoforo in Manzoni's classic nineteenth-century Italian novel *The Betrothed*. Confraternities of the Blessed Sacrament and of the Passion were lay organizations the Capuchins frequently established in their churches.

Yet the Capuchins remained within an earlier tradition, and they showed little inclination to become involved in schools. A breakthrough towards a new form of religious life took place with the foundation in 1524 of the Theatines, the first order of clerks regular, and in 1540 of the Jesuits, by far the most numerous and the most influential order in this category. Clerks regular saw themselves generally as reformed priests who were committed to pastoral activity yet lived in community with the profession of solemn vows and according to a rule which facilitated this activity more than did the traditional rules like the Benedictine or Augustinian. A new feature of the clerks regular was the total orientation of their organization to ministry, whereas the older orders retained elements of the monastic tradition which was interpreted as standing in the way of this. Especially in the case of the Jesuits, ministry constituted an essential element of their religious life from the beginning.

Ignatius Loyola's *Spiritual Exercises* left a decided mark not only on the Jesuits but on subsequent Catholic spirituality. The author was born in 1490/1 of middling nobility at the castle of Loyola in Spain's Basque country, while his father seems to have been on campaign against the Moslems around Granada. Iñigo, as he was called until a registrar at the University of Paris mistakenly translated his name into the Latin 'Ignatius', received the education of a courtier at the court of Don Juan Velázquez de Cuellar, treasurer of Ferdinand of Aragon, where he was placed when he was 15. When Velázquez lost favour and died, Iñigo entered the service of the Duke of Nájera, the Governor of Navarre, which had come under Castilian control in 1512. There he heroically but unsuccessfully led the defence of Pamplona against the French

invaders in 1521 in what was a secondary theatre of the long
Habsburg–Valois Wars. A cannonball wounded him in both legs, forcing
him to return to Loyola for an extended period of convalescence. His
secretary later wrote of Ignatius's life up to this point: 'Though he was
attached to the faith, he lived no wise in conformity with it and did not
avoid sin; rather he was much addicted to gambling and dissolute in
his dealings with women, contentious and keen about using his sword.'

It was while lying in bed recovering from his wounds that Ignatius
underwent his conversion. He asked for popular chivalric romances to
while away the time. But the only books in the house were pious works
like the *Life of Christ* by Ludolph of Saxony or the *Golden Legend*, a
volume of lives of the saints. Soon Iñigo started to notice the differing
movements within himself while reading these books. Thoughts of
great deeds that he would do for his lady, perhaps the young wife of
Charles V, gave him initial pleasure but then left a sour taste behind,
whereas reflections on the life of Christ and the saints left him with a
sense of peace and joy that endured. Here was the beginning of his discernment of spirits, a method of reading the movements within an
individual in such a way as to be able to discern the direction in which
God was moving that individual.

In March 1522, at the age of 31, Iñigo departed Loyola, 'feeling
within himself a powerful urge to be serving Our Lord', as he wrote in
his later *Autobiography*, his goal Jerusalem and a life of penance there.

But first, on his way to Barcelona to take ship, he stopped at the
great Benedictine monastery of Montserrat. There, after making a
general confession of his life, he kept vigil in the church before the
statue of Our Lady, in the manner of a knight before his knighting. As
biographer James Brodrick wrote, 'he is the only saint known to have
dedicated himself utterly to God by a vigil of arms'. Then, probably
because of an outbreak of plague in Barcelona, he made a detour to the
small town of Manresa, where he eventually remained 11 months,
undergoing the experiences that were to serve as the basis for the
Spiritual Exercises. The first four months were spent in prayer, fasting,
and penance, during which he experienced much consolation. Then
spiritual turmoil overtook him, scruples about his past life, doubts
about his capacity to lead his new life, general confusion; it was his
'dark night', and it brought him to the brink of suicide. Then, he tells
us, God gradually gave him a sense of his presence and instructed him
'as a schoolteacher deals with a child'. A high point was an intense interior illumination of the Holy Trinity, in which he saw revealed the way

God created the world and was leading all creation back to himself through Christ. This experience would ground Ignatius's world-affirming spirituality. When he finally left Manresa for Jerusalem, his outlook was outgoing and apostolic, his goal to 'help souls', as he put it.

Iñigo now carried with him the basic outline of his *Spiritual Exercises*, which he would continue to amend and rework until its formal approval by the church in 1548. Unimpressive when one reads it, the book is not meant to be read but to serve as a guide for a retreat master leading a retreatant one-on-one through a programme of prayer over four 'weeks' of unequal length or roughly 30 days. The individual is led to see his own life within the context of the salvation history of humanity. The goal was two-fold: first, to introduce the retreatant to a life of prayer and then to help the retreatant determine the vocation or choice to which God was calling him in the service of his kingdom. At the beginning, in the Principle and Foundation, the individual reflected upon his creation by and total dependence upon a loving God. The sum total of God's creatures were presented as gifts of God's goodness which were intended to lead men and women back to their source, that is, to God. But they misused or abused creatures; this was to turn away from God and to sin. Humanity's and the individual's sin and forgiveness figure prominently in the first week of the *Exercises*, which ends with the individual's experience of God's forgiveness and mercy. The second week opens with a crucial meditation which represents Christ the King calling the retreatant to follow him in his campaign to lead the world back to his Father. The retreatant then reflects on the life of Christ up to his Passion in the expectation that in the course of this prayer he will recognize, with the help of the discernment of the movements within himself, the way God is calling him individually to follow Christ or, in other words, God's will for him. After the retreatant's election or choice to follow Christ's call, the last two weeks of the *Exercises* consist in prayer over the passion and death of Christ and then over his resurrection and risen life, to confirm the retreatant in his election. The *Exercises* conclude with a Contemplation to Obtain Divine Love, in which the retreatant prays over the many gifts God has bestowed and continues to bestow on him and so is led to a generous self-surrender back to God.

The *Exercises* belong within a tradition dating from the late Middle Ages of books on methodological meditation and mental prayer for the individual. Important among these was the *Exercise of the Spiritual Life* by the Benedictine García Jiménez de Cisneros, abbot of Montserrat, which appeared in 1500. In developing the *Exercises* Ignatius drew upon this tradition, but the extent to which he did so is controverted. Unquestionably the synthesis was his own. The tradition with its concern for individual meditation and the *Exercises* in particular with their methodology to discern the individual's vocation express the individualism of the Renaissance. Subsequently, the *Exercises* were widely adapted, in accord with Ignatius's intention, for use by groups and for popular missions.

After a long journey via Rome and Venice, Iñigo learned in Jerusalem that the authorities, because of the political situation, would allow him to remain there for only 20 days. He then made his decision to return to Spain, to begin study for the priesthood; only as a priest could he hope to exercise a ministry. There followed years of study, first in Barcelona, then at the universities of Alcalà and Salamanca, while he lived from alms and engaged regularly in religious conversations. Twice these brought him into difficulties with the Inquisition, which was one reason that in 1528 he moved to the University of Paris, still the centre of the European intellectual world. There, as he pursued his studies, he gathered about him his first permanent companions, leading them through the *Spiritual Exercises*. Among these were Francis Xavier, a fellow Basque, the future missionary to Asia.

The 43-year-old Ignatius still had no intention of founding a religious order when on 15 August 1534 he and his six companions, all students at the university, vowed to live a life of evangelical poverty and to labour in the Holy Land for the good of souls. Should this latter be impossible, as turned out to be the case, they agreed that they would offer their services to the pope in Rome as the Vicar of Christ and as the figure with the best knowledge of the needs of the universal church. Yet found an order is precisely what he and his companions determined to do in 1539. It had become obvious that this was the only way they could preserve their community as the demand for reformed priests required that they scatter to different regions of Europe and throughout the world.

According to the bull of Paul III establishing the Society of Jesus in 1540 as a religious order, it was 'principally instituted to work for the advancement of souls in Christian life and doctrine, and for the propagation of the faith by public preaching and the ministry of God's Word, by spiritual exercises and works of charity, more particularly by grounding in Christianity boys and unlettered persons, and by hearing the confessions of the faithful'.[3] Noteworthy here is the general character of 'public preaching and the ministry of God's Word' and 'works of charity', the absence of a reference to Protestantism, and explicit mention of the instruction of children and the uneducated in Christian doctrine. Already it had become apparent that the formation of Christians required catechesis, especially for young people as is evident from the newly founded lay confraternities of Christian doctrine such as the highly successful one inaugurated at Milan in 1536 by Castellino da Castello. Professed Jesuits were to take a vow of 'special care for the instruction of children', and catechetical instruction was to remain an important aspect of their ministry.

In order to facilitate their pastoral activities and ministerial flexibility, the Jesuits eliminated regular prayer in choir as well as any fixed times for prayer, and they also set aside regular fasts or other austerities. These were significant departures from the traditional rules of religious orders. For Jesuits Ignatius wanted not only a new balance of contemplation and activity, but he sought to integrate the two creatively in Jesuits as 'contemplatives in action'. The Jesuit would 'find God' in his work and so in the world as much as in formal prayer, which tended to be more private and individual. Moreover, the Jesuit was to be ready to be sent on pastoral missions, so that not the monastery but 'the whole world becomes our house', as one of Ignatius's early interpreters wrote. Another feature of the Society of Jesus was the solemn vow of the professed placing them at the disposition of the Holy See for mission and so attaching the Society in a particular fashion to the pope, the result of which was to strengthen the papacy. Ignatius spent the last years of his life in Rome engaged chiefly in writing the Society's Constitutions. By his death in 1556, the Jesuits numbered roughly 1000 members with 33 colleges. Its membership peaked in the mid-eighteenth century at 22,589 with a network of over 800 educational institutions throughout Catholic Europe, Asia and America.

Initially, the early Jesuits had not foreseen work in schools or colleges. The first Jesuit colleges were residences for young Jesuit scholastics or seminarians attending universities in preparation for the priesthood. After it became evident that the university lectures were not adequate, Jesuits began to hold their own lectures in the colleges. Benefactors, however, were reluctant to support schools for young Jesuit scholastics alone, so the Society began to admit extern students too, for the first time in 1546 at Gandía in Spain, where Francis Borgia, then Duke of Gandía and later third superior general of the order, was the founder. The first college established primarily for externs was at Messina in

Sicily in 1548, and quickly a demand built up for colleges, which Ignatius interpreted as the call of God. So the Society became increasingly involved in education, which came to be recognized as a most effective way to prepare young men for an active Christian life in the world.

This evolution harmonized with both the catechetical ministry and the contemporary humanist vision of the possibilities of education. Later, other orders of women as well as men followed in this path, and so education became increasingly an activity for religious. Early on, Ignatius made a further decision that Jesuit colleges would not normally accept boys without some prior training in Latin, and this tended to make it difficult for the very poor to find a place in them. Yet it would be a mistake to see Jesuit colleges as only schools. They were also 'pastoral centres'. At the college in Loretto in 1556, of the nine fathers five were engaged in direct pastoral work such as preaching or caring for the sick. A look at the five colleges of the Milan Province in 1574 shows that, in addition to a rector and a minister in each, they included a total of 12 Jesuits occupied in pastoral work, 11 priests principally engaged in teaching along with 10 scholastics who taught. By 1600 the now seven colleges of the province comprised 42 *'operarii'* or pastoral workers as opposed to 20 teaching priests. After the foundation of the Marian Congregation by the young Belgian scholastic Jean Leunis in Rome in 1563, these and similar confraternities for many types of people were often based in Jesuit colleges and served to disseminate an active Jesuit spirituality.

None of the other orders of clerks regular came close to approaching the numbers of the Capuchins, the Jesuits, or the older orders. The Theatines, who emerged out of the Oratory of Divine Love, counted only 12 until the 1550s, but by 1650 they totalled nearly 1100, mostly in Italy. They did not take up the work of education as a principal activity. Neither did the Somaschi, who were founded near Venice by Jerome Emiliani in 1534 for the care of orphans and other victims in the midst of the Italian Wars, nor did the Camillians who were founded at Rome by Camillus de Lellis in 1584 for the care of the sick in hospitals. None of these orders expanded much beyond Italy, though the Camillians did establish houses on the Iberian Peninsula in the second half of the seventeenth century and then in Latin America. The case was different with the Barnabites, founded at Milan in 1533 by Anthony Maria Zaccaria for various pastoral and catechetical activities. They altered their constitutions in 1608 to enable them to open schools, and soon they had colleges not only in Milan but in Savoy, France, and the Habsburg lands. Their numbers peaked at 788 in 1724.

Of particular interest for their role in education are the Piarists and the Doctrinaires. The former came into existence as a congregation in Rome in 1602 under the leadership of the Spaniard Joseph Calasanz, and only became a religious order in 1621, with the purpose of providing free, elementary Christian education to poor boys, who in the early years had to bring testimonials of their poverty from their parish priests. After many vicissitudes the order numbered about 500 in 1646, and 1680 by 1724, primarily in Italy but also in the Habsburg lands and in Poland. In the course of the seventeenth century they opened colleges which often competed with the Jesuits, while at the same time maintaining their tradition of free education for the poor in elementary schools. Eventually their numbers reached 3000 in the late eighteenth century. The Doctrinaires were essentially a confraternity founded at Avignon in 1598 by César de Bus, for the principal purpose of teaching Christian doctrine. De Bus worked out his own unique catechetical method and was greatly influenced by the confraternities for Christian doctrine that had grown up in Italy and especially in Milan. The Doctrinaires too gradually began to open colleges, of which they operated 39, nearly all in mid-sized cities and towns of France, by 1690. Their number never exceeded 400.

A new phenomenon of the late sixteenth and early seventeenth century were societies of common life, that is associations primarily of priests who wished to live in community according to the evangelical counsels but without taking public vows. There were a number of reasons for the omission of vows, but the chief one seems to have been the desire to identify with and to provide a model for the secular clergy who were recognized to be in need of reform. The societies eschewed the exemptions of religious orders and placed themselves under the jurisdiction of the local bishop. Some saw their style of life as a revival of the life of the clergy in the early church, others considered formal vows an obstacle to an effective priestly ministry. Generally speaking, their spirituality focused on the priesthood itself and, not surprisingly, they became deeply involved in the education of diocesan priests.

Apart from the original Roman Oratory of Philip Neri, which first received papal recognition in 1575, these societies were concentrated in France. Pierre de Bérulle founded the French Oratory at Paris in 1611; by his death in 1629 there were 60 houses with 400 members and by 1702 there were 78 communities with 581 priests, nearly all in

France. Under pressure from Paul V, and with reluctance on Bérulle's part, the French Oratorians took up the work of secondary education and by 1631 possessed 31 colleges. Vincent de Paul's Congregation of the Mission, or Lazarists after the hospital complex of St Lazare given them on the outskirts of Paris, first came into existence in 1625, for the purpose of preaching missions in rural areas, and for the education and formation of the clergy. By Vincent's death in 1660 they counted 229 members in 25 houses, chiefly in France but also in Italy, Ireland, and North Africa. Other important societies of common life were the Sulpicians, dating from 1642, the Eudists from 1643, and the Paris Foreign Mission Society from 1664. In the 135 dioceses in France in the mid-eighteenth century, the Lazarists conducted 60 seminaries, the Sulpicians 20, the Oratorians and the Doctrinaires 14 each, and the Eudists 13. So one gets an idea of their impact on the education of the clergy in France. For a long time the Jesuits had only reluctantly accepted French seminaries, but at the vigorous urging of Louis XIV, who wanted to counter Jansenist inroads, they took on many more so that by the mid-eighteenth century they controlled 32.

Two important non-clerical male congregations originated in the sixteenth and late seventeenth centuries; the first, the Hospitallers of St John of God, who were devoted to ministry to the sick as were the Camillians, and the Brothers of the Christian Schools committed to the growing ministry of education. The former, who continued a medieval tradition of service to the sick, traced their origins to the Spaniard John of God, who has been called 'the creator of the modern hospital' after his construction of a hospital in Granada just prior to his death in 1550. The society underwent constitutional ups and downs after its recognition by Pius V in 1572, and in the early seventeenth century split into Spanish and Italian branches. By the early eighteenth century 288 hospitals spread over most of Catholic Europe, as well as Latin America and Canada, were conducted by their 2046 members. The Hospitallers took a special vow of service to the sick, and like the Capuchins they became well known for their care of the plague-stricken. Free elementary education for poor boys was the ministry of the Brothers of the Christian Schools, founded by John Baptist de la Salle, who opened their first school at Reims in 1679. Canonically recognized at Rome in 1725, they opened 116 schools by 1789, thus realizing 'the first programme of national primary education in France'. By choice they did not become clerics, and they worked out a spirituality of the Christian teacher which drew on the resources of Baptism and

Confirmation but not Orders for a pastoral mission. Other groups were to follow in both their traditions.

For France in the seventeenth century one can speak of a 'feminization' of religious life, in that for the first time female religious outnumbered male. Cloistered, contemplative nuns still were in the clear majority, especially after a considerable increase in female monastic vocations in the first half of the century. The Discalced Carmelites of Teresa's reform formed a small community in Paris in 1601, and from that beginning within 40 years 55 Carmelite convents spread across France in a 'mystical invasion'. But the many active congregations represented a new phenomenon as they sprouted up in France, and to a lesser extent in the Netherlands, the Rhineland, and North Italy. They resulted from a widespread desire among women to participate more fully in the active ministry of Christ. In France middle- and lower-class women took on religious life in large numbers, local groups often functioning spontaneously before they organized formally. The women came to constitute a professional class committed to activity in the world as care-givers and above all as teachers. So female religious life acquired a new style and a new apostolic spirituality often related to that of the Jesuits with whom the sisters were frequently associated. To be sure, there were medieval precedents, especially for care of the sick in hospitals and in homes, particularly in the Netherlands, and often associated with the traditional third orders such as the Franciscan Grey Sisters. The fact that their own Constitutions prohibited the Jesuits from officially taking responsibility for women's congregations left those congregations which the Jesuits encouraged greater independence. The new active women religious came to constitute major actors in the campaign to christianize society. Mothers usually set the religious tone in families, and they needed to be prepared to do this. Reformed Catholicism flourished in areas of female education, and by 1700 schooling was increasingly considered a social necessity for girls in the cities and towns of Catholic northern Europe.

These developments among women religious seem to have taken place if not in spite of, then certainly not because of, the Council of Trent or the papacy. At its close the Council issued reform measures for female monasteries, insisting in particular on a stricter observance of enclosure or cloister, but it ignored the many monasteries without cloister, including the various third-order religious congregations. Pius V, then, in his rigorous bull *Circa Pastoralis* of 1566 interpreting the decree of Trent, required that all female monasteries accept cloister, even where entrants had not foreseen this as part of the way of life, and that all third orders accept cloister or remain as they were, in which case they could accept no new novices and so were sentenced to extinction. Such rigour was difficult to enforce; Venetian patricians, for example, were not ready to allow their daughters either to return to the world and so claim their inheritances, or to remain walled up completely behind cloister walls. Eventually, with social change and vigorous episcopal support from some quarters, active female religious congregations with only limited enclosure came to be tolerated by Rome. The papal position wavered under different popes, with Paul V (1605–21) being particularly open to this development and Urban VIII (1623–44) much less so. The whole issue illustrates the inability of central authority to impose its policy in the face of resistance, not only of the women but of their supporters among clergy and laity.

Of all the women's congregations the Ursulines were undoubtedly the most numerous and probably the most influential. They were the first women's religious congregation vowed to the ministry of education and, under this title, called to play an important role in the grand movement of Catholic Reform. Because they did not have a centralized organization, but were divided into many separate congregations with varying numbers of affiliated convents, it is hard to determine their precise numbers. In France, where they were most heavily concentrated and where they became 'the feminine teaching congregation par excellence', there were in 1750 about 10,000 Ursulines as opposed to about 3500 Jesuits, with about 350 institutions as opposed to about 150 Jesuit houses. Altogether they may have outnumbered the Jesuits throughout Europe.

The Ursulines owed their origin to Angela Merici, an unmarried laywoman of Brescia, who could read but probably not write, and whose ideal of Christian service for women in the world obviously spoke to her contemporaries in Italy. Born in Desanzano in Venetian territory about 1474, Angela lived most of her life there and in nearby Salò until she was 40. At some point she became an active member of the Franciscan third order, which gave her an outlet for her piety oriented as it was towards charitable activity. She moved to Brescia in 1516 at the request of the noblewoman Caterina Patengola, who had asked for a companion after the sudden death of her husband and two sons; this invitation had been long preceded, according to an account, by a vision in 1506 which had foretold to Angela that she would found a society of virgins in Brescia. There she was thrust into a city which had been rocked by the social effects of the Italian Wars, as well as religious unrest partly due to the long absence of the bishop.

Angela soon became associated with the local Oratory of Divine Love, helping out in the female section of the new hospital for incurables which was under construction in 1521. Other activities claimed her attention, such as reconciling enemies, arranging marriages, caring for orphans, and instructing girls in Christian doctrine. She also undertook pilgrimages to Jerusalem and Rome. Gradually her goal evolved into a community of virgins and widows who would serve in the world as they had done in the early church, of whom the legendary St Ursula, then popularly associated in Italy with education, was chosen as patron. Angela was responding to the needs of the times as she gathered women about her, first to assist in the hospital for incurables, then to look after orphans and to visit families as they took up other care-giving activities, and then to instruct girls in Christian doctrine. Most of the young women about her continued to live with their families, though as early as 1532 some were living in community. They all committed them-selves to lives of poverty, chastity, and obedience in the following of Christ, but they took no vows, perhaps to avoid closer ecclesiastical control. Angela's associates numbered 35, mostly of lower-class origins, when the group first formally organized in 1535. The initial rule was a combination of features from third orders and confraternities. It received the approval of the Bishop of Brescia the following year, and that of Paul III in 1544. In 1539, the year before Angela's death, the group numbered about 150, but the years following were difficult ones as it gradually became a congregation.

Charles Borromeo has been called 'a second founder' of the Ursulines. In 1567 as archbishop he brought them to Milan, primarily to assist in his programme of religious instruction, thus pushing them more clearly in the direction of the teaching of young girls and so towards education. In 1576 he required that each bishop of his ecclesiastical province establish the Ursulines in his diocese, where they came under local episcopal authority. So they expanded in north Italy, frequently recruited and encouraged by local governments too. Borromeo's revi-sion of their rule became one of the variations found among the nearly autonomous Ursuline communities united only in a common attach-ment to the tradition of the first community of Brescia. Most Ursulines in Italy continued to reside with their families even as the number living in community increased, nor did they take public vows, so skirting the legislation of Trent.

The papal territory of Avignon provided the stepping stone for the Ursuline entrance into France. There, with the support of César de Bus and the Doctrinaires, a community was established in 1598. By 1600 they were in Aix, 1604 in Toulouse, and 1607 in Paris as they took root in other French cities, often with Jesuit support, as well as in Liège and Cologne, where they served the sick, worked with prostitutes, and above all taught catechism. Increasingly in France, they lived in community with a vow of chastity and the practice of poverty and obedience; gradually they came to be seen as in conflict with Trent's regulations, which had not yet been the case in Italy. Two actions of the Paris community in 1612 were then to have far-reaching consequences for the Ursulines, especially in France. That year the Paris community accepted monastic enclosure. This was the result partly of pressure from the French hierarchy, who had set out to bring all women's congregations into line with the Roman policy, partly of pressure from French society which hesitated to accept uncloistered single women living outside the home, but also partly of the desire of the women themselves who at this time of religious revival in France and the introduction of the Discalced Carmelites saw a greater value in the strict cloistered life. On the other hand, at the same time the Paris Ursulines secured papal approval of their ministry of instruction of girls and then were permitted to take a special vow committing themselves to this work of education. Indeed, this instruction was to take priority over their obligation to common prayer in choir. So the Ursulines were able to preserve their active ministry of education. The move back into the cloister was a source of conflict within the Ursulines but eventually most communities in France made the transition. This, incidentally, was not the case in Italy, where into the eighteenth century the majority of Ursulines did not live in community.

But the Ursuline schools remained, continued to multiply, and became a major factor in the efforts to christianize the population of Catholic Europe. Folks realized that young girls as future mothers would influence their families. With the sisters themselves there evolved a new form of religious life combining contemplation with classroom teaching. So, despite their cloister, the Ursulines actively reached out to the girls and women about them.

One Ursuline who did not accept cloister was Anne de Xainctonge, born in 1567 in Dijon, where she grew up in the shadow of the Jesuit college and yearned to create something similar for girls. When the Jesuits were forced to leave Dijon in 1595, she moved to Dôle in the Free Country of Burgundy, beyond the reach of the French hierarchy. There in 1606 she established an Ursuline foundation for the instruction of girls, especially poor girls, as well as for other pastoral ministry. Shortly after her death in 1621 a Jesuit completed the rule she had been writing, which included simple vows, the complete absence of cloister, and a prohibition of boarding students along with significant borrowings from the Jesuit Constitutions. Her rule was approved by the Archbishop of Besançon, but seems never to have been approved by Rome. Several autonomous communities in the Free County, Lorraine, and Switzerland grew out of Xainctonge's initiative, and in 1789 there were 200 sisters living in nine houses.

Anne's spirituality of the teacher was similar to John Baptist de la Salle's, and there was evidence that she may have influenced him. She possessed a high sense of individual vocation; that is, God's call that endowed the schoolteacher with dignity. At the time schoolteachers enjoyed little social esteem. The sister sanctified herself precisely as she carried out her ministry in the classroom with its daily grind and frequent fatigue. Just as the Christian Brother had to resist the temptation to become a priest, so Anne's Ursulines had to withstand the attractions of the pure contemplative life. For this reason they took a special vow of stability in the community. Reserve and patience were necessary with the students, obedience within the community. Both the brothers and the sisters, like the Jesuits, were to avoid severe penances and mortifications lest these weaken them for their work.

There were of course many other initiatives besides the Ursulines' to find forms of religious life that would allow more room for the ministry of women in the world. They met with varying degrees of success. In the second decade of the seventeenth century Jane Frances de Chantal and Francis de Sales were unable to avoid cloister for their new Visitandines, largely due to the opposition of the Archbishop of Lyons. The English woman Mary Ward founded the Institute of the Blessed Virgin Mary, or English Ladies as they came to be popularly known in Catholic south Germany, at St Omer's across the channel in the Netherlands in 1609. One reason her initiative enjoyed little success was that she insisted on a centralized organization with vows similar to the Jesuits, and so provoked ecclesiastical opposition. The Congregation of Our Lady, founded by Alex Le Clerc and Peter Fourier at Mattaincourt in Lorraine in 1597, principally with a view to the religious instruction of girls, evolved similarly to the Ursulines. It became a cloistered order with a special vow committing them to the education of girls. By 1640 they possessed 48 houses in Lorraine, Savoy, France, and Germany. The pattern was nearly the same for the Daughters of Our Lady, founded at Bordeaux by Jeanne de Lestonnac, the niece of Montaigne, in 1606. Widowed with seven children at age 41, she too was profoundly influenced by the Jesuits, and she intended that her foundation be as like the Society as possible. At least 30 houses stemmed from her initiative before her death in 1640, all devoted to the education of girls.

Vincent de Paul and Louise de Marillac proceeded differently in the case of the Daughters of Charity, who traced their origins back to 1629 and who grew out of small groups of women, 'charités', who assisted pastors in rural parishes. They were concerned with the care of the poor and the sick and were not involved in education. Recognized as a confraternity by the Archbishop of Paris in 1646, they took merely private vows committing them to poverty, chastity, obedience, and the service of the poor, to be renewed annually. Canonically, the Daughters were not religious, and so they were completely free from cloister. Vincent also succeeded in placing them ultimately under the authority of the Superior General of the Lazarists, so that they were internally exempt from the control of the local bishop and were able to expand more readily. By 1700 their number rose to 1000; by 1789 to over 4000, nearly all in France.

By the end of the seventeenth century uncloistered female religious congregations, at least in France and the Low Countries, and to a lesser extent in Italy, were growing rapidly. One count indicates 17 new teaching congregations in France between 1660 and 1715, and there were also congregations devoted to the care of the poor and the sick, nearly all subordinate to the diocesan ordinary. Some took vows, others avoided them in order to circumvent canonical difficulties but committed themselves to poverty, chastity, and obedience in other ways. The Ladies of St Maur, first organized as a community in Rouen about 1670, conducted four free schools for girls there seven years later and shortly afterwards opened a school in Paris. The Ladies took no officially recognized religious vows. They developed into much more than a diocesan congregation, with 102 houses in 45 dioceses and more than 20,000 students in 1789. An example of a community in the Low Countries were the Daughters of St Agnes. They could trace their origins back to the Jesuit Bernard Olivier, a companion of Ignatius Loyola himself, who in 1554 had recruited a young girl to assist in the religious instruction of girls at Tournai. The evolution of the group is unclear; it seems to have undergone a second foundation about 1600. Their great trial came in the early 1630s, at the same time as Rome took action against Mary Ward, when the nuncio in Brussels sought to suppress the group which then conducted schools in a number of Belgian towns. But the protests of the Archbishop of Cambrai in favour of the women were successful, and the community continued its activity.

The new influx of religious, especially male religious, into ministry had its effects on church structures. The foundation especially of the Capuchins and the Jesuits, who were particularly favoured by the papacy, strengthened Rome at first *vis-à-vis* the bishops and national churches. With their centralized international organizations, and with their continued widespread exemptions, the two orders were the most active protagonists of papal authority during the period. This came at the same time that Trent emphasized the role of bishops in their dioceses and sought to regulate exemptions from episcopal authority. Eventually their allegiance to Rome would cost both orders dearly as the papacy became embattled in the eighteenth century. The papacy for its part gradually became more actively involved in the affairs of religious. Sixtus V in 1586 established the first Vatican organ to deal explicitly with their affairs, and it continued its activity as the Congregation for Religious after the reorganization of the Roman Curia two years later. Generally, the Vatican fostered centralization within orders and congregations and a generic concept of 'religious' that tended to downplay the distinctive features of orders and congregations and to favour the monastic vision of religious, especially in the case of women religious.

The involvement of new religious orders in the church's pastoral mission also exacerbated rivalry and even conflict between regulars and seculars over their respective roles; in 1601 Clement VIII entrusted to the aforementioned congregation the mediation of disputes between bishops and religious, and it became the Congregation for Bishops and Religious. The privileges granted religious orders were often a sticking point for the diocesan clergy; Jesuits, for example, received from Rome widespread authority for the reconciliation of heretics.

An area of often acute conflict was France, where there developed a particularly strong sense of identity in the parish clergy, partly as a result of the formation they received in the new seminaries conducted by the various societies of common life. This rivalry between seculars and regulars contributed to the Jansenist controversy. In parts of Germany and the Habsburg lands, where the parish clergy was devastated by the Reformation and then the Thirty Years War, bishops long remained dependent on Rome and the religious orders. In these areas the Jesuits frequently represented an anti-Protestant militance which contrasted with their general tendency towards accommodation elsewhere and especially overseas. In the Habsburg lands the international character of orders such as the Jesuits and Capuchins fit well with the supranational nature of the dynasty and the imperial character of Habsburg Catholicism. But after 1648, and especially after 1700, as Trent's reforms began to have an effect on them, the secular clergy began to assert a new independence. Much later the reforms of Emperor Joseph II (1780–90) would take shape in the Habsburg lands, to the disadvantage of religious orders.

Religious were also the principal carriers of the Gospel into Asia, Africa, and America in the early modern period. There rivalries among them, sometimes growing out of different approaches to mission, occasionally hindered their effectiveness. Certainly this was a factor in the famous Rites Controversies. Nor were conflicts among religious orders limited to overseas territories, as is clear from the long contest between the Jesuits and various monastic orders over claims to monastic lands recovered for the Catholic Church during the Thirty Years War after they had been seized by Protestants.

The new religious orders and congregations with their orientation towards ministry in the world were principal agents of christianization, and confessionalism, in early modern Catholic Europe, above all as teachers. The emergence of the women's congregations represented a new presence of women in the mission of the church, and they offered new opportunities especially to middle- and lower-class women. New orders increased the spiritualities or ways of practising Christianity available to the faithful. A new individualism appeared in the interest in private meditation and in individual vocation and the means to arrive at it offered by the *Spiritual Exercises*. Especially with the Jesuits there emerged a new synthesis of prayer and activity in the world. The new orders and congregations gave impetus to the growth of papal power within the church, and greatly increased the role of religious in the church's missionary and pastoral mission.

3

THE COUNCIL OF TRENT AND THE PAPACY

On 13 October 1534, after a conclave of only two days, Cardinal Alessandro Farnese emerged as pope. As Paul III he governed the church until 1549, with one foot, as it were, in the Renaissance and the other in the movement for reform and renewal. Certainly his greatest achievement was the convocation and then the actual opening of the historic Council of Trent in 1545; this was a major step in the evolution of Catholic confessionalism. Born of a family of the Papal States, Farnese had been named a cardinal at the age of 23 by Pope Alexander VI way back in 1493, perhaps because of this pope's liaison with his sister, the legendary beauty Giulia Farnese. Earlier popes legitimized several of his children. Even after his ordination to the priesthood in 1519, and a turn to a serious moral life, he continued to enjoy a Renaissance prelate's style of life. His nepotism was flagrant. Shortly after his election he raised to the cardinalate two of his teen-age grandchildren, and a leading concern of his papacy was the acquisition of the Duchy of Parma in north Italy for his son Pierluigi, which in fact remained in the Farnese family for two centuries. His was the last successful effort of a pope to invest his family with a principality.

But Paul III realized from the beginning that the prestige of the papacy required much sharper focus on its responsibilities for the church. In early 1535 he made it clear that a council was his principal goal, and he dispatched nuncios to Germany, France, and Spain to test the waters. This was a departure from his predecessor Clement VII, who feared a council as a likely source not only of criticism of his papacy but of conciliarism, which mirrored in the church the claims to predominance by representative bodies *vis-à-vis* prince or king in many emerging states. Despite an apparent victory of the papacy over conciliarism in the course of the fifteenth century, the doctrine retained significant adherents and was occasionally invoked, especially by the King of France, as a means of pressuring the papacy. Indeed, the relationship of the bishops as a collectivity to the pope was to be an issue at the council.

As early as 1520 Luther, the imperial estates, and Charles V had called for a council. Yet there were vastly different conceptions of how a council should look. Even before Paul III, on 2 June 1536, summoned a council for Mantua the following May, the Protestant states allied in the League of Schmalkeld declared unacceptable any council outside Germany and under papal leadership. France saw in a council the means by which Charles might unite the Empire and so prove still more formidable. So it opposed a council, thus helping to frustrate efforts to deal with the ecclesiastical situation. Indeed, the pope was regularly perceived by Charles as leaning towards the French, a perception which was not entirely off target because of the papacy's fear, throughout most of the early modern period, of Habsburg dominance in Italy and in Europe. In any event, Paul III's efforts towards a council in Mantua failed.

Meanwhile, in addition to his nephews, the pope appointed to the college of cardinals a number of reform-minded figures, and from these he formed a committee to draw up a report on the state of the church. It included the Venetian layman Gasparo Contarini, the fiercely Neapolitan co-founder of the Theatines, Gian Pietro Carafa, and the Englishman Reginald Pole. The result the following year was the influential *Advice concerning the Reform of the Church*. The report was highly critical of the church's situation and especially of the secularization of the papal office and the decadence evident in Rome. It lambasted the exaggeration of papal power by canonists, the cardinals' lust for wealth, and the regular dispensations from canon law, especially from the obligation of residence for bishops and pastors, and it pointed to the abuse of indulgences. Though meant to be secret, the report soon turned up in Germany, where it elicited 'I told you so's' from the Protestants. But it demonstrated the seriousness of its authors and was to have an eventual impact on reform.

Initiatives from below received the papal stamp of approval with Paul's bulls establishing the Capuchins in 1536, the Jesuits in 1540, and the Ursulines in 1544. In addition, in 1542, the Roman Inquisition was reorganized and its jurisdiction extended, largely because of fear of Protestantism's spread into Italy, where so-called evangelical groups had appeared especially in Venice and Naples. So there came into existence a bulwark of the Counter Reformation. Initially, its direction was entrusted to a committee of six cardinals, of whom the new cardinal Gian Pietro Carafa was the spearhead.

Once it became clear that the Protestants would not attend a council outside Germany, Charles V promoted a religious colloquy or discussion among theologians under imperial sponsorship to resolve the differences between Catholics and Protestants in Germany. Religious unity there would strengthen Charles' position generally and enable him to confront more effectively the persistent Turkish threat from the southeast. Reluctantly, the papacy supported this initiative and dispatched Cardinal Giovanni Morone to represent it at Worms in 1540 and Cardinal Contarini at Regensburg in 1541, where Philip Melancthon was his principal interlocutor. Here a tenuous agreement was reached on the fundamental issue of justification, but the talks broke down over the understanding of the Eucharist, and the role of the papacy did not even come up for discussion. Eventually, the agreement on justification was rejected by both Luther and in Rome. So once again in Rome plans for a council came to the fore. The pope agreed to Charles' suggestion that it be held in Trent, a town within the Empire and so satisfying the demand for a council on German territory, but on the Italian side of the Alps. On 22 May 1542 Paul III formally summoned the council to assemble there the following 1 November. In the meantime the Turks, allied with the French, took Buda, and open war between Charles and Francis flared up once again. Only a handful of delegates turned up at Trent, so that the pope had to suspend the council. Charles, for his part, gradually prepared to take up arms against the League of Schmalkeld, especially in view of the continuing spread of Protestantism in Germany. In 1543 he intervened on the Lower Rhine against the Duke of Cleves and the Archbishop of Cologne, preventing them from taking their lands into the Protestant camp.

The Peace of Crépy of 18 September 1544 ended for a time the conflict between Charles and Francis, and a secret agreement between the two committed Francis to allow French participation in the council, a commitment that eventually would not be honoured. On 30 November the pope rescinded his earlier suspension, and set the date for the council's opening in Trent for the following 15 March. In addition, that spring Paul III promised to support Charles' projected offensive against the League with subsidies and an army of 12,500 men; the goal was to defeat the Protestants militarily and compel them to assist at the council. Yet mistrust persisted between the two allies, and the ill-timed attempt of the pope to secure the duchy of Milan for his nephew Pierluigi did not improve their relationship.

Finally, after still further delays, the Council of Trent convened on Laetare Sunday, 13 December 1545. In attendance for the opening session were four archbishops, 22 bishops, and five generals of religious orders along with the three papal legates, Cardinals Giovanni Maria del Monte and Marcello Cervini, who were both future popes, and Cardinal Reginald Pole, who was to depart early because of ill-health. During the council's first period there were never more than 70 voting participants present, and they were assisted by about 50 theologians. All in all, the council was to meet in three distinct periods at Trent over the next 18 years: from December 1545 to March 1547; from May 1551 to April 1552, and then, after a 10-year hiatus, from January 1562 to December 1563. Altogether, 270 bishops participated in the council, 187 of them Italian, though by no means were all the Italians papalists, since there were many from Venice and Spanish Naples. Representatives of the principal Catholic states were also on hand.

At the start of the council it was necessary to establish procedures. Paul III entrusted the three papal legates with the leadership of the council, with Cardinal del Monte as president. But the council was clearly not a mere papal tool; it was rather half-way between Constance, which had ended the schism and elected a new pope, and Lateran V, which had taken place in Rome. The legates quickly won the right to determine the agenda, but they allowed freedom of speech, realizing that without it the council would forfeit its credibility. Those with the right to vote were bishops and heads of religious orders; no procurators or proxies were permitted. The principal place of business was the general congregation, where votes were taken, but as one might expect, much of the work was done in deputations or committees and in conferences in which the theological consultors participated.

A major problem at the start was whether reform legislation or doctrinal definition was to have priority. Emperor Charles wanted disciplinary reforms to be taken up first and doctrinal issues postponed, because he hoped that once reforms were set in motion, Protestants would come to take part in the council and a compromise would be found in matters of doctrine. For the pope the first order of business was to clarify the Catholic position on doctrine, so as to eliminate the widespread confusion among the faithful. Paul also feared that, in his desire for an understanding with the Protestants, the emperor might attempt to force unacceptable doctrinal compromises. The upshot was an agreement to treat issues of doctrine and issues of reform alternately. Moreover, the council fathers followed the policy of not discussing theological differences among Catholics; their full thrust was towards delineating clearly the Catholic stance *vis-à-vis* the Protestants. A subsequent criticism of Trent was that it hindered the return of the Protestants, but this is to overlook the extensive Protestant confessionalism up to this time, as well as the failure of the religious colloquies.

The first period of the council saw the issuance of major doctrinal decrees. The first responded to the Protestant notion of 'Scripture alone', declaring instead that there were two sources of divine revelation, tradition as well as Scripture, without clearly establishing the relationship between them, and insisting on the right of the church to interpret the Scripture authoritatively. It asserted that the Latin Vulgate version of the Bible was free of dogmatic error and suitable for both theology and devotion, while at the same time recognizing that the text needed correction and so acknowledging humanist criticism. The council recommended that lectures explaining the Scriptures be held in major urban churches as well as in schools, and especially for seminarians, and it neither discouraged nor encouraged private reading of the Bible.

The most important decree concerned justification, which responded to the Protestant notions of 'faith alone' and 'grace alone'. After a drawn-out debate it was passed unanimously. The decree has been considered a theological masterpiece in its development. It steered a middle course between Pelagianism or an excessive emphasis on human effort on the one hand and a determinist form of predestination on the other, insisting on the absolute initiative of God as well as on the part of man's free will. Original sin and the general features of the seven sacraments were subjects of other doctrinal decrees.

Reform decrees covered a number of topics. Their general intent was to encourage the residence of bishops and pastors and so restrict, if not eliminate, absenteeism and pluralism. They also aimed to strengthen the position of bishops in their dioceses by cutting back on exemptions from their authority as well as on appeals to Rome. One justification that bishops often gave for their absence was that they were not masters in their own domain. Now they were to have clear control, for example, over who could preach and who would be ordained to the priesthood in their dioceses. The role of the bishop as pastor was emphasized, as opposed to that of an ecclesiastical office-holder with rights of jurisdiction. Bishops and pastors were to preach regularly themselves, at least on Sundays and feast days, or find substitutes to do so.

As the council fathers turned to the question of the Eucharist, the plague began to break out in Trent, spread there from the theatre of war in south Germany. This was the occasion of the vote on 11 March 1547 to transfer the council to Bologna in the Papal States. Pope Paul had for some time desired this because of the ascending military position of Charles in the Empire. The pope wanted the defeat of the Protestants and their submission to the council, not a Habsburg predominance in Germany and a greatly strengthened European imperial power; he preferred negotiations with the Protestant princes and with France, which covertly supported them, to continued war, and he had withdrawn his troops from Germany in January. But Charles won a major victory at Mühlberg on 24 April, in the process taking prisoner the two leading Protestant princes, John Frederick of Saxony and Philip of Hesse. Neither pope nor emperor wanted a complete break, and the council continued its deliberations at Bologna. In September the occupation of Piacenza by imperial troops and the murder of the pope's son Pierliugi, with the connivance of the Spanish governor of Milan, greatly exacerbated the relationship between Paul and Charles. When Charles threatened to continue the council at Trent with a minority of imperialist bishops, thus raising the spectre of a schism, the pope suspended the council on 1 February 1548. So it was left, hanging in mid-air as it were. Only Paul's death on 10 November 1549 opened the prospect to a reconvening of the council in Trent.

The cardinals needed a conclave of nearly three months before electing pope, on 8 February 1550, Giovanni Maria del Monte, a native Roman and one of the presidents of the council, who took the name Julius III. The new pope summoned the council to reassemble in Trent on 1 May 1551. Now there actually appeared representatives of several German Protestant states including Brandenburg and Electoral Saxony as Charles V guaranteed they would. There had been a misunderstanding, however, regarding the terms of their participation, and their presence amounted to little. The council fathers now issued decrees reasserting the Catholic position on the Real Presence of Christ in the

Eucharist and on the sacrament of penance with auricular confession. A reform decree regulated appeals to Rome over the heads of local ordinaries. But then there took place a sudden reversal in Charles V's fortunes. The new French King Henry II joined with recalcitrant German princes to defeat Charles, and when they threatened to overrun Trent itself in the spring of 1552, the council was forced once again to disperse. So it remained incomplete. Pope Julius turned his attention to the preparation of a bull for the reform of the curia, but he died before its promulgation. His successor, Marcello Cervini, who also had served as a president in Trent, and who was intent upon vigorous reform, died after only 20 days as pope. He is known perhaps above all as the dedicatee of Palestrina's 'Mass in Honor of Pope Marcellus'. Meanwhile, following the abdication of Charles, Emperor Ferdinand I, his brother and successor, recognized the legal existence of the Lutherans in the historic Peace of Augsburg (1555). The year before this, after the ascent of the Catholic Mary Tudor to the throne in England, there took place a reconcilation of that kingdom with Rome. It proved, however, to be short-lived.

With the election of the 79-year-old veteran reformer Gian Pietro Carafa as Paul IV in May 1555 there blew a new, harsh wind through Rome. Ignatius Loyola admitted that his bones quaked when he first learned of Carafa's election, from whom he feared efforts to alter the structure of the Society of Jesus. After the founder's death the following year, the pope did compel the Jesuits to sing the office in choir and to reduce the term of the superior general's tenure to three years, changes which lapsed with the death of the pope. Under the ascetic and autocratic Carafa, reform continued but under strict papal leadership. Paul's vision of the papacy harked back to the medieval Popes Gregory IX and Boniface VIII, and he mistrusted a council, especially one held in the Empire far away from Rome. Furthermore, as a Neapolitan whose homeland remained under Spanish rule, Paul nourished a hatred of the Habsburgs. In 1556 he even involved the papacy in a brief, disastrous war with Philip II, whose support was necessary for a successful council. The Peace of Augsburg was anathema to him, as was the election of Emperor Ferdinand I, precisely because of Ferdinand's acceptance of Augsburg and the participation of heretical princes in his election. As long as Paul occupied the chair of Peter, there would be no return to Trent.

The prosecution of heresy and the work of the Inquisition stood out as the priority of Paul IV. Even the papal historian Ludwig von Pastor spoke of a 'regime of terror' under Paul. The pope saw to an overhaul of the Inquisition and rarely missed one of its sessions. During his pontificate many moderate reformers came under suspicion. Perhaps the most well known were the Cardinals Giovanni Morone and Reginald Pole. Morone, who had undertaken a number of diplomatic missions to Germany for earlier popes and who would later rescue the floundering council, was imprisoned for alleged heresy for over a year in 1557, and Pole would probably have encountered the same fate had death not saved him. The first papal Index of Forbidden Books appeared under Paul, and the Jesuit Peter Canisius complained from Germany that its severity was a 'scandal', listing as it did all the works of Erasmus as well as all the books published by 61 publishing houses. Nor did the Jews in the Papal States escape the pope's rigour. They were compelled to move into ghettos and to wear yellow hats as a distinguishing mark. At the death of the tragic Paul, crowds stormed the palace of the Inquisition in Rome and set it ablaze.

The new pope, Pius IV of a Milanese Medici family unrelated to the Florentine Medici, recognized the need to reconvene the council, and this he did for 6 April 1561. He had left the curia in 1558 as a protest against the policies of Paul. By the time of his accession the position of the church had grown worse; in France the Huguenots surfaced as a public force to be reckoned with, and in England Elizabeth had once again broken with Rome. Pius was resolved to cooperate with the two Habsburg rulers, Philip II and Emperor Ferdinand I, thus reversing the policy of Paul. After the usual delays the council reopened at Trent on 18 January 1562. Initially it was not clear whether it was to begin anew or whether it was to take up where it had left off. Emperor Ferdinand and Catherine de Medici, the regent in France, both preferred a new start, since it would give them a free hand to negotiate with their dissident groups. But Philip II strongly advocated resumption, as did the pope himself, whose diplomacy gradually won the day. Two papal nuncios carried invitations along with a personal letter from the pope to the German Protestant princes assembled at Naumburg, but the princes declined to participate in a council under papal leadership. Altogether more than 200 bishops were to take part in this final period, where the same procedures would be followed as in the earlier periods.

Initially, the council fathers turned to the issue of reform, and of the 12 articles drawn up for their consideration, the first dealt again with episcopal residence. The first period's effort to deal with it had effected little. But the topic now brought to the fore the more fundamental issue of the relationship between a bishop and the bishops as a corporate body to the pope. At this point one came dangerously close to conciliarism, even though those who championed the position of the bishops were hardly conciliarists. In the analogous contest in most states between the ruler and representative estates for the upper hand – the major exception was England – the ruler won the day as Europe gradually headed into an age of absolutism, an absolutism which was not as complete as once thought, but which nevertheless meant the predominance of the ruler over the estates and an increasing centralization. The same was true in the church; indeed, one might say the church led the way. In both cases the desire for order characteristic of Europe as the sixteenth century progressed was certainly a factor in the outcome.

The Spanish bishops championed the position that one could only truly effect the reform of residence by declaring that the presence of a bishop in his diocese was demanded by divine right or God's law. This would make it impossible for the papacy to grant dispensations, and it would also appeal vigorously to episcopal consciences. Cardinals and other officials of the Roman curia feared this legislation, since many of them lived as absentee bishops, and they also saw in it an attempt to limit papal power, as well as a potential opportunity for Protestants to chide Rome for having contravened divine law by dispensing from residence. Pius himself was angry when he learned that the legates had permitted the issue to come to the floor. Debate was spirited in the general congregation, where the fathers were split almost evenly. Eventually the legates succeeded in withdrawing the issue, but only with the promise to return to it when the sacrament of orders came up for discussion.

Accordingly, the debate revived some months later. At this point the proposed decree failed to assert that the office of bishop existed by divine right, implying that it might have been the result of historical development rather than the will of Christ. Involved here too was papal power; if the office of bishop had not been instituted by Christ, then the source of episcopal authority was, according to some theologians, the papacy. In this context the more specific issue of residency by divine law arose again. Soon an impasse obtained, and the stress of the situation seems to have hastened the death of two papal legates in March 1563 within several days of each other. Pius now appointed Cardinal Giovanni Morone, who had languished in prison under Paul IV, president of the council and endowed him with broad authority. Morone's first move was to travel to Innsbruck to convince Emperor

Ferdinand of the firm papal intention of reform also on the residency question. After the departure of Morone, Ferdinand remarked that 'our good Cardinal Morone will see to a good reform'. Meanwhile, at the Colloquy of Poissy in France, Catherine de Medici's efforts to reach a settlement between Catholics and Huguenots had failed, as had a subsequent Catholic military campaign to subdue the Huguenots, so that French Catholic leaders realized that they needed the support of Rome and the council. Now a contingent of French bishops led by the Cardinal of Lorraine arrived in Trent, and gradually showed sympathy for the papal position. With a personal letter, Pius also succeeded in convincing Philip II of his determination to foster reform.

A satisfactory compromise was now reached and the council's most severe crisis was in the end overcome. The decree on orders affirmed that a hierarchy existed in the church 'instituted by divine appointment', and it condemned the position that 'bishops who are elevated by the authority of the pope are not legitimate and true bishops, but a human fabrication'. In an accompanying decree on reform the council declared that bishops were bound to reside in their dioceses by 'divine command', without further elaborating on the nature of the obligation, and it explicitly applied this to the officials of the Roman curia including cardinals who were not dispensed from residence by virtue of their office. The council did allow, however, that 'Christian charity, pressing need, due obedience and the evident benefit of church or state sometimes insistently requires the absence of some', and it laid down regulations for such circumstances. In the end-result the Council of Trent never did establish a Catholic position on the role of the papacy in the church or its relationship to the bishops. This is surprising since the Protestants had launched a vigorous attack on the papacy. There was simply no adequate agreement at hand. This left the issue open for discussion at subsequent councils, and in fact Vatican I in 1870 asserted papal primacy while Vatican II in 1965 balanced this by laying out the role of the bishops in the government of the church. But developments at the end of, and in the wake of, Trent made it possible for the papacy to seize the initiative and so to emerge more clearly than ever as victor over the bishops.

A number of further doctrinal and disciplinary issues came up for treatment in the final period of the council. Picking up on the theme of the Eucharist from the previous period, the council affirmed the presence of Christ under each species, bread and wine, in Holy Communion, asserted the right of the church to limit Communion for the laity to the sacred bread, but left the decision whether to allow Communion under both species or not, up to the pope. In 1564, at the urging of the emperor and the duke of Bavaria, Pius IV did concede the chalice to the laity in areas of Central Europe. But Gregory XIII withdrew the concession in 1584 after many complaints that it only served to confuse the faithful. Taking the cup had become a Protestant symbol. The council responded to one of Luther's principal attacks when it declared that the Mass was truly a sacrifice. The decree on the sacramentality of Holy Orders also included one of the most far-reaching measures of the council when it stipulated that each diocese establish its own seminary for the education of its clergy, and a structure was laid out for their preparation for ministry. This was intended to remedy the shortcomings in the education and formation of the clergy which the council recognized as a major source of the Reformation.

Provisions of the decree declaring the sacramentality of matrimony greatly influenced the life of the faithful. Prohibited for the future were the so-called clandestine marriages, which were often a source of confusion among the people. Henceforth, for a marriage to be valid in the eyes of the church, consent had to be exchanged before the pastor as the representative of the church along with two witnesses. Free consent of both parties was reasserted as essential to marriage; many of the conciliar fathers thought that parents unduly pressured their children in this regard. The council also reduced the impediments to marriage based on consanguinity or on spiritual relationships, that is, growing out of sponsorship at baptism or confirmation. The pastor was made responsible for determining whether consent was truly free and whether impediments were at hand. In addition each parish was now required – many had long done so – to keep an official register of marriages as well as of baptisms, the latter being necessary to check on spiritual relationships. So the pastor in each parish assumed a new form of record-keeping and became a bureaucratic agent.

A number of reform decrees had emanated by now from the council, calling for residence of bishops and so indicting pluralism, requiring the foundation of seminaries, and regulating marriage. Cardinal Morone still foresaw a general reform decree that would deal with many further issues. Initially, this was intended to be a reform of princes as well, that would regulate the relationship between the church and princes or governments, to protect church interests such as benefit of clergy. But the various Catholic states opposed this initiative with the result that the council never expressed itself on church–state issues, nor did it attempt to touch the privileges of princes with regard to appointment to ecclesiastical offices. There could be no far-reaching reform without the support of the princes, the conciliar fathers realized, and they did not want to forfeit this. State and church needed to cooperate.

The council issued the first of two wide-ranging reform decrees prepared under Morone's guidance on 11 November 1563. Its essential thrust again was to strengthen the position of the bishop in his diocese against restrictions from within and without the diocese. The bishop remained the first focus of reform. Norms for the appointment of a bishop were set out, which once again portrayed him as a pastor and teacher of his people and not as a hierarchical ruler. Provincial councils or meetings of the bishops of an ecclesiastical province under the leadership of the archbishop were to be held every three years, and diocesan synods or meetings of the principal clergy of the diocese were to take place annually. The bishop was also to visit the parishes of his diocese on a regular basis. He was made responsible for determining those to be ordained within his diocese, and he received increased authority over corporations or officials within the diocese such as chapters or archdeacons as well as, in pastoral matters and especially in the hearing of confessions, over exempt religious orders. But many provisions here were fuzzy and subsequently led to conflict and litigation. Furthermore, it was made more difficult to appeal from episcopal courts to Rome.

Not only were bishops to preach regularly in their churches, but pastors of parishes were to do the same. Laity were to attend their parish churches to hear the word of God; indeed, the council emphasized the parish as an essential unit of the diocese and concentrated its attention on the parish priest. In the decree on Holy Orders the fathers had inserted a section formulating guidelines for the formation and education of the diocesan clergy and requiring that each bishop establish a seminary in his diocese. This may have been the most significant reform measure taken by the council. Though the council also passed a decree on the reform of life in religious orders several weeks later, this decree assumed nowhere near the importance of the measures taken regarding bishops and parish priests, and it took little cognizance of the changes introduced by the new religious orders and congregations.

News reached Trent on 30 November 1563, when the fathers were already looking to end the council, that the pope had suffered a stroke and seemed to be near death. His demise would mean a new pope, whose attitude towards the council was unpredictable. So the fathers hastened to complete their task. They passed decrees on religious images, on the veneration of saints and relics, on purgatory, and on indulgences, in which they attempted to root out abuses while essentially affirming proper Catholic belief and practice. The council then issued a final reform decree in which it attempted to restrict the use of excommunication and other ecclesiastical censures, dealt with abuses in the system of benefices while recognizing legitimate rights of patronage, and summoned princes and rulers to support the measures taken by the council. Finally, at the conclusion of their session on 4 December, the fathers read and approved all the doctrinal decrees of the two earlier periods and then, significantly, requested the pope to confirm all the council's decrees, thus implicitly acknowledging his position. So the council came to an end amid a chorus of 'Te Deums'.

As its great historian Hubert Jedin asserted, the council's historical importance lay in two achievements. First, it drew a clear line between Catholic and Protestant teaching on most controverted issues and so clarified the situation for the faithful. This was a major step in Catholic confessionalism. Yet it neglected issues associated with ecclesiology and in particular the position of the papacy. Though many teachings were condemned as heretical, no heretics were mentioned by name, and in this sense a way to dialogue was left open. Secondly, the council marked a milestone of Catholic reform. Its decrees aimed not only at the elimination of abuses but at an updated pastoral approach that stressed the role of the bishop and the parish priest in the ministry of the church. They were to be pastors and effective preachers and catechists who lived among their people, not merely ecclesiastical officials. Yet the reform decrees of Trent did not fully encompass the Roman curia, so that the reform undertaken was not one 'in head as well as members' to the degree late medieval reformers had demanded. The religious orders, especially the new ones, who were to supply much of the resources for the Catholic Reform, received relatively little attention, and the new missionary efforts across the seas where Catholicism was rapidly expanding went virtually unnoticed. Implementation of conciliar decrees was another matter; that would require decades and even centuries.

The papacy immediately threw itself behind the implementation of the council. In doing so it succeeded in controlling the council's interpretation and augmenting its own status within the church. The result was

growing prestige and an increasing centralization in Rome which periodically came into conflict with a more episcopalist understanding of
the council. Three vigorous and highly competent personalities succeeded Pius IV in the chair of Peter: Pius V from 1565 to 1572; Gregory
XIII from 1572 to 1585; and Sixtus V from 1585 to 1590. By the end
of the century the moral stature and international political influence of
the papacy had climbed dramatically from the its nadir at the century's
opening.

In a secret consistory of cardinals of 26 January 1564, Pius IV, recovered
from his stroke, confirmed orally all the conciliar decrees. But because
of opposition in Rome the papal bull *Benedictus Deus*, which formally
approved the council's decrees, did not appear until 30 June, although
it was backdated to 26 January. Roman officials wanted to assure the
papacy the right of interpretation, and many of them also feared for
their own sources of revenue which were endangered by the conciliar
insistence on residence. Pius IV intended to implement the decrees
but wanted to keep the manner of doing so in his own hands. He
did not want to be seen as merely the executive organ of a legislature.
According to the bull, the right of interpretation was restricted to
the pope, and in August 1564 Pius established a new Roman Congregation of the Council for its interpretation. No-one was to publish
commentaries, glosses, scholia, or notes to the decrees without papal
authorization.

The closing months of the council had also seen the fathers entrust a
number of tasks to the pope, which further elevated his stature. The
Index of Forbidden Books issued by Paul IV had been obviously
unworkable, and so the council fathers undertook to prepare their own.
But unwilling to prolong the council for the sake of finishing the task,
they turned it over to the pope, and so there appeared in March 1564 a
somewhat less rigorous papal Index. At the behest of the council Pius
IV also issued a Tridentine Profession of Faith in November 1564,
which summarized the doctrinal decrees of Trent and included a
promise of obedience to the pope. This profession served as a response
to the Protestant confessions of faith and as a salient example of
Catholic confessionalism. All bishops, religious superiors, pastors, pro-
fessors, and candidates for academic degrees were required to subscribe
to it before entering upon their offices or receiving their degrees.

The council desired, too, a catechism to oppose the Protestant ones
and especially Luther's popular catechisms. The German Jesuit Peter
Canisius realized early on the need for a Catholic catechism. In 1555

he published the first edition of his *Summary of Christian Doctrine*, which was aimed first of all at university students, and in 1558 and 1566 he followed with catechisms for adolescents and then for children. These were to become the most popular Catholic catechisms, altogether undergoing more than 200 editions in various languages before the death of Canisius in 1597. But he was unable to secure any official conciliar approbation for his work either as the catechism of the council or as one approved by the council. Pius IV rather commissioned four theologians from Latin lands, who had all participated in the council, to prepare the *Roman Catechism*. Its intended audience was pastors rather than students, to serve them as a form of handbook for preaching and for the administration of the sacraments. When it appeared in 1566, endorsed by both the council and the new pope, Pius V, it was the most authoritiative Catholic catechism published until then. The tone of the *Roman Catechism* was more moderate than Canisius's, and in this sense more open to dialogue, as was the council itself. Its ordering of the material was not suggested by an anti-Protestant intent, as was Canisius's; it did not even mention indulgences and devoted little attention to Mary. Whereas Canisius's catechisms identified Christian with Catholic, the *Roman Catechism* spoke of the Christian people and Christendom in such a way as to comprise Protestants. But this tone was not to prevail.

Under Pius V in 1568 there was issued a new version of the Breviary or Divine Office, which was prayed daily by every Catholic cleric in major orders. Two years later there followed a new Roman Missal, which contained the order of Mass as it was to be celebrated throughout the liturgical year. The Missal restricted a certain flexibility in the service, such as the interpolation of prayers at certain junctures in the Mass. Both were imposed on all churches and religious orders without a tradition of 200 years to the contrary. Their appearance fostered further the tendency towards confessionalism as well as subordination to Rome. No changes were to be introduced into either without the permission of the Holy See.

A definite, general improvement in the quality of bishops eventually followed in the wake of Trent. Starting with the end of the sixteenth century, innumerable were the bishops who devoted themselves to their pastoral responsibilities and to the reform of their dioceses, independently of the manner of their appointment. Certainly not all bishops fitted this category, but that there took place a general rise in the quality of bishops is uncontestable, with France setting the tone by the later seventeenth century.

Numerous provincial councils and diocesan synods convened in the years following Trent, to translate the council's legislation into regional and local programmes. But there was a vast discrepancy in the conduct of councils and synods. In Germany provincial councils were rare; two important ones were held at Salzburg in 1569 and 1573. Yet neither a provincial nor a diocesan synod was ever held in Mainz. Triennial provincial councils or annual diocesan councils never became general features of church life. The papacy and the states sought to control provincial councils. Early provincial councils after Trent submitted their results to Rome for confirmation, in order to give them more authority. Rome then gradually introduced the requirement that provincial councils submit their decisions and decrees to the Congregation of the Council for approval, in the interests of a uniform policy throughout the church. Sixtus V formalized this requirement with a bull in 1588. Philip II of Spain urged the convocation of provincial councils immediately after Trent, and they were held in all the Spanish archbishoprics except Seville in 1565/6, but all were subject to careful oversight by a royal representative. Few were convened subsequently except in Catalonia. Perhaps 100 diocesan synods met in Castile in the wake of the council, also under tight royal control as the provincial councils had been. Conflicts among local interests, for example between archbishops and bishops, hindered the effectiveness of provincial councils and generated appeals to Rome, which in turn augmented Roman authority. The impetus towards councils and synods, then, clearly waned by the early seventeenth century, except in France where, after 1650, frequent synods became the norm in many dioceses providing the bishop with an opportunity to indicate policy and fostering a sense of identity among the diocesan clergy.

Episcopal visitations, or inspections, of parishes and other institutions of a diocese showed greater staying power as a procedure, and their many surviving documents remain a rich source for early modern church life. But here too there were vast differences in practice. The bishops of France and Italy stood out for their practice of visitation in the seventeenth century.

Despite the emphasis on bishops at Trent, they saw their authority diminished with respect to the papacy and to the secular power. The papacy firmly believed in the need for assistance from the secular power in the cause of reform and in the struggle against the Protestants, and frequently popes supported it against bishops.

Charles Borromeo, the saintly, austere, well-organized archbishop of Milan from 1565 until 1584, has long been recognized as the embodiment of the Tridentine reform bishop. More recently he has also come to represent an episcopalist interpretation of Trent that did not prevail. Having been raised to the cardinalate at the age of 22 by his uncle, Pius IV in 1560, Borromeo served in the curia during the last period of the council and conducted the papal correspondence with the legates in Trent. At first he sided with the curialists who saw in the council a threat to the papacy. But a profound conversion triggered by the death of his brother in November 1562 led to his ordination and a change of mind, whereby he saw in the diocesan bishop the foundation of the church and of Tridentine reform. This was the view he took with him when he made his formal entry into Milan on 23 September 1565, in archiepiscopal regalia rather than cardinal's robes, the first archbishop to reside there in 80 years.

Milan was then the most populous archdiocese in Italy, with more than 800,000 souls. Even prior to his formal entry Borromeo embarked on an ambitious programme of reform that resulted in tensions not only with the Spanish governor but also with the papacy as a result of his insistence on episcopal rights. Though ever loyal to Rome, he chaffed under increasing Roman supervision, especially under Gregory XIII. According to Borromeo, the task of Rome and the Roman agencies was to aid the bishops but not to meddle in the operation of dioceses. During his tenure he conducted 11 diocesan synods and six provincial councils. Pastors in every nook and valley of his jurisdiction experienced his visitation. The Jesuits, the Theatines, and the Ursulines all came to Milan at his behest, and he founded his own diocesan congregation of Oblates and fostered the catechetical efforts of the Confraternity of Christian Doctrine which dated back to the 1530s. Yet he kept the religious under his control, often at the expense of conflict with them.

Borromeo's active assertion of ecclesiastical rights also generated difficulties with the Spanish authority. Gregory XIII was more sensitive to the church's need for princely assistance, and the pope's failure enthusiastically to support him irritated Borromeo. After his Fourth Provincial Council in 1576 he dispatched the decrees to Rome, even though he was not canonically obligated to do so. Three years later he was still awaiting a supportive response from the curia. After his death Rome downplayed Borromeo's advocacy of episcopal rights, and eventually stipulated that when he was portrayed this was always to be in his cardinalatial rather than in his archiepiscopal robes. But his vigorous assertion of episcopal rights with regard to religious orders and Rome, if not the secular power, was to live on above all in France where his influence was quickly felt. One hundred copies of the *Acts of the Milanese Church*, a compendium of Borromeo's reform, were shipped to Lyons after their publication in 1582.

Pope Gregory XIII fostered and expanded the role of papal nuncios and so of the papacy in the work of reform; at the same time he was ready to make compromises with rulers, which benefited the papacy at the expense of bishops, for long-range goals of reform. His special concern was Germany, where the church was particularly weak and dependent on papal support. The Renaissance papacy had pioneered the practice of maintaining permanent representatives at the courts of Europe – one of the features of the growing state – and had always employed them for ecclesiastical as well as political purposes. Now they became active agents of reform, especially in Germany. Felician Ninguarda, who greatly abetted the efforts to implement the council in Germany, served as a roving nuncio in south Germany from 1569 to 1583, and eventually nunciatures exclusively for reform were established in Lucerne (1579), Graz (1580), and Cologne (1584). In addition, the German Congregation in Rome, founded under Pius V, was most active during the pontificate of Gregory; its strategy continued the council's: create good bishops and work from the top down.

Two actions of Gregory in 1583 showed his willingness to favour the secular authority and to bend the rules of Trent for the greater good. Here it is well to recall too that in Germany nearly all bishops were prince–bishops, that is, they held secular as well as ecclesiastical authority, a situation Trent had ignored. That year the church in Germany once again withstood Protestant efforts to secularize the crucial archbishopric of Cologne. This required the combined military efforts of the pope, Spain, and Bavaria. In order to preserve and develop this Catholic outpost on the Rhine the pope encouraged the election to the archbishopric of the young, and unqualified, Ernest of Bavaria. Already as a 12-year-old in 1566 he had become Prince–Bishop of Freising in south Germany, and subsequently Prince–Bishop of Liège and Hildesheim; later in 1585 he would become Prince–Bishop of Münster in Westphalia. So Gregory fostered the interests of the Bavarian Wittelsbachs in order simultaneously to create a bulwark of reform in northwest Germany. Though Ernest himself was not an effective bishop, his nephew Ferdinand, who succeeded him in most of the sees in 1612 and added Paderborn, would show himself an active reformer.

That same year, 1583, Gregory concluded a concordat with Duke William of Bavaria which conceded to the duke rights to tax the clergy, control many ecclesiastical appointments, and oversee the administration of extensive church property, measures which did not sit well with the local bishops. Pope and ruler cooperated over the heads of the bishops, prince-bishops in this case. Furthermore, pluralism was to become frequent in Germany, particularly in favour of the politically potent Houses of Habsburg and Wittelsbach, who supplied ecclesiastical princes able to stabilize a shaky Catholicism. Their part in Catholic Reform and Counter Reformation was highly significant. Ordinarily, the actual pastoral work was committed to the responsibility of an auxiliary bishop.

Sixtus V, the former Franciscan who occupied the See of Peter from 1585 to 1590, continued to foster the centralization of the church, especially by issuing new regulations for the periodic visits to Rome of bishops from across the world and by reorganizing the Roman curia. Depending upon the distance from Rome, bishops were expected to travel thither on a regular basis, from every three years for Italian bishops to every 10 years for those across the seas, and to bring with them a report on the state of their dioceses. This measure came increasingly to be observed in practice after the turn of the century, though bishops often enough sent proxies in their place. In addition, through the nuncios and with the help of a reorganized informative process on the candidates, the papacy took a more active part in the appointment of bishops.

More important perhaps was the restructuring of the curia under Sixtus. The demands on it had long since outgrown the administrative capacity inherited from the late Middle Ages, and the popes had turned increasingly to committees of cardinals, temporary or permanent, to handle curial business. Sixtus now established a structure of 15 papal congregations or ministries headed by cardinals, six for the government of the Papal States and nine for the government of the universal church. The nine included the Congregations of the Inquisition, the Index, the Council, and Bishops, all of which already existed, as well as Congregations for Regulars or Religious, for the Consistory of Cardinals, for the *Signatura Gratiae*, which granted papal dispensations, for Rites, and for the Vatican Printing Press, which Sixtus created to give the papacy its own publication organ. Later, in 1622, the Congregation for the Propagation of the Faith followed, to oversee and coordinate missionary efforts overseas. All these congregations were placed directly under the pope.

This reorganization of the curia resulted in the diminution of the role of the College of Cardinals in the government of the church as well as of the Papal States. The cardinals saw their quasi-constitutional position as an international representative body or ecclesiastical senate ended, so capping a development initiated by Nicholas V (1447–55). Thus from the mid-fifteenth century onwards there was a continuity of direction towards a papal monarchy, not only with respect to the bishops as a collectivity but also with respect to the College of Cardinals. The Council of Constance had limited the number of the college to 24; since then the number had grown and Sixtus now increased it to 70, thus reducing the importance of the individual cardinal. Rather than councillors of the pope, who met with him regularly in consistory, they became papal bureaucrats, with decision-making fixed more than ever in the pope himself. Sixtus's successor Clement VIII (1592–1605) refused to discuss important issues of church government with the cardinals in consistories, and turned instead to his own close advisers. After 1600 consistories declined from two or three a week to twice a month. Along with the gradual numerical increase in cardinals, there had taken place a progressive Italianization of the college.

The reform of the Roman curia that late medieval critics and many fathers at Trent called for did not come to pass. This does not mean there were no changes for the better. There were. At least from Paul IV on, the style of life of popes and cardinals in Rome underwent a change. Piety was definitely in vogue. If most cardinals and Roman ecclesiastics did not display the personal sanctity of the Jesuit Robert Bellarmine, who served as a cardinal from 1599 until his death in 1621, or of the church historian and disciple of Philip Neri, 'the Apostle of Rome' (1515–95), the Oratorian Cesare Baronius, who served as a cardinal from 1596 until his death in 1607, much more was now expected of them. Pluralism among members of the curia was greatly reduced. Yet with the underlying continuity of structural development from the mid-fifteenth century through the Reformation period towards a more monarchical papacy, came the attendant trappings of a court. Nor should we forget that the pope also ruled a principality, a situation which will be covered more fully in the next chapter. Residence requirements were often waived for papal officials, for example, nuncios who were bishops. The newly created Cardinal Bellarmine, in a paper prepared for Clement VIII in 1600, complained of the failure to implement Trent's reforms with members of the curia, including cardinals, especially with regard to residence.

Nepotism and patronage persisted, reinforced by the widespread social conviction that *pietas* or loyalty to one's family required that the cleric too advance his family's interest. Following his visit to Rome in 1580, the French essayist Michel de Montaigne noted in his *Travel Journal* that Gregory XIII 'gives advancement to his relations without any prejudice to the rights of the Church', and he saw no abuse.[1] Yet, at the expense of the church, funds on a large scale found their way into the coffers of members of the papal family, their clients, and other members of the curia, through outright gifts, through pensions, through the bestowal of non-ecclesiastical offices like commander of the Castel Sant'Angelo, which were stepping stones to church positions. Prominent offenders in this regard were Paul V (1605–21), who saw to the elevation of the Borghese from urban patricians in Rome to one of the leading Italian aristocratic, landowning, families, and Urban VIII (1623–44), who at the end of his life suffered severe pangs of remorse for his lavish gifts to his Barberini family. His nephew Francesco alone received 63 million scudi. Members of patrician and aristocratic Italian families purchased as investments offices in the curia, some of which were sinecures – the sale of offices was a principal means of raising papal revenue – and with a view to rising to the cardinalate and pos- sibly to the papacy itself. The result was a new Roman aristocracy dependent upon papal beneficence. Others sought at the papal court the opportunity for more modest social and economic advance. Thus the papacy took on features typical of the seventeenth-century European court, so exhibiting its consonance with the times. Despite attempts of other popes to do so, only at the end of the century, in 1692, did Innocent XII take effective measures against nepotism.

The popes of the late sixteenth and seventeenth centuries were determined to assert Rome's dignity as the centre of Christendom, the site of the martyrdom of Peter and Paul, and the repository of the classical heritage. To this end, in addition to a programme of urban renewal unlike anything seen in Europe up to that time, they like their Renaissance predecessors presided over a lavish patronage of the arts that made Rome the artistic centre of Europe into the eighteenth cen- tury. In Rome there came to birth around 1600 the vibrant, dramatic, and often monumental Baroque style that was suited to express the élan of a revived Catholicism. The new Basilica of St Peter's exemplifies this Baroque, as well as the papacy's use of the arts in its service. Julius II had laid the cornerstone for the new St Peter's back in 1506, and work had continued on it throughout the sixteenth century. Michelangelo took over as chief architect in 1546, agreeing to work without pay. His death in 1564 prevented him from glimpsing the finished dome which he had designed and which was set in place in 1590. Paul V decided in 1605, to change the form of the church from a Greek to a Latin cross and so to add an extended nave, in order to accommodate the crowds that streamed to papal services. St Peter's was now intended to be the grandest church in Christendom. Urban VIII consecrated it in 1626, and then commissioned Gian Lorenzo Bernini, the artistic genius of the age, to oversee the completion of the interior. Three of his magnificent creations there were the baldachin with the twisted bronze columns over the main papal altar, the dramatic statue of the centurion Longinus as he cried out 'Truly thou art the Son of God' after the death of Christ, and the alleged Chair of Peter that appeared to be suspended in mid-air in the apse held up only by the power of the Holy Spirit. In 1666, then, Bernini completed the colonnade that reaches out from St Peter's to surround the square and symbolically to embrace the world.

One institution deserves further attention, the Roman Inquisition, which was also an agent of confessionalism and of centralization of church government. Generally speaking the Inquisition was an ecclesiastical court for the discovery and prosecution of heresy. The principal aim was pastoral; that is, to lead the accused to repentance and to confession, and to protect others from the danger that heresy represented to their salvation. Four different Inquisitions stand out. The first was the Medieval Inquisition, which was originally established by the papacy in the thirteenth century to deal with the threat posed by the Albigensian heresy in southern France. The second was the Spanish Inquisition set up by papal authority on the initiative of Ferdinand and Isabella in 1478, whose initial concern was the reversion of *Conversos* or *Moriscos* to their old religious practices. The third Inquisition, the Portuguese, was created in 1536, by papal authority. Like the Spanish, it came under the control of the monarchy and took *Conversos* to be its chief concern. The fourth Inquisition was the Roman which, as we have seen, amounted to a reorganization of the Medieval Inquisition by Paul III in 1542, to counter the Protestant threat. It was listed first among the papal congregations in the curial reorganization of 1588. Originally, the Roman Inquisition was also to regulate the publication and censorship of books, but Pius V in 1571 established a separate Congregation of the Index to exercise this function.

The Roman as well as the Portuguese and Spanish Inquisitions dealt initially only with heretics. The Spanish Jesuit theologian Francis Suarez defined them in classic fashion in 1621 as those who professed to be Christian yet clung wilfully and obstinately to doctrines contrary to those of the Catholic Church. So heretics were clearly distinguished from Jews, Muslims, and other non-believers like the American Indians, who had never accepted Christianity and could not be forced to accept it, precisely because faith had to be a free act. A heretic was a baptized person who had renounced his baptismal commitment and betrayed the faith he once possessed. Suarez extended the term to second- or third-generation Protestants once they turned down the opportunity to learn about Catholicism, even though some Catholic theologians such as the Belgian Jean Vermeulen (Joannes Molanus), applying to them principles invoked for toleration of the Jews by Thomas Aquinas, had argued three decades earlier for their toleration. For Suarez force was a licit and suitable means to persuade heretics to abjure, and the death penalty was legitimate for obstinate heretics who refused to return to the faith. His position becomes more intelligible if we consider his assumption that, for eternal salvation, profession of the Catholic faith was necessary, and if we remember that for him the church had a responsibility for heretics by virtue of their baptism that it did not have for non-believers whose fate could be left to the mercy of God. Corporal and social punishments, Suarez maintained, provided an example and a deterrent to others and, apart from the death penalty, were meant to lead to correction and conversion of the heretic. Suarez argued tortuously that corporal punishment did not diminish the freedom of the heretic in any essential way, an argument in sharp contrast to his efforts to protect the freedom of Indians then being evangelized by Spanish missionaries. In any event, better that heretics were brought to faith by such methods than not at all. Sometimes, he admitted, there were false conversions, but they could be permitted in light of the greater evil to be avoided.

The original plan for the Roman Inquisition called for a network of courts throughout Christendom with its centre in Rome. They would proceed against heretics and those suspected of heresy without need of the local bishop's permission. Rome considered the courts of the Inquisition superior to either episcopal or secular courts. But Spain and Portugal already had their Inquisition, and France and other Catholic states would not permit it to function in their territories. Some Italian states greatly restricted its activity; Venice, for example, insisted on the presence of lay representatives in the court in addition to the Dominican and Franciscan friars who usually constituted it. Eventually the Roman Inquisition became a series of regional courts in Italy with a central or supreme court in Rome made up of the cardinals of the congregation. But if its ability to implement its decisions was limited to areas of Italy, these decisions, as well as those of the companion Congregation of the Index, were held by Rome to be normative for the whole church, as are the decisions of the Congregation for the Doctrine of the Faith, the successor of the Inquisition, up to the present day.

Generally speaking, courts of the Inquisition in Italy were most active in the two decades on each side of 1600, after which the number of trials slackened off considerably. Furthermore, by the 1580s heresy in the form of Protestantism had ceased to be a major concern, and a broad, undefined category, 'illicit magic', and a host of other deviations more moral than theological became the chief objects of their attention. Assisting the regional judges were *vicari*, officials who represented the court in towns and villages beyond the regional seat; in 1622 there were 43 for the court in Modena. The Roman Inquisition never staged the spectacular, outdoor *autos-da-fé* that were popular in Spain for the reconciliation and punishment of heretics, and that occasionally could last for two to three days and conclude 150 to 200 cases.

Recent research has shown that, contrary to long-accepted myths, the Roman Inquisition followed careful legal procedures and was more respectful of suspects' rights than most other contemporary courts. Anonymous denunciations were not allowed. Clear and evident proof or a confession was required for conviction, and two witnesses sufficed for proof. A defendant was not supposed to know the names of his accusers because of the very real fear of retaliation by the defendant's family or friends, but this protection of the accuser's identity seems to have frequently broken down in practice. The defendant was guaranteed a defence lawyer, a right recognized in England only in 1836. Torture was occasionally employed – in two to three per cent of the cases in Venice – but only under strictly delineated circumstances when there was solid evidence that the defendant was lying. Confessions made under torture then had to be corroborated subsequently in order to be valid. Only recently have scholars learned that many sentences were not to be taken literally; 'perpetual imprisonment' often meant, for example, three years. Arrests were made only after careful investigation. Figures indicate that there were roughly 100 executions by the Inquisition in Rome between 1542 and 1761, the most famous perhaps being the burning at the stake of Giordano Bruno on the Campo dei Fiori in 1600. The majority of penances were light, such as public abjuration before the church on Sunday or the regular saying of prayers. All but the most ordinary cases were subjected to the scrutiny of the cardinal inquisitors in Rome who, for example, determined upon leniency for a provincial grocer accused of denying the immortality of the soul because he seemed to have come to this opinion 'through ignorance and passion and ... had not learned it consciously from others'.

The most harmful effects of the Roman Inquisition seem to have been the fear it generated because of the secrecy of its proceedings and the intimidation of intellectual life that it, along with the Index, provoked. The extent of both of these is hard to measure and remains controversial, especially since the main archives of the Roman congregation have remained closed for practical purposes until very recently. Also in question still is the degree to which the three early modern Inquisitions contributed to the disciplining of the populace as increasingly in the later sixteenth century they turned away from the prosecution of strict heresy – whether of *Conversos* or *Moriscos* in Spain and Portugal, or Protestants in Italy – to moral conduct and alleged magical practices.

4

THE CHURCH, THE STATES, AND RELIGIOUS WARS

The gradual emergence of the states and the decline of the Christian commonwealth or *respublica christiana* was a feature of late medieval and early modern Europe which the church, and especially the papacy, had to confront. The challenge of the states to the papacy dated from at least the fourteenth century, and it grew more intense as it became intertwined with conciliarism and Italian politics. The sixteenth-century papacy, in light of European expansion across the seas along with the Reformation, reaffirmed its universalist claims, and theologians pursued a new synthesis around the term 'the indirect power of the pope', that would, it was hoped, integrate papal claims with the advance of the state. The church and the papacy accepted the new world of the sovereign states, and for a time the papacy succeeded in operating within it, only to be excluded in 1648 at the Peace of Westphalia largely because of its own policy. By that time the wars of religion were coming to an end.

Throughout the whole period from the mid-fifteenth through the seventeenth century states increased control of religion within their borders, especially in the three key areas of ecclesiastical appointments, taxation, and jurisdiction. Rulers also intervened increasingly in issues of clerical reform and popular christianization, often enough out of a sense of responsibility as Christian princes in the absence of action by the church. Initially, the papacy acquiesced in these developments because of its desire to secure princely support against conciliarism, and it negotiated concordats with a number of states prior to the Reformation with a view to regulating church–government relations.

70

These directions then became more pronounced under the pressure of the Reformation. Only after its outbreak and the initial formation of confessions can we properly speak of the confessionalization of the state and of society. Princes often took the lead in the fight against heresy, issuing measures to prevent its spread into their lands and taking up arms to defend against it. Many were the conflicts between papacy and states over issues of competence, but the papacy often welcomed princely incursions into religious matters, aware as it was of its dependence on governments in the struggle against Protestantism both within states and internationally, and in the mounting of missionary initiatives overseas. The increasing assumption of a religious role by the state contributed to the state's consolidation; the state was confessionalized and the confession was politicized. A result in the long run was the decline of the papacy and the coming of the state churches of the Old Regime. The direction was the same in the Protestant states, especially in the German territories and in England where government acquired an even stronger hold on the church. In Catholic lands the bond with Rome, though occasionally stretched to the limit, preserved the church from becoming fully subordinate to the state. Confessionalization also meant that many political and social conflicts were intertwined with religion. Hence the wars in which religion was a significant, though not always the dominant, issue.

The first state the papacy had to deal with was the Papal States, a medium-sized state which straddled central Italy. It exhibited a peculiar admixture of spiritual and temporal power in the papal ruler. Here there was a rough continuity of movement from Nicholas V through Urban VIII, from Renaissance through Catholic Reform into the seventeenth century, towards the consolidation of the Papal States as an absolute principality and the embellishment of Rome as residence of the pope. So the Papal States shared in the general evolution of the modern state, in some respects leading the way. Many of the Reformers' complaints about the secularization of the papacy were rooted in this development of the Papal States rather than in individual abuses. There were two basic reasons for the papal policy of consolidation. One was the recognition that the Papal States had to play a part in the search for a balance of power on the Italian Peninsula; for this an effective government apparatus as well as an army was necessary. The second reason for consolidation was the realization that after widespread dismantling of the papal financial system developed at Avignon, and with the rising reluctance of the European states to allow funds to flow to Rome, the papacy needed to draw much more on the Papal States for its revenue. Only a well-organized state could meet these demands. The loss of the Protestant states further diminished income. Whereas previously revenue from the universal church supported the Papal States, by 1600 three-fourths of papal income came from the Papal States themselves. Warfare and construction costs in Rome demanded funds. From the least-taxed Italian state in 1500, the Papal States became perhaps the most heavily taxed by 1600. Yet substantial revenue still flowed to Rome through papal claims on ecclesiastical lands in Italy and in Spain.

Two landmarks in the consolidation of the Papal States stood at the beginning and the end of the sixteenth century: the reconquest of Bologna by Julius II in 1506 and the recovery of Ferrara under Clement VIII in 1598. Gradually a recalcitrant nobility was tamed and, with less success, measures were taken to end the banditry endemic in regions of the Papal States. The reduction of the role of the cardinals and the reorganization of the Roman congregations under Sixtus V contributed to the growth of an absolute principality just as it did to the centralization of authority in the church. The cardinal-nephew and/or secretary of state assumed direction of foreign affairs, and the camerlengo was entrusted with the administration of the Papal States themselves. A bureaucratic reorganization put cardinal-legates – usually represented in the provinces by vice-legates – in charge of the provinces, and papal governors or *podestà* were installed in the cities and towns, thus greatly reducing municipal self-government. By 1600, according to Jean Delumeau, 'the popes disposed of a state that administratively was the equal, if not the superior, of any other state in Europe'.

Its principal weakness lay in the relative neglect of social and economic growth, and this explains its failure to evolve into an effective modern principality. There emerged no merchant middle class, nor a civil servant middle class because, as we shall see, all major administrative positions came into the hands of clerics. Nor did nepotism by any means die out. The Barberini Pope Urban VIII practised it as energetically as any pope of the Renaissance, and at the end of his pontificate he engaged the Papal States in a disastrous and futile war in order to secure the small principality of Castro for his family. An additional drain on funds was the necessity of keeping the ecclesiastical and secular aristocracy happy with gifts and pensions.

Further anomalies characterized the Papal States. There took place here the same expansion of government authority at the expense of the church as elsewhere. As a uniform law took effect, it seriously infringed on canon law and ecclesiastical immunity. Government officials usually held the upper hand over church functionaries. Archbishop Gabriele Paleotti of Bologna, a staunch advocate like Borromeo of Tridentine reform, complained bitterly of the papal governor's interference in his dispute with a cathedral canon who refused to carry out his obligations, and again of the cardinal legate's prosecution of priests accused of banditry without any reference to ecclesiastical jurisdiction. In a letter to Borromeo in 1581, during the papacy of Gregory XIII, he lamented that he was being reduced to a bishop with mitre but no crosier. One reason for the intense clericalization of the Papal States' bureaucracy seems to have been to obviate the charge from other European courts that in the Papal States themselves clerics were subordinate to laymen.

Another feature of the growth of the Papal States was the development starting in the late fifteenth century of a diplomatic corps, which was later greatly enhanced by Gregory XIII, as we have seen. Popes preferred, even in ecclesiastical matters, to deal with princes through the nuncios, who initially were more officials of state than church, rather than through the local bishop or clerical assembly. So the papacy regulated ecclesiastical affairs through concordats over the heads of the local churches.

First England in the fourteenth century during the Avignon Papacy, and then Sicily, France, Castile, and Naples in the fifteenth required a governmental *placet* or approval before a papal document could be published in their realms. Fourteenth-century parliamentary decrees in England restricted appeals to Rome, and other legislation limited payments to Rome as well as papal provisions for English benefices. In one respect the eventual break with Rome in 1534 was merely a further step in this development, a fact clouded by the general agreement between Rome and the usually weak English kings during the fifteenth century.

In France the Pragmatic Sanction of Bourges was issued in 1438 by Charles VII with the vigorous support of the University of Paris and the *parlements*. It laid the foundation of the Gallicanism of the Old Regime, which was characterized by insistence on the liberties of the French Church *vis-à-vis* Rome. This measure asserted the conciliarist position that a general council was superior to the pope, and it greatly restricted the payment of taxes to Rome, as well as judicial appeals. In addition, it limited Roman influence on ecclesiastical appointments while asserting the rights of electors and patrons in filling benefices. Subsequent relations between the papacy and France, especially after the French invasion of Italy in 1494, were coloured by developments in the Peninsula. The French king was not above using the threat of a council to intimidate the pope, as when Louis XII supported an abortive council summoned for Pisa in 1511.

Finally, in 1516, Pope Leo X and the young French king, Francis I, signed the Concordat of Bologna which served as a bulwark against the movement that erupted in Germany the following year and regulated relations between the papacy and France until the French Revolution. It exemplified the procedure whereby pope and prince arrived at an agreement apart from the local church. For his part, the pope secured the formal renunciation from France of the conciliarist position expressed in the Pragmatic Sanction of Bourges, and so warded off the threat of a French schism; royal concessions here were not congenial either to the University of Paris or to the *parlementaires*, the traditional supports of Gallicanism. Nor was the king's yielding on the payment of annates to Rome, which were maintained at a time when the papacy suffered financial need. The crown, for its part, was granted the right of nomination to all the major benefices in France, including 93 bishoprics and 527 abbeys, in addition to its control of many lesser benefices by virtue of practice or privilege. To be sure, the pope retained the right to refuse appointment to nominees who failed to meet certain criteria of age, education, and conduct, but still the concordat endowed the king with extensive control over the French Church. The French lawyer Pierre Pithou was to write in 1594 that 'the king, in practice, is more the head of the church in France than the pope'. In the course of the seventeenth century the French kings, especially Louis XIV, tightened their control of the church, and the French Church asserted its position *vis-à-vis* Rome most aggressively in the Four Gallican Articles issued by the Assembly of the Clergy in 1682.

A similar situation obtained in Spain. The *Patronato Real* or royal patronage of the Spanish Church, as well as other features of the monarchy's control of religion, had roots in the long Reconquest and reached a critical stage under the 'Catholic Kings' Ferdinand and Isabella. The Inquisition came into existence in 1478, and it functioned in virtual independence from Rome. That same year the rulers convoked a Council at Seville that in a later missive to Rome insisted that the crown required control of all the major benefices of the country for political reasons: the political lordship of ecclesiastics, their social influence, and the often precarious situation of the church lands on the frontier. Sixtus IV did not accept this argument in principle, but he yielded in fact, appointing to office the monarchs' candidates. Only in 1523, during the reign of the Habsburg Charles V, did the crown secure a settlement similar to the concordat with France, conceding it the right of presentation to all the major churches in Spain. Meanwhile, Julius II in 1508 had granted the *Patronato Real de las Indias* to the crown, which established nearly complete royal control over the church in the Spanish New World while at the same time requiring the crown to assume the responsibility for the financial support of the church in the Indies. A later amendment gave the crown the right of veto over foreign missionaries to be sent across the seas.

Though technically, as a result of agreements made among the Spanish Church, the papacy, and the crown, the church in Spain remained exempt from taxation, in reality, by the latter part of the reign of Philip II it provided approximately 20 per cent of the royal revenue. The principal sources of this income were what came to be called the 'Three Graces'. The first was the *cruzada*, initially a tax on the faithful approved by the papacy in the fifteenth century to help finance the Reconquest and subsequent campaigns against the Turks. By the middle of the reign of Charles V, this had lost its emergency character and become a standard triennial imposition. The second tax, the *subsidio*, was paid regularly on nearly all church income, and in 1567, with the approval of Pius V, a third tax, the *excusado*, came to be levied on each parish to help pay for the war in the Netherlands. The acting Archbishop of Toledo complained to the king in 1574 that Philip took for the crown more than half the church's income, and in this respect he was no better than Lutheran princes. Regarding the immunity of the clergy, royal courts early on exercised jurisdiction over ecclesiastics in civil matters, and in other matters the crown oversaw the church courts. In 1572 the government declared null and void all appeals to Rome in ecclesiastical cases and, of course, the Inquisition remained all-powerful in its jurisdiction.

In Germany there was to be no national church as in France or Spain, but rather a number of territorial churches. Only in the eighteenth century, after the storm of the Reformation had passed over, did there emerge consciousness of an Imperial Church or *Reichskirche* founded on the emperor and the peculiar German institution of the prince–(arch)bishoprics where the ecclesiastical princes possessed secular as well as spiritual authority. The Concordat of Vienna between the papacy and Emperor Frederick III in 1448 was fundamental for the later constitutional structure of the church in Germany. It stipulated that the election of the imperial prince–(arch)bishops would continue to be in the hands of the cathedral chapters, though ultimately subject to papal veto should the candidate not meet certain criteria. This confirmed for the German chapters a competence which most chapters elsewhere had lost either to pope or ruler. By virtue of the concordat the papacy also retained the right to appoint to a number of German benefices in the uneven or so-called 'papal months', and to collect levies, especially the annates. On the eve of the Reformation, proportionately more funds flowed to Rome from Germany than from France or Spain, a situation of which the Germans were aware.

German secular princes, on the other hand, acquired considerable control over the church in their territories well before the Reformation, often on condition they abandon conciliarism. The same process was at work in many imperial cities. By the Concordat of Vienna itself Emperor Frederick secured the right of appointment to six bishoprics in his hereditary lands, as well as to nearly 100 other benefices. The right to visit and reform most of the monasteries in the same area was also his as a result of the agreement. In a concordat with the Hohenzollern Elector of Brandenburg in 1447, Nicholas V conceded the right of appointment to the three bishoprics Brandenburg, Havelberg, and Lebus, as well as to a number of canonries. In the Saxon lands the dukes acquired similar rights, and the Duke of Cleves considered himself 'pope' in his lands where he restricted ecclesiastical jurisdiction and clerical immunity while pursuing a policy of monastic reform. Luther's appeal in his *Address to the Ruling Class of the German Nation* that the emperor and princes undertake the reform of the church, inasmuch as church authorities failed to act, was in this tradition.

The Peace of Augsburg of 1555, with its principle 'whose the region, his the religion', assigned to the German secular rulers the responsibility for the regulation of religion in their territories. The papacy neither sanctioned nor formally disapproved of the Peace, but it did urge the German Catholic princes to take advantage of the legal situation to reform and consolidate Catholicism in their lands. In Protestant lands the church came even more under the control of the state. Generally speaking, Catholic rulers did not attempt to tamper with matters of dogma or belief as did Protestant princes.

Increasingly in the late Middle Ages princes intervened in matters of religious discipline, with a view to fostering the welfare of their subjects of which the primary element was their advancement in virtue and in religion. Contemporary mirrors of princes stressed the responsibility of the prince for the salvation of his subjects. Once the Reformation broke out, the prince's obligation to protect and advance religion included more prominently the duty to protect his people from heresy. This was true of Protestant as well as Catholic rulers, both of whom assumed increasing responsibility for ecclesiastical discipline. Calvinist authorities were legendary in their efforts to impose a godly life on their fellows. In 1598, the first year of his reign, Duke Maximilian of Bavaria issued a Law for Morality and Religion. Among other things it directed the people to receive the obligatory Easter Communion, to attend church regularly, and to kneel and pray at least one 'Our Father' and one 'Hail Mary' for the deliverance of Christendom from the Turkish danger when the bell rang daily reminding them to do so. Those guilty of cursing were liable to penalties as severe as the amputation of a limb. Crossing the border to attend Protestant services or to get married before a Protestant pastor was strictly prohibited. Another abuse singled out was the retention of concubines by priests. Such legislation was typical in German territories, both Catholic and Protestant, in the sixteenth century. Princes were as instrumental in fostering religion as popes and bishops.

Certainly rulers profited from intensified involvement in church affairs. It enhanced their power and authority, expanded their jurisdiction, and facilitated access to the resources of the church. They gained not only financially but in manpower too when clergy came to function as civil officials, for example, in the keeping of registers as required by the Council of Trent. Princes also benefited in terms of a religiously unified, loyal population, with a clearer identity and a greater degree of discipline. Machiavelli pointed out the importance of unity of religion for the élan of a state, while disdaining Christianity as this religion. Contemporaries realized the value of this unity, the Spaniards in the later sixteenth century attributing their relative freedom from civil war to the absence of heresy. In Germany, where there was basically one language, religion came to serve even more as a source of territorial identity, and certainly a predominant element in holding together the evolving multi-ethnic, multi-lingual Habsburg Monarchy in Central Europe was Catholicism. Confessionalization in this form advanced the state-building process.

Yet it would be a serious mistake to see in princes' desires to foster and advance religion merely the pursuit of political advantage, or to smile cynically when they claimed to recognize an overlap of their obligation as Christian princes with their political advantage. Here one must look at each individual case, Protestant or Catholic. Many princes acted out of religious conviction. There existed, in fact, a whole literature arguing the coincidence of princely obligation, and especially the duty to foster religion, with political advantage. Perhaps most influential in this genre was the *Reason of State* of the Italian Giovanni Botero, first published in 1589 and probably the most widely circulated book on state-building in the first half of the seventeenth century. The good and the useful went hand in hand; this was a Catholic attitude typical of the period, as we shall see later.

Despite its weakened position *vis-à-vis* the emerging European states, the papacy maintained its universalist claims in the temporal as well as in the spiritual order. One medieval tradition, perhaps best represented by the thirteenth-century canonist Cardinal Hostiensis and the four-teenth-century Pope Boniface VIII, held that all authority, temporal as well as spiritual, proceeded from Christ in the form of the two swords or the keys that he handed over to Peter, his vicar, who in turn passed them on to his successors, the popes. Spiritual and temporal authority were distinct, but they were both possessed by the pope, who in turn was the source of the authority of temporal rulers. By virtue of this tradition, for example, Pope Nicholas V in 1455 conferred on the Portuguese crown rule over areas of Africa as their ships pushed further down its west coast. Alexander VI acted in the same spirit when in 1493 he bestowed on the Catholic Monarchs rule over the lands to the west that had been discovered and would be occupied in their name, with the obligation of christianizing the native peoples. By later granting the *Patronato* to the Spaniards, and the analogous *Padroado* to the Portuguese, the papacy effectively limited its own reach with respect to intervention in these areas.

Yet there was another, more realistic, medieval tradition associated with Thomas Aquinas that was to have a greater impact on the relationship between church and governments in the early modern period. For Aquinas, following Aristotle, the state had its own proper end based in human nature, which was the common good or temporal happiness of the community; in pursuing this goal the state was autonomous. But this temporal happiness was ordained to the further transcendent happiness of eternal life, which was the goal of the church. A ruler's obligation was to lead his people towards both goals. Should he govern so as to obstruct the attainment of the spiritual goal, the church might intervene in the ruler's affairs to set matters aright. Here was the root of what came to be called 'the indirect power of the papacy in temporal matters'.

Furthermore, Aquinas distinguished between Muslims and other gentiles or non-believers. The former, as a group, had explicitly rejected faith in Christ, and they had seized territory from Christians, for the reconquest of which Christians were entitled to make war. Hence the legitimacy of the Crusades. But as contacts with Asia evolved, and then as the Iberians first ventured to the Atlantic islands in the fourteenth century and eventually across the Atlantic, a new type of nonbeliever became increasingly familiar, who knew nothing of Christ and who had not seized Christian territory. The first theologian to deal with this issue systematically was the Italian Dominican Thomas De Vio, Cardinal Cajetan. He argued that it was legitimate to wage war against the Muslims only because of their seizure of Christian territory, not because of their unbelief. As to other non-believers, they retained their natural rights and neither king nor pope was allowed to attack them with a view to securing temporal authority over them.

But the thinker chiefly responsible for elaborating a theory of the relationship between church and state that incorporated the recently discovered peoples across the seas, and laid the groundwork for a new international order, was the Spanish Dominican Francisco de Vitoria. He has been rightly called 'the father of international law'. After long study in Paris, where he breathed in the spirit of a revived Thomism, Vitoria returned to Spain in 1522 and became professor of theology at Salamanca in 1526, a post he held until his death in 1546. No major work of his was published until his lectures appeared posthumously in 1557 at Lyons, but he exercised great influence through his students and the many leading figures who consulted him. According to Vitoria, writing with a special view to the New World, there existed an international community of sovereign states, some Christian, others composed of non-believers or pagans, but all of which were based in the natural law, which in principle was knowable through human reason apart from faith. So he accepted the emerging sovereign state. Neither the pope, much less the emperor or another ruler, had any right to interfere in the temporal affairs of these states, except under specific circumstances when a ruler violated the rights of his own people or of others. Then outside intervention was allowed and perhaps even demanded.

What did this mean for the Spanish situation in the New World? Alexander VI as pope could legitimately grant the Spaniards the exclusive right to preach the Gospel in the New World, that is, the *Patronato*, but he could not concede them sovereignty there. Nor did the fact of discovery carry with it sovereignty, since native rulers had long exercised it in their territories. But there were other titles that did justify Spanish intervention. According to Vitoria, each human being was endowed with the right to travel, do business, and settle where he wanted; should the Indians deny this right, then other rulers might intervene. Oppressive tyranny that resulted in the seizure of innocent victims for human sacrifice or the practice of cannibalism served to justify intervention. This clearly applied to the Conquest of Mexico, as did Vitoria's argument that a ruler might intervene in order to assist an ally in a just cause, as Cortés claimed to do in his campaign against the Aztecs. Furthermore, by virtue of Christ's mandate, Christians had the right to preach the Gospel everywhere; should a state refuse this, another ruler might intervene to enforce compliance. Oppression or persecution of believers then could also trigger intervention. All in all, Vitoria's position served to justify fundamentally the Spanish position in the New World while at the same time supporting those who advocated a just and humane treatment of the natives.

At the end of the sixteenth and into the early seventeenth century, two Jesuit thinkers, Cardinal Bellarmine and the Spaniard Suarez, developed further the thought of Aquinas and Vitoria, especially with respect to the indirect power of the pope in temporal affairs and the nature of the international community. Bellarmine's treatment of the subject appeared most fully in his *Controversies*, which were first published between 1586 and 1593, and Suarez's in his *On the Laws and God as Legislator*, which was published in 1612. Sixtus V actually censured Bellarmine for unduly restricting the temporal power of the papacy. The cardinal was more concerned with the situation in Europe after the Reformation than with the world across the seas, and both he and Suarez further elaborated their positions in an international war of words with James I of England after his imposition of a new Oath of Allegiance on the English Catholics in 1606.

Both Bellarmine and Suarez argued for the right of the pope, by virtue of his indirect power, to intervene against a prince who seriously hindered the transcendent goal of the state, a condition which was especially applicable to heretical rulers, and even to take measures to depose him, though they cautioned about the practical wisdom of such a course. In this context there arose the perennial, more general, issue of the right of subjects to rebel against an unjust ruler, which both Bellarmine and Suarez upheld under certain circumstances but from which Bellarmine seems to have retreated in his later years, largely for much the same reason that Jean Bodin rejected a right of rebellion: the need for civil order in a society where civil and religious war, especially in France, was tearing society apart. The last instance where a pope excommunicated a ruler and released subjects from their bond of obedience was the excommunication of Elizabeth of England by Pius V in 1570. The measure proved to be counter-productive, only raising the level of anti-Catholicism in England and dividing the English Catholics themselves. The indirect power of the pope, as well as the right of rebellion against an unjust oppressor, which was often associated with it, continued to be inflammatory issues into the period of the Thirty Years War.

Bellarmine and Suarez, building on Aquinas and Vitoria, succeeded in further laying a foundation for an international society of sovereign states. They found two bases for this international order, the one specifically Christian, the other arising out of the human solidarity that followed from the universal natural law. The former was more prominent in Bellarmine, whose approach was more historical and theological and for whom Christendom, or the essentially European *respublica christiana*, remained the guiding concept. Suarez's approach, like Vitoria's, was more philosophical and universal because of his interest in the Spanish territories across the seas. Both dealt with issues that remain with us today: international order among sovereign states and the right, or obligation, of outside intervention against unjust governments.

Two rulers stand out as Counter Reformation princes: the Habsburg King Philip II of Spain who ruled from 1556 until 1598 and, a generation later, the Wittelsbach Duke Maximilian of Bavaria, who reigned from 1598 to 1651, and in whom many contemporaries recognized characteristics of Philip. Both were intent upon the triumph of Catholicism and the advancement of their political interests, goals which they tended to identify. Both took seriously their obligation before God for the welfare, spiritual and temporal, of their subjects. They saw themselves as instruments of God's providence in the cause of his church, and they undertook religious or holy wars to defend or advance its interests. Philip came into conflict with the pope over policy while remaining firm in his allegiance to the papacy. His father, Emperor Charles V, instructed him always to respect the pope but also warned him that he might have to oppose the pope in defence of his rights. As it turned out, at the very start of his reign Philip waged a brief war with a virulently anti-Spanish Paul IV in 1556–7, a step he undertook only after consultation with theological advisors.

When Philip returned from the Netherlands to Spain in 1559, he established his capital in Madrid. From there he was to rule the vast Spanish Monarchy, the first empire on which the sun truly did not set. It comprised the kingdoms of Castile and Aragon on the Iberian Peninsula, the duchy of Milan and the kingdom of Naples in Italy, Sicily, the free county of Burgundy, the 17 provinces of the Netherlands, the Spanish colonies in the New World, and, in the Far East, the Philippines. Added to this in 1580, after the direct line of succession there died out, was the kingdom of Portugal with its colonies in Asia and the Americas. During his long reign Philip was the predominant European ruler, partly because of the descent of France into intermittent civil war from 1562 until the issuance of the Edict of Nantes in 1598 by the new Bourbon King Henry IV granting limited toleration to the Huguenots.

Born at Valladolid in 1527, from his early years Philip was educated in his religion, and he remained throughout his life a man of personal piety. Daily he attended Mass, and during Lent he usually withdrew to a monastery for a brief retreat. Saint Teresa of Avila, after meeting the king in the late 1570s, remarked about his 'deep spirituality', and Philip for his part venerated her, shielded her from all charges of heterodoxy, and after her death made sure that all her writings and papers came to the library of the Escorial. This magnificent, austere palace that Philip constructed about 30 miles northwest of Madrid served not only as a royal residence; as a mausoleum it housed the mortal remains of Charles V and at Philip's death 15 other members of his immediate family, and as a monastery it was the home of Hieronymite monks who prayed for the monarchy and in whose liturgical services Philip could participate as he wished. From his modest bedroom, through a small window which looked down on the chapel, he could view the altar and follow the Mass. From his faith he drew consolation in the public and private tragedies he suffered; he buried three wives and eight children.

Contemporaries asserted that 'there was no pope in Spain', and we have seen already the control Philip exercised over the church. He accepted the decrees of the Council of Trent, with the proviso 'without prejudice to the rights of the crown'. Philip made determined efforts to catholicize his subjects, a policy dictated not only by the responsibility he bore as a Christian prince but also by the conviction inculcated by his father that the terms 'heretic' and 'rebel' were interchangeable, a belief common enough in early modern Europe and not wholly off the mark. Catholicism was fostered as the common bond uniting the diverse regions of the monarchy. Philip publicly supported the Inquisition, whose tribunals probably heard about 1000 cases per year during his reign. In the 1560s the Inquisition undertook a concerted campaign against the *Moriscos*, concentrated in the kingdoms of Granada and Valencia in the southeast, who were considered Turkish sympathizers. Provoked by the new aggressiveness of the government, *Moriscos* around the city of Granada did revolt at Christmas 1568. After their suppression the government forcefully resettled them throughout Castile, thus contributing to the depopulation of Granada and the transfer of the *Morisco* problem elsewhere. It would remain for Philip's son and successor, Philip III, to expel them from Spain in 1609.

Philip's efforts to christianize the native populations in the New World and in the Philippines met with more success. Indeed, Geoffrey Parker concludes that '"the taming of America" during the second half of the sixteenth century was unquestionably Philip II's greatest achievement'. To this we shall return in Chapter 7.

Philip II's foreign policy was essentially conservative. He aimed basically at the maintenance of the *status quo*, not at expansion. Apart from his acquisition of Portugal, and with it the Portuguese Empire, and perhaps apart from his involvement in the French wars in the 1590s, his goal was to preserve his vast monarchy and to defend Catholicism. But as Giovanni Botero argued in his *Reason of State*, certainly with the Spanish Monarchy in mind, the preservation of a powerful political entity posed a more difficult challenge than did its creation, especially one composed of units separated by water. After he returned to Spain, Philip focused on the Mediterranean. He was conscious of his responsibility for the defence of Christendom against the aggressive Ottoman Turks, especially in the western Mediterranean. Religion and the common Turkish enemy were bonds binding Spain to Sicily, Naples, and the papacy.

In 1565 Philip dispatched a Spanish fleet to help defend the strategic island of Malta against a Turkish invasion, successfully as it turned out. When the Turks invaded Cyprus in 1570, Pius V took the lead in organizing the Holy League composed of Spain, Venice, and the Papal States to repel the aggression. The following year their combined naval forces decisively defeated the Turkish fleet off Lepanto in the Gulf of Patras in Greece, in what was undoubtedly a sterling victory and a boost to Christian confidence. But there was no effective follow-up, partly because Philip with the emerging crisis in the Netherlands was unwilling to commit Spanish forces to further activity in the Mediterranean. The Turks held Cyprus and controlled most of the North African coast up to Morocco. But then they became involved in war to their east in Persia, and in 1578 Philip concluded a truce with them that was subsequently prolonged. Henceforth the main theatre of the long Christian–Turkish conflict was to be the Balkans and the plains of Hungary.

By the late 1560s Philip's priority had become the mounting rebellion in the Netherlands, which was to consume enormous funds, continually imperil the monarchy's finances, and so limit the effectiveness of his government. As was frequently the case in early modern Europe, the issues were at the start a mixture of the religious and the constitutional. His and the rebels' refusal to compromise on religion was one reason for the prolongation of the conflict.

Philip's initial goal was to reorganize the church hierarchy and to strengthen his government in the 17 provinces. His plan was to add 14 bishoprics to the four existing (arch)bishoprics, which were unusually extensive territorially. Philip, of course, would enjoy the right of appointment to these bishoprics, and the new bishops would sit in the Estates-General, thus bolstering his political position. Furthermore, after Philip's accession in the Netherlands in 1555, Calvinism began to spread there; a Calvinist confession of faith was drawn up for the Netherlands in 1561. Philip was determined to implement the Tridentine decrees and to enforce the heresy laws. To this end he revived the local episcopal inquisitions; he did not attempt to introduce the Spanish Inquisition, though the population, including many Catholics, feared the resort to 'Spanish' measures. Other points at issue were taxation and the composition of the Council of State which Philip established to advise his half-sister, Margaret of Parma, who served as his regent after his return to Spain; on these he was willing to compromise.

Trouble broke out in the Netherlands in 1566 when nearly 300 members of the lesser nobility presented a petition to Margaret calling for the abolition of the inquisitions, non-enforcement of the Tridentine decrees, and the convocation of the Estates-General. Margaret dismissed them with little result, and when one of her entourage disdainfully dubbed them 'beggars', they proudly assumed the name for themselves. There followed popular tumults accompanied by a wave of Calvinist-inspired iconoclasm which horrified Philip. This outburst brought many leading nobles back to his allegiance, but William of Orange departed for Germany in order to prepare for war. He was to be Philip's chief antagonist.

Philip now dispatched the veteran duke of Alba with 10,000 troops to restore order, consolidate the government, and enforce religious uniformity. Alba took rigorous measures. His Council of Troubles executed approximately 1000 and confiscated the property of another 9000. He almost succeeded in his task, receiving help from the St Bartholomew's Day Massacre of Huguenot leaders in France on 24 August 1572, which eliminated the threat of French intervention in support of the rebels. But meanwhile Calvinist seamen, who had been expelled from England as pirates, landed at Brill and gradually seized control of the towns in the two northernmost provinces of Holland and Zeeland, which were to become the heart of the revolt. William of Orange allied with them. These developments, and Alba's efforts to introduce new taxes on the Spanish model, provoked a renewed rebellion. Complaints to Madrid from all sides brought about the appointment of the more moderate Don Luis Requesens in Alba's place as governor in 1573. But neither side would accept toleration, and Requesens learned that indeed religion rather than taxation lay at the heart of the revolt.

Debts accumulated by his many international commitments compelled Philip to declare bankruptcy in 1575. Inability to pay his soldiers led to the infamous Spanish Fury at Antwerp the following year, where the mutinous army plundered, raped, and murdered nearly 6000 victims before they were brought under control. This disaster served as a catalyst to unite briefly all the Netherlanders, Catholic and Calvinist, against the Spaniards. But the unity did not endure, largely because of the Calvinists' refusal to tolerate Catholics in Holland and Zeeland and because of another iconoclastic outbreak. Philip now named his nephew, Alexander Farnese, Duke of Parma, as governor. With his extraordinary military and diplomatic skills, Parma was able by 1578 to win back most of the southern provinces. For their part the seven northern provinces formed the Union of Utrecht in 1579, and then two years later, having deposed Philip, declared their independence and began to look more aggressively for assistance from France and England. Philip put a price on the head of the rebel William of Orange, and indeed he was assassinated in 1584, thus depriving the Dutch of their leader.

But the United Provinces, as they were now called, succeeded in obtaining the promise of effective help from England in the Treaty of Nonsuch in 1585, which rescued the Dutch Republic and helped push Philip towards the mounting of the Spanish Armada. By the death of Parma in 1592, the borders were more or less drawn between what would become the Spanish Netherlands and the Dutch Republic. In 1598, the year of his death, Philip saw to the provisional transfer of sovereignty in the Netherlands to his favourite daughter Isabella, and the son of Emperor Maximilian, Archduke Albert. The two married in 1599 and became known in the Spanish Netherlands as the 'Archdukes'.

But the war continued until the Twelve Years Truce of 1609, which granted the United Provinces *de-facto* independence. Neither side conceded religious toleration. Under the Archdukes a Catholic culture flourished in the Spanish Netherlands – it was the age of Rubens – but war broke out anew after the lapse of the Truce in 1621 and merged with the broader conflict of the Thirty Years War. Only at its conclusion did the United Provinces acquire formal recognition of their independence.

Philip's policy towards England, and to a lesser extent France, can only be understood in terms of the Dutch rebellion and the Spanish Empire in America. England, and France less so, aided the Dutch rebels, rendered sea communications with the Netherlands difficult, and preyed on Spanish shipping with the New World. By the 1560s English seadogs were harassing Spanish Atlantic traffic, a pursuit that was to intensify in the coming decades. The English, for their part, felt threatened by the presence of Alba's army in the Netherlands. Increasingly, English volunteers fought there, and in 1585, as we have seen, Elizabeth in effect allied with the United Provinces.

Philip's eventual response was the storied Armada of 1588. Its maximum goal was the conquest of England with the help of an uprising of English Catholics in the north. The alternative, more realistic objective was toleration for the English Catholics and withdrawal of the English from the towns they held in the Netherlands. Philip was convinced that the Armada sailed on a divine mission, which would receive God's help; he even seems at one point to have counted on a miracle if this were required for victory. So much the more profoundly was he shocked by his defeat, especially a defeat in which the weather played a major role.

He is said to have remarked, 'I sent the fleet against men, not against wind and water'. God's providence appeared to have abandoned Spain. Philip and much of the nation went into a period of soul-searching and mourning. To this the Spanish Jesuit Pedro de Ribadeneira responded in an ascetical classic, *A Treatise on Tribulation*, that the defeat was a mystery of God's providence, to be borne as a punishment for sin, and he called for reform of life and trust in God's inscrutable designs. The war with England continued until 1604.

The French too intermittently aided the Dutch, and Huguenot corsairs raided Spanish shipping. But Philip's intervention in the French wars was dictated also by the old dynastic rivalry with France, and in the 1590s by imperial designs when for a time he hoped to place his daughter Isabella on the French throne. Twice Parma received orders to march into France when his troops could have been used more effectively in the Netherlands. Philip staunchly opposed the reconciliation with the church of the new Bourbon king, Henry IV. He doubted the sincerity of Henry's second conversion to Catholicism, and he foresaw that absolution for Henry would lead to a regenerated France, as indeed it did. Both Sixtus V and Clement VIII were ready to welcome Henry back, happy to restore a counterweight to Spain. By the Peace of Vervins in 1598, the year of his death, Philip withdrew from France, constrained by financial and economic realities. The population of Spain paid heavily for his defence of monarchy and church, but he seems rarely to have doubted his priorities.

Philip II expired at the Escorial early on the morning of 13 September 1598, after a long illness and 53 days lying flat on his back in bed where he could scarcely be touched without pain. He bore this ordeal with a patience and surrender to God's will that stirred admiration at the court and among his people. Philip intended to instruct them in the Christian art of dying, and his peaceful, composed death was interpreted as fixing the stamp of divine approval upon his reign as Catholic King. From Clement VIII, with whom he had had his differences, Philip sought and received a papal blessing. The pope recognized after Philip's death that 'the entire life of this king was a continual struggle against the enemies of our holy Faith', and he went on, 'when it comes to matters of piety and zeal, I can say that no one can compare with His Majesty, except for those saints who are enjoying heavenly bliss forever'.

Maximilian of Bavaria came to power in 1598, the year of Philip II's death, after his father Duke William V abdicated, and he governed until 1651, three years after the Peace of Westphalia ended the Thirty

Years War. He was not a prince of European, much less of world, stature as was Philip, but he was the leading German Catholic prince during much of the drawn-out war. Genuine religious ardour and political ambition were the forces that dominated this highly self-conscious prince throughout his lifetime. More than three hours of each working day Maximilian devoted to prayer, according to one report, and he rationed out with exactness the remainder of his time among work, sleep, recreation, and meals. After his death there was found in a small strongbox he always carried with him on journeys, and for which he alone had the key, not the expected jewels but a scourge and a hair-shirt, both worn by use. But a profound sense of the realities of this world also characterized Maximilian. In the first year of his reign, after Bavaria had failed to secure the bishopric of Passau for its candidate, Maximilian wrote to his father, 'I see now that ecclesiastics as well as secular men of influence look only to *ragion di stato*, and that he is respected who possesses many lands or much money. Since we have neither, we will enjoy no influence either with the Italians or others until we improve our financial situation.'

Administrative structures had deteriorated and governmental finances were approaching the point of bankruptcy under Duke William. Within 10 years the young ruler turned Bavaria into the best-administered and most powerful territory in the Empire. Maximilian was an advocate of benevolent but absolute rule. He was deeply conscious of his responsibility to God for the temporal and eternal welfare of his subjects, but he gave little indication that he was accountable to any mortal being. Maximilian actively promoted the practice of religion and morality and took measures to prevent any Protestant inroads. We have already seen the detailed Law for Morality and Religion of his first year in office. Rome had early recognized in Bavaria a champion of orthodoxy, as well as a Catholic alternative to the Habsburgs in Germany, and was ready to grant privileges to the Bavarian dukes in exchange for their vigorous support of Catholicism. Thus Gregory XIII concluded the Concordat of 1583 with Duke William. William and Maximilian both realized that the religious improvement of their subjects depended on a supply of educated and devout priests, and so the new religious orders of the Catholic Reform, especially the Jesuits and Capuchins, found in them diligent supporters and generous benefactors. In Munich in 1597 St Michael's Church, the leading Renaissance church north of the Alps, was consecrated, the crown of the Jesuit college complex under construction since 1583.

Maximilian's concern for religion did not end at the Bavarian border. His responsibility as the first secular prince of the Empire and his own territorial interests combined to encourage him to promote the defence and advancement of the church in the Empire. He watched with foreboding during his early years in power as the storm clouds gathered that were to darken Germany during the Thirty Years War. The Peace of Augsburg had succeeded in bringing a period of peace to Germany, but increasingly in the 1580s divergent interpretations of the Peace put forward in a spirit of confessional militance not only provoked prolonged litigation, but boiled over into political and then military confrontations. The Elector Palatine became the leader of an aggressive, generally Calvinist group of German states. Catholics and Calvinists clashed in the brief War of Cologne in 1583. The dispute over the fate of the imperial city of Donauworth resulted in the collapse of the Reichstag of 1608 and the eventual formation of Protestant and Catholic defensive alliances, with Maximilian taking the initiative in the organization of the Catholic League.

On 23 May 1618, members of an assembly of Bohemian Protestants meeting in Prague pushed their way into the Hradschin Palace and heaved three Catholic government officials out of the window, thus igniting the Thirty Years War. Miraculously, as Catholics interpreted the event, all three were able to walk away, having landed on a compost heap. But the rebellion quickly spread to the Austrian and Hungarian lands of Archduke Ferdinand, who nevertheless was elected Emperor Ferdinand II in October 1619 in Frankfurt. Both Philip III and Maximilian came to Ferdinand's help, and on 8 November 1620, at the critical battle of the White Mountain outside Prague, the troops of the Catholic League, led on by the fiery Carmelite preacher Domenico à Jesu Maria and under the banner of the Blessed Virgin, overwhelmed the rebels, thus setting the stage for the consolidation of Habsburg government in Bohemia and the Austrian lands.

But the war spread to the west and north, largely because Frederick, the Calvinist Elector Palatine, had accepted the Bohemian crown from the rebels. After their conquest of the Palatinate, the armies of the Catholic League and the emperor brought under their control, after a series of unexpected military victories, much of northern Germany.

This development provoked a lively debate over policy at the courts of Munich and Vienna. On the one hand there were the militants, in Munich led by Maximilian's Jesuit confessor, Adam Contzen. For them the war was a holy as well as a religious one; that is, it was fought not only to advance religious interests but at the behest of God and with promise of his assistance. They discerned in the Catholic triumphs the call of God's Providence, and his promise of aid, to reclaim the ecclesiastical lands seized by the Protestants since 1555 in alleged violation of the Peace of Augsburg. To fail to respond to this summons was sinful pusillanimity and a shameful blotch on princely reputations. Help could be expected eventually from Catholic France, an expectation not so naive as hindsight might suggest, since Cardinal Richelieu, the king's first minister, was then under considerable pressure from the *dévot* party who opposed his anti-Habsburg policy. The moderates, on the other hand, were willing to make some concessions to the Protestants in order to consolidate the gains made up to that point. By pressing their advantage, the moderates feared, the Catholics would overreach themselves and provoke Protestant Saxony and Brandenburg, hitherto neutral in the war, to take up arms against the Catholics. They also questioned the theological position of the militants with its appeal to Providence and its analogy between the current conflict and the holy wars of the Old Testament where God had indeed fought alongside the Hebrews.

The militants won out, and with Maximilian's support Ferdinand issued in early 1629 the Edict of Restitution which embodied the Catholic understanding of the Peace of Augsburg. With this measure, more than at any other time, the religious character of the Thirty Years War came to the fore. The result was, as the moderates had foreseen, the alienation of Saxony and Brandenburg and then the intervention, with French support, of the Swedish King, Gustavus Adolphus, the Lion of the North, on the Protestant side. A combined Swedish–Saxon army routed the Catholic forces at Breitenfeld near Leipzig in 1631, reversing the whole course of the war and raising many of the same questions about God's Providence that had surfaced after the defeat of the Spanish Armada. At the battle of Nördlingen in 1634 the military balance was restored, and at the Peace of Prague of 1635, Maximilian, and Ferdinand II, retreated from the militant position and made concessions to the German Protestant states in an effort, successful in large part, to win them back to the side of the emperor. So the most religious phase of the war came to an end.

The concessions made by Maximilian and Ferdinand did not mean that they were less concerned about religion. Rather they came to see that in the long run the good of Catholicism was better served by limited concessions to the Protestants in the Empire. Continued war only barbarized the people and bankrupted the governments. Maximilian moved further in this direction in the years after the Peace of Prague, which anticipated the Peace of Westphalia.

A sharp contrast to Philip II and Maximilian as a figure of the Counter Reformation was the enigmatic and controversial French statesman Cardinal Richelieu, who was Louis XIII's first minister from 1624 to 1642. Like them he tended to identify the church's interest with the state's. His approach to Protestants and to foreign policy, however, differed drastically from theirs. Still, he saw himself, not without reason, as a reformer and champion of the church. Recent research has shown that, much like a Renaissance prince of the church, Richelieu amassed for himself and his family an enormous fortune, but that he also was in many respects a genuinely pious and devout man.

Born in 1585, probably in Paris, the future cardinal's father died when he was only five years old, and his mother then moved back to the family manor in Poitou. Originally, Armand-Jean was destined for a military career, but when his older brother decided to become a Carthusian monk, plans were changed and Armand-Jean was chosen to occupy the local bishopric of Luçon, which had come into possession of the family in 1584. After a brief, intensive period of study, and the necessary dispensation because of age, he was consecrated bishop in early 1607. The young Richelieu turned out to be a model shepherd. He quickly summoned a diocesan synod as required by Trent, where he issued a number of regulations aimed at revitalizing the clergy working in a region with a substantial Huguenot population. He undertook pastoral visitations, and he began to prepare the foundation of a diocesan seminary. From his pen there came a short catechism, *The Instruction of a Christian*, which was subsequently published and translated into a number of languages.

But the diocese of Luçon could not satisfy Richelieu's ambition, and he soon began to make contacts at court. At the Estates-General of 1614 he was chosen as spokesman for the clergy, a task he performed with a brilliance that drew him to the attention of Marie de Medici, widow of Henry IV and Regent of France. After King Louis attained his majority, increasing tension between the son and his dominating mother several times broke out into civil war. Richelieu proved adept at reconciling mother and son. With Marie's backing he became a member of the king's council in early 1624, and in August he was named chief minister. Meanwhile, he had received the cardinalate and resigned his bishopric of Luçon.

Louis XIII was not a figurehead king, and one of Richelieu's achievements during his long ministry was to retain the support of this diffident, upright monarch upon whose favour he utterly depended. As a general principle, Richelieu stated later in his masterful *Political Testament* that 'the first foundation of the welfare of a state was the establishment of the reign of God'. This he subsequently seemed to identify with the rule of 'reason', a position essentially similar to the Thomistic harmony between grace and nature. Both the reign of God and reason dictated as the basic principle submission to the laws of the Creator from whom the ruler received his authority. There are few grounds for doubting the cardinal's sincerity in this regard. From the beginning, then, he pursued a policy which he considered consistent with this principle. Two of his goals were the destruction of the Huguenots as a political faction, and the elevation of Louis as King of France to his rightful preeminence in Christendom.

The Huguenots, who constituted about 10 per cent of the French population, had received in the Edict of Nantes of 1598 limited toleration and freedom of worship along with the right to fortify up to 50 towns and to build another 200 forts. During the regency several Huguenot revolts broke out in southern and western France. Richelieu was determined to destroy their political power as detrimental to the king's authority. But he also intended to tolerate them as a religious group, a policy that brought him into conflict with the *dévots*, who included Marie de Medici in their ranks. From his years at Luçon, Richelieu was familiar with Huguenots, and he worked towards their conversion, introducing Capuchin missionaries there and writing a book of his own with this goal in mind, *The Principal Points of the Faith of the Catholic Church*. But he did not make the clear connection between heresy and political sedition that Philip II and Maximilian did. The king's reduction of the great Huguenot fortress of La Rochelle in 1628, after a year-long siege directed by Richelieu himself, was followed by the Edict of Alais which ended the Huguenots' political and military privileges but allowed for continued toleration. The king was obliged to work for their conversion, but this was to be done chiefly by persuasion. The use of force risked, in scriptural terms, tearing up the wheat with the chaff and, in the process, generating upheaval in the kingdom, as the wars of the previous century had shown. So Richelieu represented a view of toleration that eventually many Catholics would accept. Not only the welfare of the state but also the good of religion itself in the long run required toleration.

Richelieu's foreign policy was certainly guided by hostility to the Habsburgs, and it caused even more consternation among the *dévots*. Many scholars since have interpreted it as a naked pursuit of French interests and grandeur. But this does not do justice to the complex cardinal. To be sure, he organized alliances with the German Protestant states, with the Dutch, and with Denmark and Sweden against the Spanish and German Habsburgs, and in 1635 he took up arms against them. In doing this he has been accused of frustrating the Counter Reformation in the Empire, especially by his alliance with Gustavus Adolphus. There is much truth to this. Yet Richelieu contended that the Habsburgs used religion as a cloak for their ambition for universal monarchy and the subjection of Europe. Whether the Habsburgs in fact intended this or not, Richelieu seems to have believed it, and it fits the pattern of the long Habsburg–French rivalry. Richelieu's goal was 'the peace of Christendom', free from Habsburg domination. By this he seems to have meant a structural arrangement among the Christian powers that would permit them to co-exist in peace and liberty. Involved in this were systems of alliances comprising Protestant as well as Catholic states and a primitive sense for a balance of power and collective security. France, of course, would be the arbiter and protector of the programme. In what Richelieu seems to have thought was a divinely dictated order, French, European, and church interests all coincided. Nor was the papacy unsympathetic to his view, traditionally suspicious of Habsburg intentions as it was and especially so under Urban VIII, who tended to tilt in the direction of Paris. Richelieu's vision foreshadowed aspects of the Peace of Westphalia.

Throughout most of his ministry Richelieu clashed with the *dévot* party. The contest between the *dévots* and Richelieu's supporters, the 'good Frenchmen' or *bons français*, was analogous to the struggle between the militants and the moderates at the courts of Munich and Vienna. The *dévots*, led by Marie de Medici, favoured a pro-Spanish foreign policy in the interests of Catholic solidarity. Peace with Spain would enable the government to concentrate on the defeat and conversion of the Huguenots. The *dévots* vigorously opposed Richelieu's support of heretics in the German war. They also argued that the government should concentrate on the relief of the peasants at home who were being crushed by taxes levied to finance the war. Richelieu won a major victory over the *devôts* in November 1630 when Louis, forced to choose between the cardinal and his mother, opted for his minister. Soon afterwards Marie was exiled to the provinces. She then fled to the Netherlands, never to return to France.

Richelieu worked steadily to improve the situation of the church in France. The qualifications of new bishops appointed during his ministry rose slowly. As with the conversion of the Huguenots, Richelieu believed in gradual progress rather than radical reform which could easily backfire. With the second generation of *dévots* such as Vincent de Paul and the Oratorian Charles Condren he worked well, largely because they were non-political. Though he had differences with the Jesuits, and feared their growing power in France, he protected them from the hostility of the Gallican *parlementaires* and University of Paris, a fact recognized by the Jesuit superior general in Rome.

Pope Clement VIII had functioned as a mediator between Spain and France in the Peace of Vervins in 1598. After the Swedish victory at Breitenfeld in 1631, Urban VIII sought to play this role for which he claimed the title of Christendom's *padre commune*. In 1632 he dispatched extraordinary nuncios to the courts of Vienna, Paris, and Madrid with a view to reconciling the three major Catholic powers and forming a joint front against the Protestants. But the papacy refused to negotiate directly with heretics, a stance which, understandable as it might be, greatly undercut its political effectiveness. At the time of the Peace of Prague, in 1635, Urban in effect told Ferdinand II to make as advantageous a peace as he could, but not to expect the papacy officially to sanction concessions to heretics. In 1636 Urban summoned a peace congress for Cologne, but little resulted from his initiative.

Subsequently, Fabio Chigi, later Pope Alexander VII, served as papal delegate to the Westphalian peace negotiations under both Urban and his successor Innocent X. Chigi generally represented a hard line against concessions during the talks, and he followed his instructions to abstain from official negotiations with the Protestants. The papacy's position was juridical rather than political; it did not want to surrender alleged rights of the church which might in the indefinite future be reasserted. Innocent X waited nearly two years after the conclusion of the Peace of Westphalia, that is, until most troops had been demobilized, before lodging a formal protest against its concessions to heretics. The long wait was dictated by the intention to avoid responsibility for a possible resumption of hostilities. Negotiations at the peace congress, having foreseen such a protest, wrote into the treaty itself a provision invalidating it.

By taking the position it did, the papacy further excluded itself from the European political stage. At the Congress of Westphalia the moderate position now represented by Maximilian and Ferdinand III prevailed. Further concessions were made to the Protestants in the Empire, especially the legalization of Calvinism, additional relinquishment of ecclesiastical property, and the sanctioning of toleration in some places. Essentially, these concessions were made for the same reason that Richelieu tolerated the Huguenots. The common good, which included the progress of religion, required it. The alternative was enduring conflict, barbarization of the populations, and political collapse.

This does not mean that Ferdinand and Maximilian allowed Protestants in their own territories as opposed to the Empire; they did not. Indeed, Louis XIV revoked the Edict of Nantes in 1685. But still the general movement towards toleration had set in. International toleration was a fact. Religious wars between Catholics and Protestants were coming to an end. Toleration would come at a different pace in different countries, and for the most part slowly. But most Catholics, if not the papacy, recognized that Protestantism would be an enduring reality.

5

EVANGELIZATION AND POPULAR
PIETY IN EUROPE

The Catholic Reform as well as the Protestant Reformation took as a primary goal to evangelize, or christianize, ordinary people. This always implied adaptation to their situation. Evangelization meant raising the level of religious knowledge and practice, and it was closely related to confessionalism. Ultimately, both Catholic Reform and Reformation sought to deepen religious belief, but belief is still more difficult to measure than knowledge or practice, and in the last instance is known only to God. Yet knowledge and practice probably do usually reflect belief. Evaluated from the perspective of christianization, the Catholic Reform was undoubtedly successful by the early decades of the eighteenth century, especially if one also considers its educational efforts, to be taken up in the following chapter.

Another matter is the degree of success. Realism is in order about expectations of religious change. Improvement decidedly took place in knowledge and practice. Clearly it varied from place to place, from region to region, but the overall picture in 1700 is surely brighter than it had been in 1500. Changes in the style of piety and religious practice accompanied it as a new confessional Catholic consciousness developed, which authorities, both ecclesiastical and civil, actively fostered. Piety became more personal while retaining its communal character. More folks now knew their catechism and could recite basic prayers. The faithful approached confession and received Holy Communion more regularly, and matrimony and confirmation became more prominent as sacraments. A sense of the universal church combined with awareness of the local community, as saints venerated throughout the church took their place alongside local ones. Features of late medieval Christianity – such as processions, pilgrimages, and confraternities, which Protestants had criticized vigorously – revived after a brief lull, gradually shedding many if not all of their more profane or raucous elements. A new emphasis on charitable good works and the needs of the poor and unfortunate was evident, especially in the many confraternities, though this did not result in a questioning of social structures. Catholics, like Protestants, learned that they could live their faith within their particular states of life in the world, a development to be treated in Chapter 8.

Just as cities and towns were the early focal points of the Reformation, so was this the case with the Catholic Reform. Cities such as Munich, Lyons, and Barcelona first felt its effects, often with the foundation of a Jesuit college. Gradually, the movement encompassed the hinterland and over decades extended beyond into the countryside, and finally into mountainous areas. Ironically, as some have observed, rural areas which were the last to be reached by the Catholic Reform remained firmly Catholic into the twentieth century, whereas larger cities began to show signs of de-Christianization already in the eighteenth. Regionally, north Italy, the Spanish Netherlands and the Rhineland, Alsace, Lorraine, and surrounding lands of the 'Middle Kingdom', Bavaria, and parts of the Iberian Peninsula felt its effects among laity as well as clergy by the late sixteenth century. Much of France did so in the first half of the next century, and only in its second half did the Catholic Reform take firm hold in the Austrian and Bohemian lands, where extensive areas were forcibly recatholicized. Eventually, Catholicism, along with the dynasty and the aristocracy, came to constitute the three pillars of the Habsburg Monarchy.

Government as well as church actively promoted the advance of religious knowledge and practice. Like their Protestant counterparts, Catholic rulers and municipal authorities recognized the usefulness of religion in terms of the promotion of order, loyalty, and industry among subjects or citizens. But Philip II, Maximilian of Bavaria, and Emperor Ferdinand II also clearly believed in the religious values they promoted, as did many other authorities. For them, and indeed this was a feature common to many early modern Catholic figures, the good and the useful coincided. Religious practice contributed to the common good and to the power of the state. To this end authorities felt justified in the use of many forms of pressure and force. We have already looked at the Inquisitions.

Preaching as a mode of evangelization and confessionalism was as important to Catholics as it was to Protestants in the sixteenth century. As we saw earlier, the fifteenth century witnessed a new wave of preaching activity that was carried along by the mendicant orders, and that produced charismatic preachers known over Europe. This activity continued to expand in the sixteenth and seventeenth centuries. New was a further systematization or rationalization of method. This was applied above all in the popular missions undertaken first by Jesuits and Capuchins and then, chiefly in France in the seventeenth century, by the Lazarists, Eudists, and Oratorians. These missions were preached first in towns and then later in the countryside, which local Jesuits in both Italy and Spain characterized as their 'Indies' because of the religious illiteracy and uncouthness of the population. The Jesuits used their colleges as bases from which to support missionary tours, and both Jesuits and Capuchins established residences to serve these internal missions. The second half of the seventeenth century then became the age of great popular missions which took on the nature of 'happenings'.

Jesuit missions were usually adaptations of the *Spiritual Exercises* of St Ignatius, in which the missioners concentrated on themes from the *Exercises* First Week, especially sin and forgiveness, and sought to lead their hearers to confession and Holy Communion. Missions might last days, weeks, or even months, and they often incorporated considerable catechetical instruction. At the request of the duke, four Jesuits made a missionary swing in 1564 through a part of Lower Bavaria which was threatened by Protestant incursions from nearby Ortenburg. It took them six months to complete their tour as they passed through numerous parishes where they often found the people hostile to their message. Two Jesuits making a missionary journey in the Archbishopric of Cologne in winter 1646–7 spent an average of two to three days in each parish, giving six to 10 sermons and garnering between 80 and 300 Communions. Often the missionaries introduced the Confraternity of Christian Doctrine to the parish with a view to maintaining the effects of the mission through systematic catechetical instruction.

Most famous of the seventeenth-century missionaries was perhaps the Italian Jesuit Paul Segneri (the Elder, to distinguish him from his nephew), who preached over 500 missions in north Italy and the Papal States between 1665 and 1692. Adapting to his audiences, he developed his own distinctive, theatrical method. Legendary for his austerity, Segneri traversed the countryside in the manner of the apostles, barefoot, staff in hand, clothed in a torn cassock with a crucifix hanging across his chest. His regular associate, Giovanni Pietro Pinamonti, accompanied him. Usually the mission's centre was a small town to which folks from the surrounding villages came. Segneri's arrival was well staged. He approached the church on a path strewn with flowers. The assembled congregation prostrated themselves as he passed, those closest to him kissing his cassock and receiving his blessing. The local clergy came forward to welcome him, presenting him with a crucifix before which Segneri and his companion prostrated themselves. Then all processed to the parish church as they sang the 'Come, Holy Spirit'. Upon leaving the church Segneri mounted a platform erected outside it or in the town square. There he preached the opening sermon.

Normally, his mission lasted eight days, and all was carefully planned: the daily schedule, the songs, the processions, the placement of men and women around the platform. Implicit throughout was a dialogue between the terrifying Segneri threatening the pains of hell and the mild Pinamonti showing the way to repentance and peace. Each day began at dawn with a catechism lesson by Pinamonti followed by a Rosary in the parish church. Chanting the Psalm *Miserere* the crowd then processed to the platform where Segneri was to preach. Topics were set for each day: Monday, the need to respond to God's call; Tuesday, the price of each individual soul; Wednesday, mortal sin and its effects; Thursday, the obstinate sinner; Friday, the need to forgive one another; Saturday, the eternity of hell. There followed this first sermon instructions given separately to different groups, especially parents and children. Next there was a procession to another church, usually in a neighbouring village, where a sermon followed on similar topics. The crowd then returned to the principal church chanting the Litany of the Blessed Virgin for another sermon, this time dealing with the life of Christ and the mission of the Apostles. The celebration of Mass followed. On Wednesday, Thursday, and Friday nights there were penitential processions after which the men, led by Father Segneri, retired to the church to scourge themselves with the discipline. Friday, preparations began for the grand closure of the mission on Sunday. A temporary chapel was constructed and decorated for the closing Mass and ceremonies on the outskirts of the town or village. Most of Saturday was given over to individual confessions. Sunday began with a grand procession to the temporary chapel in which men, women, and children were all clothed in penitential garb. There they heard Mass, received Holy Communion, and then listened to a final dramatic exhortation to perseverance which was also meant to communicate the peace that followed upon forgiveness of sins and reconciliation with God.

Segneri's method, of course, was not for everyone. Even fellow-Jesuits doubted the long-term effectiveness of such spectacles, which were not immune to parodies, and they urged a return to the simpler style of the previous century. Vincent de Paul and his associates labouring in France in the seventeenth century eschewed such dramatic, brief missions. They preferred to remain in a parish or village for a month, which they filled with instructions, catechism lessons, the hearing of confessions, and perhaps an occasional simple procession. They frequently organized a confraternity to maintain the spirit of the mission after their departure, and they often assembled the local clergy for what we today would call adult education or professional development. The Eudists active in the west of France tended to prolong their missions still more. Out of these missions in France there emerged the first 'retreat house', founded by a Jesuit at Vannes in 1660. To it laymen would resort usually for eight days for a further schooling in prayer and the ways of the spiritual life. Shortly afterwards a lay woman, Catherine de Francheville, opened a similar retreat house for women nearby. By the 1720s there were seven retreat houses for men and five for women in France, and they began to appear in Italy, Spain, and Central Europe.

Important as these missions were for evangelization as preachers penetrated further and further into the villages of Catholic Europe, still more crucial was regular preaching in city and village parishes. Trent insisted that the principal task of bishop and pastor was the preaching of the Word. The two decades following Trent saw the publication of a number of works on preaching. Here too in the pursuit of method the effort at systematization is at work. Three books of particular importance for subsequent Catholic pulpit oratory were: *On Ecclesiastical Rhetoric* (1574) by Agostino Valier, Bishop of Verona; *Ecclesiastical Rhetoric or the Manner of Preaching* (1576) by the Portuguese Dominican Luis de Granada; and *The Manner of Preaching* (1576) by the Spanish Franciscan Diego de Estrella. They and subsequent Catholic treatises suggested a variety of rhetorical styles, in particular aspects of humanist oratory. As its chief source, Catholic preaching drew upon the Scriptures. Nor were Catholic treatises on preaching hesitant to draw occasionally from Protestant manuals, especially Philip Melancthon's. In addition, sermon collections were published, in order to help pastors meet their obligation to preach on Sundays and feast days. One of these was a 600-page volume by Andreu Capella, Bishop of Urgell, which he published in 1593 in Catalan, so that the pastors could more easily read them to the people.

Yet it would be a long time before pastors, especially in rural areas, would be adequately equipped and willing to preach regularly. In 1574 the town of Salmerón near Cuenca in Spain sued its pastor because he failed to preach, arguing that it should not have to pay Franciscans from the local monastery for this service. At least up to the end of the sixteenth century authorities in the Archbishopric of Lyons seem to have expected little more than the recitation of prayers and short expositions of *The Roman Catechism* from their rural pastors, but the situation improved in the course of the following century. Visitors of the Archbishop of Trier in the last third of the seventeenth century considered it excessive to expect a pastor to both preach and give cate-chetical instruction on Sundays. The brunt of preaching remained with the religious orders throughout the seventeenth century, especially for the popular series of sermons given regularly during the Advent and Lenten seasons in the cities and towns. Indeed, pulpit oratory emerged as a distinct literary form as practised by the great preachers of the seventeenth century, who often held appointments at court. Such was the case with the Jesuit Louis Bourdaloue and Jacque Benigné Bossuet, Bishop of Meaux, both of whom preached at the court of Louis XIV, as well as the Portuguese Jesuit António Vieira (1608–97) who was a favourite of John IV of Portugal. Johann Ulrich Megerle, the son of a tavern-owner in Baden, better known by his religious name with the Augustinians, Abraham a Santa Clara, stirred, criticized, and delighted the Habsburg court and the common people of Vienna from 1666 until 1709 with his common, often coarse style of speech, which was to have an impact on the evolution of modern German. Upon being compelled to apologize for a remark in a Sunday sermon that the ladies at court, because of their suggestive attire, did not even deserve to be prodded by the barnyard pitchfork, the preacher declared the following Sunday that the ladies did indeed deserve to be so prodded.

Regular religious instruction or catechism was a prominent method of christianization; it is hard to separate it from preaching and from religious schooling. All three overlapped in reality. Enthusiasm for catechetical instruction antedated 1500 in Spain, stirred by the need to catechize the *Moriscos*, and it was evident in Spain and in Italy in the 1520s and 1530s. Several Spanish synods called for religious instruction for all the faithful. The tireless priest Juan de Avila, having seen a catechetical school in operation in Seville in 1526, took up the cause of religious instruction and himself composed a rhymed catechism. From 1540 on a number of catechisms were available in Spain. Soon the monarchy supported the movement. By mid-century in parts of Spain enthusiasm to disseminate catechetical instruction amounted to a craze. Over in Italy, the priest Castellino da Castello launched the initiative in Milan in 1536 which resulted in the Confraternity of Christian Doctrine. The reasons for this upswing in catechetical activity were multiple. A new awareness of popular religious illiteracy was coupled with a rising sense that not merely a general assent to the church's teaching, but explicit knowledge of the faith, was essential for salvation. Printing and the resulting availability of catechisms undoubtedly fostered the movement. Increasingly, then, the challenge of the Protestant Reformation required that Catholics know their faith. Indeed, the Reformation era elicited from both Protestants and Catholics a decisive attempt to institutionalize religious instruction and formation.

The Council of Trent in its first period in 1546, and again at its end in 1563, vigorously supported the move for religious instruction, imposing upon pastors the obligation regularly to teach catechism to children, at least on Sundays and feast days. This measure, it should be noted, shifted some of the responsibility for Catholic upbringing from parents and godparents to the church in the form of the pastor. Often also understood under 'children' were servants and unattached adults up to the age of 40, who appeared deficient in their religious knowledge. Many diocesan and provincial councils followed up on the Tridentine decrees with more specific legislation usually prescribing that the pastor, the schoolteacher, or the sacristan teach catechism for one hour in the early afternoon on Sundays and feast days, hence 'Sunday school'. Implementation of this requirement was another matter.

A number of catechisms in Latin and the vernacular languages now came on the market in order to assist pastors and others involved in the work of religious instruction. We have already discussed the *Roman Catechism*, which was intended for the use of pastors, and the catechisms of Peter Canisius, one of which was intended for students and another for children. His catechisms remained the most popular in Germany into the nineteenth century. Several Spanish and Italian catechisms antedated Trent, including one by the Spanish Dominican theologian Domingo de Soto, but eventually Robert Bellarmine's two volumes published in 1598, one for adolescents and the other for children, predominated in Italy and circulated widely elsewhere. In 1588 the Catalan bishops prescribed for their sees the catechism of the Spanish Jesuit Diego de Ledesma. An early popular French catechism was that of the Jesuit Emond Auger, published in the 1560s. Religious instruction was slower to take hold in France, but by mid-seventeenth century many dioceses there saw to the composition of their own catechisms.

The content of most catechetical instruction was traditional. First of all, it was the learning of prayers, the Our Father and Hail Mary, and frequently the Salve Regina or Hail Holy Queen and the Confiteor, a prayerful formula for the general confession of sins that was said at the start of Mass. Secondly, it included learning the Apostle's Creed, the Ten Commandments, and the seven sacraments, presumably with some accompanying instruction. Heavy emphasis was placed on memorization. Ideally, parents or householders were to accompany children and servants, but this rarely seems to have been the case. In fact, it was unusual for any adults to come for the lessons; for them it was too embarrassing to sit in class.

Catechism instruction faced considerable resistance, often from the diocesan clergy themselves, who argued against keeping children indoors on Sunday afternoon; pastors in Bavaria sometimes preferred to teach the prayers after the homily at Mass. Some argued that instruction had always been the responsibility of parents and godparents, not the pastor's. One Catalonian pastor responded to an episcopal visitor in 1611 that he was well aware of the regulation calling for catechism on Sunday afternoon, but since he knew no-one would come at that time, he conducted the lesson during Mass. In outlying parish chapels, especially during the winter months, authorities agreed to less frequent instruction, and a diocesan synod in Regensburg in 1650 allowed for instruction only twice a month, and even for a half-hour instruction in place of the homily at Mass during Advent and Lent. Following a suggestion made at Trent, some dioceses came to require a level of religious knowledge before admittance to a sacrament. The Archbishopric of Tarragona, for example, required that couples exhibit adequate religious knowledge before their wedding, and other dioceses insisted that prospective godparents do the same before they could participate in a baptismal ceremony. Such measures were often unpopular with local clergy as well as laity. More successful was the effort at systematic instruction in preparation for first confession and First Communion which was introduced at this time.

Most successful in the teaching of catechism were the Jesuits, who employed the pedagogical methods of their colleges in local and out-lying parishes as well as in elementary schools. In the early seventeenth century they conducted catechism classes in the chief parishes of Cologne as well as in the parishes around Ingolstadt. Their goal was to make the memorization involved in catechism more palatable by introducing into the lessons stories, songs, dramatizations, dialogues, and processions, and by fostering competition among the students in recitation and awarding prizes to the winners. In Cologne they composed a special catechism for preparation for First Communion, and in their colleges they made First Communion into a major event to be celebrated appropriately after adequate preparation.

How successful was this drawn-out catechetical campaign? Results were obviously mixed, with greater success in urban than in rural areas, as was the normal pattern. Reliable figures are not available for many places, Catalonia for one. Nor should we forget that many young people learned their catechism in elementary schools and colleges. Popular missions increasingly incorporated a significant element of religious instruction into their programmes. For Vincent de Paul there was no mission without catechism. Records of the Spanish Inquisition for the diocese of Cuenca show that, from 1580 to 1589, 80 per cent of those appearing before it, women as well as men, could recite the fundamental prayers by heart, a percentage that increased after 1600 for rural folks as well as town-dwellers. This was remarkable. Sunday schools in Lille in the Spanish Netherlands enrolled about 2000 children in 1580, roughly one-fourth of their part of the population. Many French pastors taught catechism regularly by mid-seventeenth century, and Sunday instruction in Christian doctrine seems to have been almost general by the early eighteenth century in France, with many parents now being incorporated into the process.

Closely associated with preaching and catechetical instruction was reception of the sacraments. Shortly after Trent, as we have seen, Rome issued a new Missal which standardized most texts for the Mass and for the liturgical year, while also allowing for the celebration of local saints' cults. The Roman Ritual, which comprised the texts for other sacraments such as matrimony, as well as for a plethora of sacramentals or pious practices such as prayers, blessings, anointings, or processions left room for considerable adaptation, so that a certain variety was present. The Mass, especially the Sunday and feast-day Mass in the parish, remained the centre of Catholic worship, above all in the countryside. For many this was as much a need as an obligation, as can be seen from demands for a second parish Mass on Sunday, so that those who had to remain home during the principal service to watch the house, might have the opportunity to attend. In towns and cities, churches of the religious orders competed successfully with the parish churches. By the early seventeenth century the practice of the devout was confession and reception of Communion monthly, or at least four times a year; there were theological disputes about the desirability of even more frequent Communion. Confession and Communion in the course of Lent and the Easter Season, mandatory since the Lateran Council of 1215, came to be nearly universally observed, a development fostered by the requirement of church or government in many areas that each parishioner receive a certificate indicating that he had fulfilled his obligation.

The introduction of the confessional by Charles Borromeo in Milan, and then gradually across most of Europe, rendered confession both more individual and private. It was a box-like structure, usually open in the front, with a chair for the priest and a grille to his side, on the other side of which there was a space for the penitent to kneel. The confessional provided greater opportunity for a conversation between confessor and penitent, and it came to serve as a forum for individual spiritual direction. Many confessional manuals issued from the press, to assist both confessor and penitent in confession. Some historians have seen in the careful examination of conscience prior to confession an aid to the development of systematic, ordered thinking. The popular handbook for confessors written by the long-time secretary to Ignatius Loyola, Juan Polanco, which first appeared in 1556, pointed out that the spiritual consolation of the penitent was a principal fruit of the sacrament. Greater frequency of confession also brought the faithful more regularly into contact with the clergy and increased the clergy's role.

The sacrament of confirmation had fallen into widespread neglect in the late Middle Ages, but gradually reappeared during the Catholic Reform. Late in the sixteenth century the Bishop of Augsburg once confirmed 30,000 people within two months; one wonders about the quality of instruction provided by the Jesuits who accompanied him on his way. St Margaret Mary Alacoque, the French Visitandine mystic, did not receive confirmation until 1659 when she was 22, instead of as a young girl. Yet by the end of the century the figures for France showed great improvement.

Governmental as well as church authorities, not only Catholic but Protestant too, wanted to end the so-called clandestine marriages, that is, marriages contracted by a private exchange of promises and copulation. The medieval church had recognized these as valid but long frowned upon them because of the confusion they generated. The resulting Tridentine legislation, which we have seen, clearly made marriage a public ceremony, brought it more under ecclesiastical control, and elevated the role of the parish priest in the ceremony by insisting on his presence as the principal witness. Gradually it became the Catholic practice across Europe. Furthermore, church practice showed an increasing attention to the obligations of the husband towards his wife.

A heavy diet of printed materials supported preaching, catechetical instruction, and participation in the sacraments in the work of evangelization. Catholics had learned to put Gutenberg's invention to good advantage, though for a time at the start of the Reformation the Protestants outdid them. Trent had neither fostered nor hindered the reading of the Bible, but Catholic authorities subsequently were wary of vernacular translations as a potential source of misunderstanding, and they were not easy to come by. But catechisms, manuals for preparation for confession and Holy Communion, lives of the saints, prayer and meditation books and other inexpensive religious publications streamed forth from the press, to be read by all groups in society including those with only a minimum of education. Books of devotion helped to foster the growing practice of meditation and mental prayer. Just as fly-sheets and pamphlets exercised much influence on the course of the German Reformation, so they played a significant role in the Catholic Reform. Especially popular in Catalonia, for example, were *goigs* or fly-sheets which usually advertised, often in verse and with an illustration, the merits of a local saint. Encouraged by Maximilian, the Bavarian Jesuits established in 1614 a foundation and a distribution system to make Catholic books widely available at no cost. Thomas à Kempis's *Imitation of Christ* remained a favourite. Other popular devotional reading included the works of Luis de Granada, Peter Canisius, and the Flemish Jesuit Francis Coster. Aegidius Albertinus, a Flemish immigrant at the court of Maximilian, was kept busy translating Spanish religious works into German, including those of Antonio de Guevara. The Jesuit Jeremias Drexel, a convert and Maximilian's court preacher from 1615 to 1638, was one of the most widely published religious writers of the seventeenth century. His 28 books appeared in more than 160 Latin editions and 40 German translations, with many of them also published in French, English, Italian, and other languages. Peter of Alcántara's inexpensive publications circulated widely in Spain.

New and revived devotional practices characterized sixteenth- and seventeenth-century Catholicism, many of them associated with confraternities. Often they involved practices or doctrines that distinguished Catholics from Protestants and so contributed to the formation of confessional identity. Such were adoration of Christ present in the Eucharist, veneration of the Blessed Virgin Mary and the saints, or prayer for the souls in purgatory. Older medieval traditions were frequently elaborated and expanded upon, so that a continuity with the earlier period was evident, for example, in Corpus Christi (Body of Christ) processions which dated back to the thirteenth century. Alongside this was the attempt to banish from processions, pilgrimages, and other observances what smacked of the profane or the superstitious. Catholics were generally much more tolerant than Protestants of customs and folk ways, and often enough tacit compromises were reached between authorities and popular pressures. With regard to the saints, there was a general tendency to combine with the veneration of local holy figures more attention to saints recognized by all the church, and so to bring out more effectively its universality.

The feast of Corpus Christi, in honour of the Real Presence of Christ in the Blessed Sacrament, was the most prominent, and is certainly the most studied, of the popular religious celebrations. It began in the Netherlands in the thirteenth century, and was effectively extended to the universal church by Pope John XXII in 1317, for the Thursday following the second Sunday after Pentecost. Thus it fell in late May or early June, at the height of spring. Very early the predominant feature of the feast came to be the procession, which grew richer in the late Middle Ages and then came to full bloom during the early modern period. The Council of Trent in its decree on the Eucharist defended and encouraged the customary festivals in honour of 'this sublime and venerable sacrament', whereby it was 'carried with reverence and honour in processions through streets and public places'. Roman norms for the procession first appeared in 1600 and then again in the Roman

Ritual of 1614, but by then local practices had long outstripped them. The Corpus Christi procession became a distinctive confessional observance asserting the community's Catholicism.

A 1588 Corpus Christi sermon delivered in Vienna by the Jesuit preacher Georg Scherer explained the feast and procession for the benefit of Catholics and non-Catholics alike. It was both a profession of faith and a celebration of the Real Presence, which called for expression not only in word but in external, bodily actions, in music, song, and dance. The greater the faith, the more joyful was the occasion. Scherer reminded his audience of the Jewish celebration of God's Presence with his people – had David not danced before the Ark? – and the acclamation of Jesus by the people at his entrance into Jerusalem. The procession expressed adoration and thanksgiving for the gift of the Eucharist, and it did so in a visible manner, so summoning bystanders to faith and to reception of Holy Communion. Alluding perhaps to the Roman triumph, Scherer saw in the procession the representation of the church's victory over the heretics who refused to acknowledge the Real Presence, and he also found in it an anticipation of Christ's final victory and the ultimate coming of God's Kingdom.

Elsewhere the procession shared in the nature of older, traditional observances, in that by bearing the Eucharist through the town and into the fields it invoked God's blessing on the community and prayed for a bountiful harvest. Its route was usually dictated by the contours of the countryside or by places significant for the identity of a town or village. Thus the procession rendered the area it traversed holy or sacred in addition to invoking a blessing, and in doing so it sometimes expressed ecclesiastical claims. Traditionally, there were four stops or stations, representing the four corners of the earth and so symbolizing the universal claims of the church. At each station the initial passage of one of the four Gospels was read; this represented a quasi-magical belief that the proclamation of the Gospel warded off demons and evil spirits. Eventually platforms were erected at the stations, for sermons or for simple dramatic presentations.

In many cities the annual Corpus Christi procession became a major civic event. The city of Barcelona made participation mandatory as early as 1320. Civic and ecclesiastical officials took the lead; guilds and confraternities marched clothed in their distinctive garb, as did faculty and students in university towns. In Munich personifications of the four administrative districts of Bavaria paraded together, expressing the participation of the whole principality. Floats bore representations of religious scenes, usually drawn from the Bible but also from the lives of saints or from traditional lore. One year a float in Munich portrayed the legend that Emperor Rudolf I (1273–91) earned God's blessing for the Habsburg dynasty by kneeling reverently when a priest passed by carrying the Body of Christ to a dying man.

Ecclesiastical authorities became more concerned about propriety and decorum during the early modern period, and they seem to have succeeded in banning from within the church itself features of the festival which they considered objectionable. This was the case in Spain. There fabulous figures took part in the celebration: dwarf-like figures with oversized heads, and giants, huge figures representing the four continents (Europe, Asia, Africa, America) who danced, and were accompanied by acrobats, clowns, and musicians. Dragon-like figures, reminiscent of the dragon of the Apocalypse, came on the scene, only to be thrown to the ground in defeat by figures of the saints. These features were simply moved outside the church. The great Spanish dramatist Pedro Calderón de la Barca composed more than 80 plays, often allegorical in character, which were initially meant for performance on Corpus Christi. 'Humility Crowned by the Plants' (*La humildad coronada de las Plantas*) featured two personifications as protagonists, the ear of wheat and the winestock, both of which were obviously associated with the Eucharist. The two emerged from the dramatic action as the most humble of the plants, and so received the triumphal crown. The lesson: the virtue of humility and the Eucharist belonged together.

Renewed devotion to Mary, the Mother of Christ, also characterized the piety of the Catholic Reform. Here, too, there was evident continuity with the medieval tradition as well as a supplementary anti-Protestant feature which sometimes rose to militance, as in the designation of Mary as *Generalissima* of the Catholic armies by Maximilian of Bavaria at the Battle of the White Mountain. According to a 1657 survey by a Dominican author, nearly one-third of the 166 Marian shrines in Catalonia dated from the period of the Catholic Reform. These were usually associated with images of the Blessed Virgin, rarely if ever with alleged Marian apparitions. In the course of the fifteenth century the Rosary had emerged as a form of prayer popular because of the manner in which it combined vocal prayer with reflection on the mysteries or events of the life of Mary and Jesus. Both Dominicans and Jesuits fostered the devotion and encouraged the formation of confraternities of the Rosary. Pius V gave it a great impetus in 1572 when he attributed the Christian victory over the Turks at Lepanto to the intercession of

Mary invoked by the praying of the Rosary. Pius established the feast of Our Lady of Victory, which was changed by his successor to the feast of the Most Holy Rosary and fixed for 7 October. The praying of the Angelus, that is, three Hail Marys followed by a versicle and concluding prayer three times a day to commemmorate the Incarnation of Jesus in the womb of Mary, became a regular practice in the course of the seventeenth century.

Pilgrimages had long been popular as a way of seeking favours from God through the intercession of a saint, expressing thanks, and undertaking penance. They as well as Marian piety had come under ringing criticism from the Protestant Reformers. But after a sharp decline in the first half of the sixteenth century, pilgrimages and especially Marian pilgrimages revived in the later sixteenth century and flourished anew in the seventeenth. Two of the most popular goals of Marian devotion were Loreto near Ancona in Italy, which drew an international following, and Altötting in Bavaria near the border with Salzburg, to which pilgrims journeyed chiefly from Bavaria and the Habsburg lands.

A Marian shrine had been located at Loreto since the late twelfth century. But only from the 1470s did there begin to circulate the legend that made Loreto distinctive, nearly two centuries after the events it purported to report. According to the story, the house in Nazareth in which the Angel Gabriel had announced to Mary that she was to become the Mother of God was now located there and known as the Holy House of Loreto. In 1291, after the reconquest of the Holy Land by the Muslims, angels miraculously transported the House first to one and then to another location in Dalmatia, and finally deposited it at Loreto in 1295. Two publications popularized the story. The first appeared in 1472, authored by Pietro di Giorgio Tolomei, better known as Teramano, a priest who had long served at the shrine. The second was an elaboration of Teramano's work, published in 1531 by Girolamo Angelita, secretary of the nearby town of Recanati. Angelita saw himself as the historian of the Holy House and personally presented his book to Pope Clement VII.

Meanwhile, miracles at the shrine and the first cautious and then energetic support of popes encouraged the development of Loreto as a pilgrimage site. The famous composer at the court of Munich, Orlando di Lasso, set to music in 1575 the Litany of Loreto, a series of invocations of Mary prayed every Saturday at Loreto. Francis Xavier, Charles Borromeo, and Francis de Sales all made their way at one time to the Holy House. Montaigne left a votive offering when he stopped there during his Italian tour in 1580. New impetus was given the pilgrimage and its final form given the legend by Orazio Torsellini, rector of the Jesuit college at Loreto where the Society had assumed care for the shrine, in his *History of Loreto*, which was published in 1594 in Latin and enjoyed wide circulation in many translations and editions. Torsellini did not avoid exaggerations if not pious fraud in his volume, and the locality benefited from the steady influx of pilgrims.

German pilgrims in particular made their way to Loreto, the young Maximilian of Bavaria journeying there in 1593 and the future Emperor Ferdinand II stopping on his way to Rome in 1598. Loreto chapels, that is, chapels modelled after the one in Italy, came to be popular in Catholic Germany. Altogether by 1753 one could count 52 such chapels, of which roughly two-thirds themselves became centres of pilgrimage to Our Lady of Loreto. The Habsburgs constructed an imitation of the Holy House for the church of the Augustinians in Vienna. So the devotion to Our Lady of Loreto influenced both popular piety and church architecture. Nor should we fail to note that one reason for the attraction of the Holy House, as well as the chapels in imitation of it, was the desire to participate more fully in the sacred action of the Annunciation which had allegedly taken place there. Furthermore, folks frequently journeyed to Loreto in connection with a Roman pilgrimage, so that the devotion fostered an orientation towards Rome.

Despite a sharp decline due to the Reformation, the Marian shrine at Altötting flourished as a pilgrimage site with the aid of prominent benefactors such as Duke William of Bavaria and the support of several religious orders. A small statue of Mary with the Child, probably dating from the thirteenth century, drew pilgrims to the shrine in the late fifteenth century from France and Italy, as well as from the German lands. Following the outbreak of the Reformation the number of pilgrims declined drastically, and in 1522 the Protestant Wolfgang Russ preached there against both Marian devotion and pilgrimages. Peter Canisius drew attention to the shrine once again in 1570 when he carried out a highly publicized exorcism at Altötting on Anne Bernhausen of Augsburg. In 1579, the first year of his reign, Duke William founded in Munich an archconfraternity of Our Lady of Altötting; members pledged a pilgrimage every four years. The duke established the Jesuits at Altötting in 1591 alongside the canons who were in charge of the shrine. The Jesuits in turn founded a college in 1640, which soon served as a centre for a confraternity, dramatic performances, and missionary activity in the region. The Franciscans set up a house in 1653, to assist in the ministry to the pilgrims, and they numbered 26 by 1687. In 1600 the Jesuits reported 7600 Communions at Altötting, in 1648, 94,000, and between 1700 and 1740 an average annually of 115,000 confessions. The number of regional group pilgrimages rose to an average of 160 annually, until a decided drop-off at the end of the eighteenth century.

Both public and private concerns brought pilgrims to Altötting. Pilgrimages contributed to the development of both territorial and civic unity, as is clear from both the triennial pilgrimage from the Bavarian city of Landshut, which first took place in the 1490s, and from the quadrennial Munich pilgrimage, which in the second half of the seventeenth century drew an average of 1600 to 1700 participants. Their prayers and offerings reflect the history of the times. The Landshut pilgrims in 1607 asked for deliverance from the plague of that year, not only for themselves but for all Bavaria. In 1610 and 1613, as war threatened, their primary request was for peace in the Empire; then following the early Catholic victories in the Thirty Years War, there was gratitude for these, which surely had come about through the intercession of the Blessed Virgin, and petition for preservation and increase of the Catholic religion. Swedish invasions prevented pilgrimages in 1634 and 1648. In 1654 pilgrims gave thanks and petitioned for the maintenance of peace for both town and territory. By the 1680s attention turned to the impending Turkish threat. The significant increase in value of the offerings, from an average of 100 to 200 florins, to nearly 700 florins in 1684, shows a growing prosperity in Landshut in the years after the Thirty Years War. But the burdens of the wars in the following years brought a substantial cutback.

The votive offerings left at Altötting reflected also the private concerns, the joys and sorrows of contemporary men and women. Frequent gifts were the bridal crowns, then worn at weddings by the groom as well as the bride, or other wedding symbols, even wedding rings. These were offered sometimes with a prayer for a happy life together, sometimes in gratitude for a long and happy marriage, and they came from folks of all social classes. Dorothea Müllnerin of Mürnau had, under pressure from her companion, murdered her baby. While in prison she beseeched Mary to obtain from God the opportunity to do penance for her sin on this earth, and she promised to make a pilgrimage, barefoot, to Altötting, there to offer a wax image of the Blessed Mother for which she would beg the funds. Unexpectedly, she was released from prison, and she then fulfilled her vow. Franz Stiller from the area of Rottenburg shot to death a judicial official in 1681. His promise was his share of a silver dish that he and his brothers and sisters had inherited from their mother. He too was unexpectedly pardoned. The family sold the silver dish, and Franz sent his share as an offering to Altötting as he had promised.

Many local and international saints came to new prominence at the same time as the church sought to end the abuses associated with their veneration while reasserting their intercessory power and emphasizing their role as models of Christian life. The Council of Trent took up the matter, and Urban VIII in 1634 streamlined the liturgical calendar and laid down new requirements for canonization procedures which Rome was to control henceforth. St Benno, a medieval bishop of Meissen on the Elbe River, had seen his cult flower in the fifteenth century to be crowned by canonization in 1524. Once the Reformation reached the territory, zealots desecrated his tomb, but the relics were saved and eventually brought to Munich where they were solemnly installed in the cathedral and the saint was declared a patron of both city and the territory. In 1603 80 parishes made pilgrimages to his tomb. In Augsburg the prince–bishop sought to revive the cult of St Ulrich, an early bishop there. Maximilian of Bavaria, then, commissioned the Jesuit Matthäus Rader to compose a book that would tell the story of the Bavarian saints, to the glory of the dynasty and territory and the edification of the faithful. Rader had already published his *Garden of the Saints* in three volumes between 1604 and 1614, biographies of the leading saints in the church's calendar, and between 1615 and 1627 he followed with his four-volume *Bavaria, Holy and Pious*, a work which combined history and hagiography in the typical fashion of the times, and which was to be imitated by similar volumes for Bohemia, Swabia, and other territories.

Across the whole church, St Joseph, whose cult had developed in the fifteenth century, became increasingly popular in the following two centuries, perhaps as a result of new interest in him as model father, and 'Joseph' emerged as a name frequently given Catholic boys, as did 'Francis' after Francis Xavier, the Jesuit missionary who was canonized along with Ignatius Loyola in 1622 and enjoyed greater appeal across the church. The thirteenth-century Franciscan Anthony of Padua enjoyed new prominence, as did the fourteenth-century Bohemian martyr John of Nepomuk, who was not formally canonized until 1729. Of both of them the tongue was the symbol, for Anthony's eloquence and for John's silence in the face of immense pressure to break the seal of confession.

For this John became known as the martyr of confession, and so attention was directed to this sacrament.

In 1578 workers in a Roman vineyard discovered previously unknown catacombs, an event which stirred renewed interest in the early martyrs and resulted in the posthumous publication in 1632 of Antonio Bosio's *Underground Rome*. Catholic churches across Europe now sought bones as relics from the catacombs, all of which were deemed to be the bones of martyrs. Usually these were given names before they were translated across the Alps and installed with great solemnity in local churches. On 7 November 1621 the bones of Sts Sulpicius, Charilaius, and Aurelia were received amidst great ceremony in the court church of the duke of Neuburg. This cult of the early Roman martyrs confirmed the bonds with both the early church and with Rome.

Concern with death and with the souls in purgatory was a distinctive feature of Catholic and especially of Spanish piety during the sixteenth and seventeenth centuries. This was another mark distinguishing Catholics from Protestants, who had eliminated purgatory as a place where folks were purified of their sins before admittance to heaven. Most people passed through purgatory after death, few went to hell, and few immediately to heaven; so it was commonly believed. Spaniards in their wills looked increasingly to the number of priests and religious who would be present at their funerals to pray for their souls and so hasten their passage through purgatory. Prayers and especially Masses were what Spaniards sought, for their own souls, for those of their families and friends, and for the poor souls in purgatory generally. A bond existed between the living and the dead, and the former could help those who had gone before them. The demand for Masses for the dead to be said, especially by the religious orders, steadily increased. Since a stipend was given as an offering for each Mass, more and more funds were invested in Masses. In 1585 69 testators in the city of Cuenca left money in their wills for 11,874 Masses, in 1645 44 testators left money for 14,319 Masses. There seems to have been an eight-fold increase in the number of Masses requested in Barcelona between the sixteenth and seventeenth centuries. Parishes and chapels came to be overwhelmed by the demand, and the money expended for Masses diverted funds from more economically profitable ventures. Indeed, investments of this kind may have been a contributing factor to Spain's economic decline. Elements of superstition sometimes persisted in this regard despite the efforts of Trent. This is evident, for example, in the trentals of votive Masses in honour of St Amador, popular in parts of Spain, which nearly assured swift passage through purgatory. The practice originated in the Middle Ages. It called for Mass to be celebrated on 30 particular feast days in the course of a year, with a different number of candles on the altar at each Mass. On the three days prior to All Souls Day, on 2 November, three more Masses were added. Trent criticized this practice vigorously, and to a large degree, it seems, effectively. As a result it died out in Madrid, and probably in other parts of Spain, but continued in Catalonia.

Confraternities came to play an even more vital role in Catholic life in the course of the sixteenth century just as ecclesiastical authorities sought to submit them to greater control. Their expansion in both number and in membership, and a new emphasis on works of charity, represented in part a response to the rising number of poor and unfortunate. In the larger urban areas of Italy by 1600, it has been estimated, every third or fourth male belonged to a confraternity at least at some point in his life, as did a lesser number of women and adolescents. In Perugia, with a population of 19,000, there were perhaps 2000 confraternity members at the end of the century. Sixty-two per cent of the men and 40 per cent of the women of Cuenca belonged to at least one confraternity in the 1570s, and many double-dipped. Most brotherhoods dated from the later Middle Ages, having been formed for devotional and social goals. They brought together folks, sometimes of similar social groups sometimes across social lines, for mutual support, spiritual and material. They provided welfare and funeral benefits plus participation in common meals and festivities, under the patronage of a particular saint or mystery in the life of Mary or Jesus which they cultivated, and they usually possessed their own chapel or at least an altar in the local church.

At the end of the fifteenth century, and first in Italy, there was a decided new outreach towards service of the poor and sick and an activist spirituality. This continued into the sixteenth century and focused on a great variety of activities: hospitals for the sick and for pilgrims; visitation of prisons and the accompaniment of condemned men to their death; the raising of dowries for poor girls; nursing care in homes; financing loans for the poor; teaching of catechism. Preachers from the religious orders frequently organized confraternities to keep alive the spirit of their missions and the practical exercise of charity. Two new popular devotions around which confraternities were increasingly formed were the Rosary and the veneration of Christ present in the Blessed Sacrament. Though both of these devotions originated in the late Middle Ages, they now underlined features of Catholicism under attack by the Protestants, devotion to Mary and belief in the Real Presence of Christ in the Eucharist.

Ecclesiastical authorities adopted an ambivalent attitude towards this proliferation of confraternities. On the one hand they wanted to encourage lay participation and even initiatitive; on the other they sought to control these associations more completely and to eliminate abuses, such as the expenditure of excessive sums on banquets and festivities. Trent empowered bishops to visit confraternities within their jurisdiction and especially to take measures to see that funds were used properly. The Confraternity of the Blessed Sacrament in one town near Cuenca, it seems, existed for little more than an occasional festive dinner together. A papal bull of 1604 determined that all new confraternities required the approval of the diocesan authorities. Another way of exercising ecclesiastical control was through the creation of archconfraternities, to the norms of which the confraternities would have to conform; most of these, as with the Archconfraternity of Christian Doctrine, were located in Rome, but by no means all of them. Many bishops encouraged the foundation of at least one confraternity in each parish, even remote ones, as a way of securing assistance from a parish elite for the pastor. They seem to have been successful, at least in Italy and Spain. Certainly, there was friction between pastors and lay leaders of the confraternities, but it is not at all clear that this was the rule. Many confraternities were associated with religious orders and their churches, and they offered an alternative to the urban parish. This created another source of friction between parish priests and religious orders. Until well into the seventeenth century the confraternities seem to have held their own, at least in many urban areas and in southern Europe.

In 1563 a young Jesuit from Liège studying in Rome, by the name of Jean Leunis, began to gather together students at the Roman College for special devotions. From this beginning was to spread into many cities of Catholic Europe the influential Marian Congregations, the most distinctively Jesuit confraternity. Usually based in a Jesuit college and not in a parish, they came to encompass many folks in a town: nobles, priests, married men, younger unmarried men, women, as well as various professional or occupational groups. Initially, people of different social ranks made up the congregations, thus emphasizing the equality of all, but fairly soon, in an accommodation to the tendency of the time and with growing membership, different social groups had their own local congregations. The Marian congregations differed from most confraternities in that they demanded more from their members: weekly confession and at least monthly Communion; daily Mass; weekly meetings; ascetical practices; and an increasing apostolic commitment, usually in terms of assistance to the poor, the sick, and prisoners or perhaps of teaching catechism or accompanying Jesuit fathers in their missionary activity. At entrance members consecrated themselves to the Blessed Mother and affirmed the Tridentine Profession of Faith. The congregations often manifested both a puritanical and a confessional militance, for example, advocating restrictions on Carnival activities or helping to ferret out suspected heretics. In the War of Cologne of 1583 they helped to mobilize the Catholic population in the defeat of the archbishop's attempt to turn the electorate into a Protestant territory.

Pope Gregory XIII's bull of 1584 designated the congregation at the Roman College as the primary Marian Congregation in the manner of an archconfraternity, to which all others were to be affiliated and to conform their organizational structure. By 1600 a network of congregations was in operation communicating with one another and offering mutual hospitality. The Antwerp congregation of married men counted 320 members in 1612, 1000 in 1664. In Lille and Cologne, each with a population of about 45,000 in the early seventeenth century, there were 2000 members in the local congregations. In the smaller Catholic towns of Douai and Ingolstadt there were 2000 and 3000 members respectively. In Munich first on the list of members of the *Congregatio major* was Duke Maximilian, and the Society generally sought to incorporate men of power and influence into the memberships.

According to the papal bulls, all the congregations were subject to the superior general of the Jesuits in Rome, and the Society appointed the directors of the local congregations. But otherwise the prefects and other officers were chosen by the membership in democratic elections, so that the lay leaders exercised considerable power and the membership gathered organizational experience. In the early seventeenth century, when some felt that the congregations were losing their élan, secret groups were formed, called the 'Aas', whose function was to rekindle the spirit and promote greater union, but some Jesuits were unhappy with this development of a secret elite. The promotion of a family life which equated women with men within marriage and moved away from the hierarchical model of family became a prime intention of the congregations, resulting in the admittance of more women, though usually in separate local congregations. In Ingolstadt in 1656 more than 700 women made their consecration together. The effects of the congregations were thus felt in politics, in charitable activity, in family life, but perhaps in the long run they, and many confraternities, were most significant for the schooling of lay people in organization and in governance. The course of the eighteenth century saw the congregations decline in many areas, only to revive at its end in some. Regions where they remained strong or recovered their vitality, like the southern Low Countries, the Rhineland, Alsace and Lorraine, and Bavaria did not subsequently become de-christianized. Louis Châtellier has argued that there was a carry-over from them through the nineteenth century Catholic social movements into the Christian democracy of the twentieth century.

Church and government often combined to employ forms of pressure and force, or discipline, to achieve results in evangelization, and they felt justified in doing so. Adam Contzen, the influential Jesuit confessor of Maximilian of Bavaria, discussed the issue of force or pressure at length in his *Ten Books on Politics* (1621). Faith, to be sure, must be voluntary if it is to be genuine, he recognized. Not even God compelled human beings to accept their own salvation. In leading folks to faith, good example, clear and persuasive preaching, effective catechesis, attractive liturgy, and education were the ordinary means to use. But if these failed, pressures might be applied, Contzen argued following Augustine, such as the requirement of attendance at sermons and church services, and the concession of privileges to those who complied and the imposition of penalties such as exclusion from office, or fines, on those who did not. He did not deal with more severe actions, such as exile or the death penalty which other Catholic authors such as Suarez and Bellarmine defended as suitable punishment for obstinate heretics. The psychological theory behind Contzen's position was that folks who performed external actions under pressure, such as attending Sunday Mass or sermons, would gradually take on the appropriate internal attitudes and so eventually perform the actions freely. This type of thinking was a part of both Catholic and Protestant pedagogy, and it was more applicable to young people than to adults. This was one reason for the concentration on education, and it helps to explain why both the Reformation and Catholic Reform were 'youth movements'. Religious authorities often gave up on adults and hoped for change with the younger generation.

A systematic, sometimes brutal, and eventually successful method for the re-catholicization of areas were the reformation commissions employed by the Austrian Habsburg rulers in the seventeenth century, when the principal enemy was heresy. These commissions developed out of the ecclesiastical procedure for visitation of parishes, and both Protestant and Catholic German rulers had made use of them previously.

Archduke Ferdinand, later Emperor Ferdinand II, commissioned Bishop Martin Brenner of Seckau in 1599 to lead such a reformation commission in his territories of Inner Austria, where Protestantism had made considerable inroads. Accompanying the bishop was a privy councillor, a treasury councillor, a secretary, and a band of 200 to 300 soldiers for protection. The commission's initial action upon arriving in a village or town was to expel the Protestant preacher if he still remained. Then the local community was summoned, and the bishop began a series of instructions on the Catholic faith, the evils of Lutheranism, and the advantages of conversion. Non-Catholics were then given a fixed period of time, usually a month, to decide whether they wanted to convert or not. In fact, the period was often extended and recalcitrants long tolerated. Exile was the alternative, but it was often in practice denied to peasants so as not to lose their labour. A Catholic pastor was installed by the commission and the appointment of a schoolteacher reserved to him. The commission then inspected the church building, looked into parish finances and, before leaving, drew up a set of regulations for the parish.

After the suppression of the Bohemian rebellion, Ferdinand followed similar procedures there, where the government played an even more prominent role. 'Piety can only be restored in Bohemia by a powerful authority', wrote Ferdinand's Jesuit confessor, William Lamormaini, in a memorandum of 1627 in which he recommended detailed procedures to be followed in Bohemia's recatholicization. Opposing him was the Capuchin Valeriano Magni, whose plan for Bohemia represented greater mildness and warned against the simulated conversions and resentment that excessive pressures would inevitably generate. Limited toleration would be more effective in the long run, and would allow for preaching and good example gradually to win over those who were hostile. The Jesuit proposal won out.

Both Ferdinand II and Ferdinand III made use of similar reformation commissions in Upper and Lower Austria, but none of these commissions seems to have enjoyed much success in rural areas until after the Thirty Years War, except for Inner Austria. In the early 1650s, then, Ferdinand III undertook a General Reformation in the Bohemian lands as well as in Upper and Lower Austria. Leopold I continued the project and brought it to a conclusion by the end of the century. In the process many folks were forced into exile, from Upper and Lower Austria perhaps 50,000 people altogether between 1620 and 1660, and from the Bohemian lands as many as 200,000. But Catholicism was restored, and it became a distinctive feature of the Habsburg Monarchy, even though a crypto-Protestant remnant remained for a time. Authorities well realized that the work of the reformation commissions was only the start of a long process of evangelization and education that, it was hoped, would lead to genuine conversion. In fact, there did evolve in the Monarchy, eventually to flourish, a Habsburg brand of Catholicism with deep popular roots. A weakness, however, perhaps unavoidable, which only became evident in later centuries, was its excessive attachment to the government and the dynasty.

Yet though it was undoubtedly a significant factor, one must be wary of exaggerating the element of compulsion in the Catholic Reform and in the Reformation. This is to overlook the attractiveness of methods of evangelization, the extent of popular religious devotion, and the widespread desire for a more profound religious life. On the other hand, there were undoubtedly many folks who were not firmly committed to either side of the religious divide and who simply shared the general desire for order. They were the ones most susceptible to pressures and most likely simply to follow the dictates of authority. The hope was that, in the long run, they would become convinced Catholics, or at least their children would.

6

EDUCATION

Few historical movements have taken education as seriously as the Catholic Reform or the Protestant Reformation. Both Catholics and Protestants saw the school as a principal instrument of inculcating the Christian message, and both realized the need to win over youth. Schooling was to become an essential part of the process of confessionalism; education was the most prominent instrument of the Catholic Reform. Preaching alone was inadequate to overcome popular religious ignorance and to instill the religious knowledge that the leaders thought necessary. We have already seen that members of the new religious orders served as schoolmasters or schoolmistresses. Perhaps adults and the elderly were set in their ways, but young people remained malleable and open to formation. Moreover, the church needed educated clerics and ministers; Catholic leaders saw the principal cause of the Reformation as the lack of formed and educated clergy. At the same time, government required a growing supply of officials and magistrates at every level. Parents realized that education was the way for their children to advance. So the demand for education was great. Hence the huge investment in schools by both Catholics and Protestants: Latin schools in the cities and towns with a view to the preparation of future leaders, priests or ministers and civil servants, and elementary schools in villages as well as cities and towns.

In the Latin schools Catholics and Protestants took over much of the educational programme of contemporary Renaissance humanists with their emphasis on the ancient classics. This was an obvious accommodation to the times, conscious or unconscious. Reading of the ancient authors was seen not only as the way to develop eloquence in the spoken and written word but also to foster growth in the moral virtues.

Apart from religious instruction, the curriculum of the programme of the Protestant educator Jean Sturm for his Latin school in Strasbourg overlapped surprisingly with the curriculum of the rapidly increasing Jesuit colleges. The new availability of printed books, especially catechisms, made the teaching of reading a high priority in the elementary schools.

Schools, of course, in most literate societies have served as instruments of socialization, social control, or social discipline; the lines between the three terms are not easily drawn and all of them can be taken in a positive sense. Catholic pioneers of education in the sixteenth century, such as Ignatius Loyola, Angela Merici, or Castellino da Castello (the Milanese diocesan priest chiefly responsible for the foundation of the Schools of Christian Doctrine), saw as the primary goal of their educational efforts the christianization of young people. Christianization engendered a more disciplined and civilized population. Civil authorities considered this an important gain for both society and government. Christianization and an ordered, disciplined society belonged together. For both purposes authorities supported the schools.

In Italy at the start of the sixteenth century there appears to have been little formal religious instruction in either elementary schools or the municipal Latin colleges. One initiative in this direction was undertaken by Niccolò Albergati, Bishop of Bologna back in 1417, when he began to organize catechism classes on a small scale. By 1425 he founded a lay confraternity with 24 members to support his goal. But the venture that was to result in widespread success started with a Milanese diocesan priest, Castellino da Castello, in 1536, when he probably was a man in his 60s. That year, on 30 November, the feast of St Andrew and a holiday in Milan, Father Castellino dispatched a lay colleague to lure young boys to a local church with the gift of an apple. There he taught them to make the sign of the cross properly and then promised more apples if they returned for further instruction. From the beginning Castellino made catechism attractive, employing a solid principle of Renaissance paedagogy.

Despite early opposition and ridicule, Castellino's project flourished first in Milan and then across northern Italy. In 1539 a lay Confraternity for Christian Reformation in Charity was formed to carry on the work; Castellino's initiative thus belongs in the tradition of the confraternity movement in Italy. A year later, due to ecclesiastical objections to the word 'Reformation' and to the teaching of religion by lay people, the Confraternity was suspended, but it reappeared in 1546 with ecclesiastical approval and eventually become the Confraternity of Christian Doctrine. By 1563 the Confraternity numbered 200 members who conducted 33 Schools of Christian Doctrine, as their schools were called, enrolling over 2000 children. From the start Castellino seems to have envisioned teaching girls too, and he recruited laywomen to instruct them, in separate classes to be sure. So laymen and laywomen were entrusted with ministry.

As places of religious and moral instruction as well as reading and, to a lesser extent, writing, these schools were an attempt to form a new style of Christians, who in turn would educate their children in the Christian way of life. Sessions were usually held on Sunday and feast-day afternoons, thus about 85 days in the year, so that children of all social classes from roughly six to 14 years of age could attend, even though in fact few children from noble families ever took part. Classes usually lasted about two hours. To avoid boring the students, the time was divided into short segments of drill, recitation, prayer both personal and communal, songs, and competitions. Instructors made use chiefly of two catechisms, which the students were taught to read. For beginners there was the *Summary of the Christian Life*, a booklet dating from 1537 and attributed to Castellino himself. For the more advanced there was the *Interrogations*, a much longer book using a question-and-answer format, whose standard edition, after some evolution, appeared in 1560. Both works aimed at a simple presentation of the Christian way of life, avoiding both polemical material and theological explanations. In contrast to Lutheran catechisms, they said little about sin and stressed the importance of works in addition to faith. The schools also used other printed materials, such as the popular *Little Office of the Blessed Virgin Mary*, a brief office in honour of Mary, modelled on the Breviary.

The Council of Trent, then, in 1563 insisted on the duty of parish priests to instruct children on Sundays and feast days in the truths of the faith. Pius V reiterated this in a bull of 1567 which called for the formation of confraternities in all dioceses in order to assist the parish priests in this task. When Charles Borromeo took up residence in Milan in 1565, he fostered the work of the Confraternity. He attempted to establish a school in each parish of his huge archdiocese, increasing clerical control over the schools but without attempting to alter the content of instruction. By 1579 there were 40 schools in Bologna, and by 1596, 740 schools in the archdiocese of Milan, one in nearly every parish, with almost 5000 teachers instructing close to 40,000 boys and girls. These catechetical schools became the first institution of mass education in the modern era. For a long period laypersons played a significant role in the movement. The Milanese layman Giambattista Casale kept a diary from 1554 to 1598 which recounted his labours and those of his wife and two sons in the catechetical schools, 'for the honor of God, the salvation of souls, and the common good', as he wrote. But especially as religious instruction was increased in the regular elementary schools under direction of the pastor or one of the new teaching orders, the part of laypersons diminished. Paul V raised the Roman branch of the Confraternity, which had been founded in 1560 by a Milanese layman, to an archconfraternity to which all other confraternities were expected to affiliate and conform. As we shall see, catechetical instruction spread, but nowhere was the Confraternity as significant as it was in Italy.

Elementary schools proliferated in the sixteenth and seventeenth centuries. Their goal was to integrate religious instruction with reading and writing, as in the Schools of Christian Doctrine. The foremost purpose was to make good Catholics. But it is very difficult to generalize about the percentage of children in city or country who attended school. There was a great variety of schools. Some were private, most were communally controlled, that is, conducted by a municipality or village in association with the parish or parishes. As time went on, increasingly in the towns, schools were entrusted to a religious order or congregation as was usually the case with schools for girls. Another division was between schools which taught Latin and those which limited themselves to the vernacular. Members of religious orders usually brought with them a spirituality and some paedagogical preparation whereas other schoolmasters did not. Especially after the Council of Trent, bishops sought to control the communal schools more effectively, and schoolmasters often had to make the Tridentine Profession of Faith and to secure an episcopal licence. Locally, the pastor was expected to oversee the schoolmaster, who himself might well be a priest or, in some cases, the sacristan. Spain seems to have lagged behind Italy and perhaps Germany in providing elementary education, though recent research indicates that literacy rates there were equal to those elsewhere. A new emphasis on elementary schools was evident in France from the early seventeenth century, where poor relief was sometimes conditional upon school attendance. The new religious congregations were to do more for schooling there than elsewhere, and this for women as well as men.

As early as the 1540s the Jesuits made their turn towards education. They were the first religious order in the history of the Catholic Church for whom formal education became a leading ministry. By the time of their suppression in 1773 they conducted more than 800 institutions in an international educational network unparalleled before or since. Their involvement in the schools was to have a significant impact on early modern European culture and to exemplify the consonance of faith with literature, art, and science. Jesuit colleges frequently served as centres of local cultural life.

Despite the earlier foundation of a college at Gandía in Spain, the network of Jesuit educational institutions traces its real origin to the opening in 1547 of the college at Messina in Sicily, which was the first college principally for non-Jesuit students. At the suggestion of the Spanish viceroy, Don Juan de Vega, who knew Ignatius personally, the city fathers of Messina requested that the newly founded Society establish a college there. Ignatius responded by dispatching 10 Jesuits to open the school, including the young Dutchman Peter Canisius, who was later to serve for many decades as the leader of the Jesuits in Germany, and Jerome Nadal, who already in 1548 outlined a curriculum for Messina which was the first step towards the later Jesuit *Ratio Studiorum* or *Plan of Studies*. The following year saw the opening of another college in Palermo, and then on 22 February 1551, the Roman College welcomed its first students, the sign over its door reading 'A School of Grammar, Humanities, and Christian Doctrine, free'. Rapidly it grew into a university, and it came to serve as the model for Jesuit educational institutions around the world. Later in 1551 Ignatius himself issued a circular letter to the whole Society encouraging the foundation of colleges, and in the last years of his life four or five new colleges were opened each year, so that when he died in 1556 there were approximately 33 colleges. Shortly before his death, an aide wrote on his behalf to the young Philip II that 'all the well-being of Christianity and of the whole world depends on the proper education of youth'. For many early Jesuits the dictum '*Puerilis institutio renovatio mundi*' (the education of youth [brings about] the renewal of the world) held true.

In the 1550s decisions were made about the development of the Jesuit ministry of education. In 1551 Ignatius decided that Jesuit colleges would not offer beginning instruction in Latin. The principal reason for this was that the nascent Society simply did not have the manpower to undertake the task. Students, when they started in a college, usually at about age 10, would have to come with some preparation in Latin. The effect of this was widespread exclusion of the poor from the schools and the direction of the educational ministry towards the middle and upper classes. But there were many exceptions to this. Ignatius and the early Jesuits do not seem to have followed a clear plan for the location of colleges, but they seem to have waited for invitations which soon streamed into Rome. They did prefer large cities, and especially cities with universities, because that is where people were to be found who exercised influence and so would be able to support the christianization at which the Jesuits aimed. Ignatius himself, however, did take the initiative for a college in Florence, and the establishment of the first Jesuit college in France at the small town of Billom in 1556 seems to have been dictated by the desire to secure the support of the local bishop, an influential figure in Paris, Guillaume Duprat, for the college that Ignatius envisioned for Paris. Antonio Possevino in the 1560s worked out a strategy for a network of schools in Piedmont and Savoy.

Some of the early colleges failed and had to be abandoned, often because of inadequate financing or staffing. The Second General Congregation of the Society, its highest legislative body, attempted to check the growth of colleges in 1565. In 1593 the Jesuit superior general, Claudio Acquaviva, laid down norms regarding the minimum endowment and the minimum number of Jesuits required for the acceptance of a college, but these were frequently ignored in practice. By 1600 there were 236 colleges in existence. In Italy and Sicily there were 56; in Portugal and the Portuguese colonies, 21; in Spain and the Spanish New World, 77, including 15 in Mexico and Peru; and 82 in the rest of Central and Western Europe of which 21 were in France. Estimates of the number of students in the Jesuit colleges in about 1630 in France alone range from 25,000 to 40,000. The social composition of the Jesuit schools in the seventeenth century differed from country to country and from region to region, and it fluctuated accordingly as times were good or bad. In Italy, where the Society conducted several colleges for nobles, the number of students from the nobility may have been disproportionately high. But the sons of office-holders, merchants, and some tradesmen or peasants vastly outnumbered the sons of the nobility elsewhere. Figures are most available for France. In the mid-1640s at the college of Bordeaux, site of a *parlement* and a port city, of the 664 students 300 came from the homes of bourgeois office-holders, 138 from merchant families, 54 from noble households, and 38 from peasant or artisan families. A couple of decades earlier the 1500 students at Billom, located in a rural area, included more than 250 from more prosperous peasant families and at Châlons-sur-Marne, a centre of the wool trade, more than 120 of 600 students were sons of artisans and nearly 200 sons of merchants.

How can we explain the success of the Jesuit colleges? Certainly there were a number of reasons which were not at all mutually exclusive. One clearly was that they offered instruction free of charge. The colleges were endowed, by municipalities, wealthy families, upper clergy, ruling princes. Particularly in Italy and in France the Jesuits took over recently founded municipal schools, often stirring the resentment of lay teachers who lost their positions. Many families undoubtedly saw in the colleges the first step towards social advancement for their sons. In 1617 the recently elected superior general, Mutius Vitelleschi, in a letter to the whole Society, echoed a lament which he attributed to Francis Borgia, who had been superior general from 1565 to 1572, 'how many come to us in order to become rich, how few in order to become better'. Civil and ecclesiastical benefactors saw in the schools a source of well-prepared government officials, as well as diocesan and religious priests. Many folks, benefactors, students, and their families were sold on the Jesuit educational programme. After much reflection and experimentation, starting with the first venture at Messina back in 1548, the programme was elaborated in the Jesuits' *Plan of Studies* which was finally promulgated in 1599. One characteristic feature was the allowance for adaptation to local circumstances.

The Jesuit programme combined classical humanist, Christian, and at the higher levels scholastic elements towards the formation of young men of 'learned and eloquent piety', or better, character (*docta et eloquens pietas*). There were basically three kinds of Jesuit educational institution: the college, the academy, and the university. The line between them was often blurred. The boy entering a Jesuit college at nine or 10 years of age could normally count on five years of study: first, second, and third grammar classes followed by a year of humanities and rhetoric each. Many colleges added courses in philosophy and in moral theology, so enabling the student to begin his university studies while still at the college. These colleges were often given the name 'academy', and usually required study of another two to three years. A small Jesuit college might number 150 to 200 students, a college of middle size up to 500. The college in Munich had 900 students in 1600, when it had already begun to offer courses in philosophy, as well as one in moral theology and one in controversial theology. By 1631 it reached a total of 1500 students, only to sink back to about 1000 for most of the eighteenth century. Beyond that the university comprised the study of scholastic theology, canon law, and Scripture in what was a four-year programme. Generally, the Jesuits avoided involvement in law or medicine and stuck to theology at the university level.

Usually at Jesuit institutions there was also a residence for live-in students, who might make up a quarter of the total student body, and, as we shall see, seminaries were often attached to Jesuit colleges. The famous college of La Flèche near Paris constructed a dormitory in 1612 to accommodate 200 students, about one-sixth of the student body. Ignatius initially prohibited corporal punishment in the colleges. When complaints forced him to relent, he allowed colleges to hire an outsider to administer such punishment when absolutely necessary, but strictly forbade Jesuits ever to do so.

One strong point of the Jesuit programme was its use of the *modus Parisiensis*, that is, the structured curriculum used at the University of Paris, familiar to the early Jesuits from their days of study there. It provided the order so dear to the age. The students were divided into clearly delineated classes which were to be taken in a particular order and which provided for promotion when the student had mastered the material of a class. This contrasted sharply with the practice in much of Europe, especially Italy. The emphasis on the humanities aimed at articulate expression of written and spoken Latin, the emotional and imaginative formation that good literature provides, and the adaptability or capacity to accommodate to one's audience that rhetoric teaches. The Jesuits also generally shared the belief that the study of classical authors, select ones to be sure – Cicero was the favourite – fostered growth in the natural virtues and a sense of civic responsibility. A feature of the Jesuit colleges not found in most contemporary schools was the study of Greek, which began as early as the first year of study.

Classical theatre had experienced a revival in the late fifteenth century as a part of the contemporary recovery of ancient culture. Germany's University of Heidelberg was central to this development, and it was exploited by Luther and especially Melancthon in Lutheran schools as a means to the *pietas litterata* that they too desired. As an extracurricular activity in Jesuit colleges theatre complemented the humanist curriculum with its development of dramatic and declamatory skills as well as its opportunity for music and ballet. The missionary thrust of the Society then brought the drama out of the school to court or into the town square for performances before a larger public. Jesuit theatrical productions became in many places major social and cultural events, above all perhaps in Germany and especially in Munich, where casts of hundreds performed. The stage came to represent the world or even the cosmos on which the great struggle for salvation between Christ and the forces of evil was played out dramatically before the audience. *Festspiele* occasionally lasted two or three days. The Jesuits themselves produced a number of playwrights whose works avoided the indecency and immorality often found in classical dramatists such as Terence, who were considered unsuitable for the students except in expurgated editions. Perhaps the most famous Jesuit dramatist was Jacob Bidermann, whose 'The Doctor of Paris' or '*Cenodoxus*' was first performed in Munich in 1609. Calderòn and the great French comic dramatist Molière were Jesuit students.

Christianity permeated the atmosphere of the college and Christian observances punctuated the daily, weekly, and annual schedule, though there seems to have been only one formal class in Christian doctrine per week. The diary of Pietro Antonio Adami, a student at the College of Saint Lucy in Bologna in the 1670s, fleshes out the prescriptions of the *Plan of Studies*. At the start and finish of the school day, students were encouraged, 'out of devotion not obligation', to make a visit to the Blessed Sacrament in the school chapel. In each classroom there was an altar with an image of the Blessed Virgin; when the student entered, he reverenced the altar and prayed a Hail Mary before taking his seat. Each class meeting opened with a prayer, and at the end of morning classes all students attended Mass together, during which they often prayed either the Rosary or the *Office of the Blessed Virgin Mary*. Saturdays there was usually a spiritual conference for the students, and during Mass they were led in an examination of conscience and given the opportunity for confession. Monthly confession and reception of Holy Communion was expected, and students sometimes approached these sacraments more frequently, bi-weekly or even weekly. On Sundays and feast days there was Mass with a sermon in the morning and then vespers in the evening, with major feasts often marked by processions and other demonstrations of faith. Carnival and Lent brought series of sermons, usually on Wednesdays or Fridays when school began a half-hour earlier than usual. Altogether, these practices introduced a certain order or cohesion into the religious life of the students, which it was hoped they would continue once they left the school.

A peculiar feature of the Jesuit college was the Marian Congregation, which aimed to foster the growth of a spiritual elite and provide students with an opportunity to develop further their devotional lives. A circular letter of 1564 encouraged Jesuits in all their colleges to introduce it. Congregations quickly reached out beyond the college students to many other groups within towns and cities, as we have seen. The collegiate congregation enjoyed a fair amount of self-government through elected officers, but a Jesuit director was the ultimate authority.

The Marian Congregation at the College of St Lucy was perhaps typical. Organized under the Marian title of the Annunciation prior to 1585, it was aggregated to the Roman congregation in 1587. Its rapid growth led to the formation of a second congregation in 1596, and a restructuring in 1608 resulted in the formation of four congregations, one now including students at the University of Bologna as well as the Jesuit college. Further reorganizations took place, and the congregations continued not only to exist but to function reasonably well, continuing after the suppression of the Jesuits in 1773 under other religious orders. At one point the congregations included nearly all the students in St Lucy's, which leads one to believe that new branches were created in order to maintain the spirit of an elite. Meetings were held weekly, and focused intently on devotional exercises. There were special celebrations on feasts of the Blessed Virgin Mary and of Jesuit saints, and particularly on the patronal feast of the individual congregation.

As we have seen, the Barnabites and the Piarists, the Oratorians and the Doctrinaires all founded colleges in turn. The former pair located their schools in Italy and in Central Europe, whereas the latter two did so chiefly in France. The Piarists and the Oratorians were to show themselves more open than the Jesuits to the changes in science of the seventeenth century.

Two male religious congregations came into existence in the course of the Catholic Reform with the initial goal of providing elementary education to the poor. The first were the Piarists, founded by the Spanish priest Joseph Calasanz, who arrived in Rome in 1592 at age 35 with a view to advancing his career. The charitable activities of several confraternities attracted his participation, and the Confraternity of Christian Doctrine particularly engaged him. Soon aware of the need for education for Rome's poor boys, Calasanz opened in 1597 a free elementary school to which students flocked. For a long time they were required to secure a testimonial from their pastor that they were indeed poor. By 1612 there were 800 students, and in 1616 a second school opened in Frascati. Benefactors including the pope were won over. Although dissension within the order marred its beginnings, the number of schools increased. Twelve more were added in Italy by 1630. The following year saw the foundation of a house at Nikolsburg in Moravia. So the Piarists' activity extended into the Habsburg Monarchy where they were introduced by Catholics who wanted an alternative to the Jesuits. The controversial *condottiere* Wallenstein attempted to secure a Piarist house for his principality of Friedland. Later in the seventeenth century the Piarists expanded into Hungary, Poland, and Spain.

In addition to free instruction for the poor, new with Calasanz was the attempt to combine instruction in arithmetic with catechism and with reading and writing in both the vernacular and Latin. Instruction was to enable students to find jobs, and for this practical subjects were necessary; but it was also to introduce them to a culture to which Latin provided the key. Many students left school at the age of 12 to seek employment, whereas others stayed on, especially for the Latin. As the order expanded, schools evolved frequently into colleges, and though they generally maintained their orientation towards the poor, the Piarists did open several colleges for nobles. This led to competition and some conflict with the Jesuits. Piarist schools paid more attention to mathematics, and they were more sympathetic to the new physical sciences than were the Jesuits; indeed there emerged a group later called the 'Galilean Piarists' (*Scolopi Galileiani*). Calasanz, who personally found mathematics fascinating, maintained contact with Galileo in the latter's late years, and one of Galileo's disciples, the scientist Giovanni Alfonso Borelli, spent two years as a Piarist. Here was another source of friction with the normally Aristotelian Jesuits.

France was the country where the most significant advances were made regarding primary education. As we saw earlier, there John Baptist de la Salle's Christian Brothers realized the first national programme of primary education. Through much of the seventeenth century, and especially after 1650, there were many initiatives for the education of the poor, at first more for girls than for boys. Normally responsibility for the organization of primary education according to episcopal directives rested with the parish priest, and in 1654 there appeared a widely circulated manual, *The Parish School*. Peter Fourier, a co-founder in the first years of the century of the Congregation of Our Lady, had failed to secure Rome's approval for an order of male teachers. Charles Demia in Lyons and Nicholas Barré in Rouen and Paris had organized elements of a school system, but their work did not survive them. De la Salle, on the other hand, effectively institutionalized in the Christian Brothers his vision of a professional teacher who was neither priest nor sacristan as were many instructors.

Born in Rheims into a family of the nobility of the robe in 1651, de la Salle studied for the priesthood there until 1670, when he began nearly two years at St Sulpice in Paris. There he came under the influence of the priest Adrien Bourdoise and spent time teaching the poor in the parish schools. Upon his return to Rheims he assumed his position as a cathedral canon, was ordained priest, and by 1680 completed his doctorate in theology at the University of Rheims. But an event of 1679 turned his life in its definitive direction. That year in Rheims he met Adrian Nyel, a priest who had come there to start up two schools for the poor. The young schoolmasters Nyel brought with him encountered problems. First, de la Salle rented a house for them, then he took them into his own house, and finally he moved into a new house with them. Gradually, the group formed a community, of which de la Salle was the natural leader. In 1683 he surrendered his canonry and its income, so committing himself and the group to a life of poverty and trust in God. By the time of his death in 1710 the Brothers conducted schools in 22 different locations – in some cities they had several schools – including one in Rome founded shortly after the turn of the century. By 1789 they had opened 116 schools, all organized in the same fashion. They often faced opposition, especially from organizations of schoolmasters who feared for their jobs, but the Brothers concentrated on the poor. De la Salle was a prolific writer in addition to being an efficient administrator, and he left behind spiritual writings, textbooks, and hymn books, as well as the *Rule*, which he worked over much of his life and which received papal approbation in 1725. Most significant was his *Conduct of Christian Schools*, completed in 1695 but only published posthumously in 1720.

The Brothers took a vow to teach their pupils without taking any payment from them. Private benefactors, municipalities, or the church provided the funding. Their curriculum included first, religion, then reading, writing, and arithmetic, and finally vocational training to be determined by local needs. De la Salle dismissed Latin from the primary school and taught only French, which was a significant change. Another innovation was the normal school or school for teachers, first for the Brothers themselves and then for lay schoolmasters serving in rural parishes. De la Salle restricted the Brothers themselves to work in cities and towns. If they were to assume responsibility for schools in the country, Brothers would have to live alone or in couples, and so there would be no community life. More importantly, perhaps, for de la Salle, they would become subordinate to the parish priest and involved in parish pastoral work. This would detract from their vocation as teachers. The Brothers also offered continuing education, in that they taught not only religion but other subjects on Sundays and feast days to those who worked during the week. Delinquent boys gained their attention, and they opened several schools for them too.

The instruction of girls lagged well behind that of boys. Most girls of aristocratic or patrician families were placed in cloistered convents for their formation as well as for the preservation of their virginity until the time came for them to marry or to take the veil in the convent. Generally, the Sunday schools of the Confraternity of Christian Doctrine sought to provide catechetical instruction for girls as well as boys. France, along with the Catholic Netherlands and the Rhineland, was the area where the education of girls advanced the most. In 1584 the Provincial Council of Bourges called for the instruction of girls in catechism and reading, and entrusted it to widows and matrons. Yet in 1673, of the 270 parishes in and around Paris, only 44 sponsored a school (*petite école*) for girls, as opposed to the 223 parish-sponsored schools for boys. There was a great difference across the dioceses of the country in the number of parishes that sponsored a girls school. For example, on the eve of the Revolution, 6 per cent of the parishes in the diocese of Albi maintained schools for girls, compared with 60 per cent in Arles. Even more than for boys, the schools were concentrated in the cities and towns.

The rapid expansion of the Ursulines and other congregations dedicated to the education of girls showed that they met a real need in French society. Starting with their first foundation in Avignon in 1598, the Ursulines had over 300 houses in France in the 1670s. The church realized that young girls as future mothers would influence their families, and so could contribute in a major way to the christianization of the people. Usually the Ursuline colleges ministered to three groups of girls or women. First, there were the boarding students who tended to be of the upper classes and who in a medium-sized school might amount to 30, but at Lille and Tournai numbered over 100. Then there were the extern students, of whom there might be from 300 to 500, although at Brussels in 1700 they numbered nearly 900. For them school was free, so that there were many girls from the middle and even lower classes. Finally, there were the adult women, along with girls, who came for catechetical instruction each Sunday and feast day, perhaps as many as 200. Beyond that, a confraternity was frequently associated with an Ursuline college.

The educational programme of the Ursuline colleges differed from that of the Jesuit colleges, further emphasizing religious instruction and the living of the Christian life. From the schools were to come women who would be pious Christian mothers and efficient household managers. The girls were taught to read and write French, in some cases to read Latin too, and to do arithmetic; domestic skills such as sewing were also part of the curriculum. Besides this, instruction in a trade was frequently a part of the programme, so that the girls could find work if necessary. By the eighteenth century some science was being taught. The Ursuline schools in Italy seem to have had a less ambitious programme, teaching only reading.

Many other foundations sprang up in France and the Low Countries in the seventeenth century for the education primarily of lower- and middle-class girls. There was the Congregation of Our Lady, established by Alex Le Clerc and Peter Fourier in 1597, and the Daughters of Our Lady of Jeanne de Lestonnac, dating from Bordeaux in 1606. Other congregations began as groups of schoolmistresses who then banded together under diocesan auspices, such as the Daughters of the Cross of Mme de Villeneuve, who were recognized by the Archbishop of Lyons in 1642. Seventeen new women's teaching congregations appeared in France between 1660 and 1715. Without formal vows, and so not bound by cloister, they were able to move more easily into rural areas, and some of them combined education with charitable activities. Many of the 'charités' of the Daughters of Charity of Vincent de Paul and Louise de Marillac also taught catechism to girls. In Paris they contracted with 25 parishes to conduct centres for the distribution of food and alms, medical assistance, and the education of girls. In some cases the congregations assisted the internal missionaries by visiting homes and by conducting catechetical lessons for women during missions. Others conducted a form of normal school for schoolmistresses who were to return to their villages to teach the girls. Most of these congregations were active within a particular diocese, but one, the Ladies of Saint Maur, were an exception; they spread from Rouen to Paris and then throughout the realm, partly because of the favour of Mme de Maintenon, the friend of Louis XIV.

For both Catholics and Protestants university education ranked as a high priority. Fifty Catholic universities were founded between 1550 and 1700, and 33 Protestant ones. In both cases the principal function of the university came to be the preparation of young men for service in the church and in the state. Theology was the dominant faculty in the sixteenth century; it yielded to law in the seventeenth, a sign of the increasing need for functionaries at various levels of government. The Iberian universities stood out in the Catholic world during the sixteenth century for their study of theology, philosophy, and law. Early in the century the University of Salamanca assumed the leading position previously held by the University of Paris. The great Spanish master Francisco de Vitoria studied at Paris before returning to Spain in 1523 and assuming the first chair of theology at Salamanca three years later. There he introduced Aquinas's *Compendium of Theology* in place of Peter Lombard's *Sentences*, thus inaugurating a new school in which his pupils and fellow Dominicans Domingo de Soto and Melchior Cano were major figures. The great moralist and canonist Martin Azpilcueta taught there in the 1530s, and much later, in the 1630s, a distinguished group of Carmelite theologians published a widely circulated *Course of Theology* which was an extended commentary on the *Compendium* of Aquinas. Suarez's *Metaphysical Disputations*, which he published in 1597 while teaching at Coimbra in Portugal, greatly influenced the study of phil-osophy and the understanding of Aristotle among Protestants as well as Catholics, this in addition to his writings on law. Yet by the middle of the seventeenth century the Iberian universities were in obvious decline, partly because of the setbacks to Spain's economy. In general the seventeenth century saw the importance of the European university diminish and cede leadership in intellectual life to the new scientific and literary academies.

In the Netherlands, the University of Louvain stood throughout the early Reformation as a bastion of Catholic orthodoxy. There in the second half of the century under the influence of Michael Baius and later of Cornelius Jansen himself, both of whom saw themselves as the legitimate interpreters of Augustine, the university became a centre of early theological Jansenism.

In contrast to Louvain, where they were kept out of the university, the Jesuits secured for themselves a strong position in the German Catholic universities and so an influence in German Catholic academic life well beyond what they enjoyed in Spain, France, or even Italy. In Ingolstadt, Cologne, Freiburg, and Erfurt a certain number of faculty positions came to be reserved for them, and in Trier, Mainz, Würzburg, and much later Heidelberg, Jesuits fully staffed some faculties, usually arts or philosophy and theology. Most attractive to the Jesuits were the theological faculties, because of their influence on the education of the clergy. Law and medicine were only rarely their concern. Dillingen, Molsheim, Paderborn, Osnabrück, Bamberg, and Graz all became Jesuit universities; that is, where the whole university was under Jesuit control. Of these, Dillingen was the only previously existing university, the others having grown out of Jesuit colleges. In addition, in the 1620s under Ferdinand II the Jesuits took over the faculties of arts, philosophy, and theology at the University of Vienna where they remained in charge well into the eighteenth century. At roughly the same time, after the defeat of the Bohemian rebellion, there began a bitter contest over the future of the venerable Charles University in Prague, which had been a centre of Protestant activism, and its relationship to the Jesuit academy founded by Ferdinand I. This stuggle eventually pitted Ferdinand II and the Jesuits against the Archbishop of Prague, the new Roman Congregation of the Propaganda Fide, and other religious orders, especially the Capuchins, who wanted to limit the expanding influence and near-monopoly of higher education in Bohemia of the Jesuits. Only in 1654, long after the death of the principal protagonists, was the conflict resolved with the formation of the Carolo-Ferdinandine University, which represented a partial victory for the Jesuits and the Habsburgs. Meanwhile, partly out of fear of Jesuit predominance in the area, the Archbishop of Salzburg summoned the Benedictines to found a university there. It opened in 1628 with a completely Benedictine faculty supported by the Benedictine monasteries of South Germany and Austria.

The Jesuits' Roman College had first opened its doors in 1551, with a faculty of 15 for 60 students. Ignatius wanted it to stand out as the model for Jesuit colleges, but he also foresaw from the beginning that it would evolve into a university at the service of the Holy See to which students would come from all over the Catholic world. Higher studies were initiated as early as 1553, and in 1556 it received from the papacy the right to grant doctorates in philosophy and theology as the universities in Paris, Salamanca, and Louvain did. But out of deference, it seems, to the *Sapienza*, the older Roman university dating from Boniface VIII and reorganized by Leo X in 1513, the Jesuit institution never took the title of university. The Roman College struggled with barely adequate financing, until Gregory XIII paid off its debt in the early 1580s, established an endowment for 200 students, and underwrote the construction of a magnificent new structure by Bartolomeo Ammanati, who had earlier drawn up the plans for the Pitti Palace in Florence. The Society summoned its luminaries to teach at the Roman College. The Spaniards Juan de Mariana and Francisco Suarez both lectured there early in their careers. The Italian Robert Bellarmine was called from Louvain by Gregory XIII in 1576 to assume the chair of controversial theology, a position he held until his appointment to the cardinalate in 1599 and during the tenure of which he published his *Controversies*. For 47 years, starting in 1565, the German Christopher Clavius (Klau) was professor of mathematics at the Roman College. He was a key figure in the calendar reform which resulted in the new Gregorian Calendar in 1583, and both he and Bellarmine were still on the scene to play ambivalent parts in the nascent Galileo Affair. The presence of the Roman College in the Eternal City gave both Rome and the papacy a new academic respectability. After his visit to Rome in 1581 Montaigne wrote in his *Travel Journal*, 'It is a marvel how much of a place this college holds in Christendom ... it is a nursery of great men in every sort of greatness.'[1]

In association with the Roman College, the papacy now for the first time in its history intervened to help educate diocesan clergy for local churches, first for Germany and then for other areas of Europe and the world. In the early 1540s curial officials in Rome, in particular Cardinal Morone, came to realize that Rome would have to assist in the preparation of priests for Germany in order to prevent the complete collapse of Catholicism in the Empire. The same idea came to Ignatius Loyola at a time when the fathers at Trent were discussing the need to provide a new programme of clerical education. Pope Julius II was won over to the project, and in August 1552 a papal bull was issued calling into existence the German College as a papal institution which was to be administered by the Jesuits. Students would come, principally from Germany, and they would live at the college while taking most of their courses at the Roman College. The doors opened in the autumn of 1552, and in the first eight years of its existence the college welcomed 68 students. But financial shortfalls soon intervened, and for a time the college housed a number of young Italian noblemen, few of whom were on the way to the priesthood.

Again Gregory XIII took the initiative. He gave the college a solid financial base. Under him also the goal of the institution shifted. Ignatius's intent had been to prepare diocesan priests who would be missionaries, pastors, and theologians in Germany. But in the 1570s, and especially after the War of Cologne in 1583, the need for well-educated and reform-minded cathedral canons in Germany became evident, largely because they were the ones who elected the prince–bishops and eventually were elected prince–bishops themselves. In order to be appointed to a chapter, however, one needed to be a noble. So after the 1580s the German College devoted itself in particular to the preparation of German nobles for positions in the chapters and eventually for bishoprics. From 1600 to 1800 nobles made up about half the number of those who matriculated and, for the whole period from 1560 to 1803, 22 per cent of the German bishops (including those in the Habsburg lands where they were especially well represented) were *Germaniker*, which did not guarantee, however, that they were always friendly to Rome. The papacy then subsidized a number of pontifical seminaries located in the Empire itself for the education of diocesan priests: in Vienna (1574), Prague (1575), Graz (1578), Fulda (1584), and Dillingen (1585). The seminaries in Braunsberg (1578) in Prussia and in Olmütz (1579) in Moravia were oriented more towards the Scandinavian countries, and the latter was open to young men other than seminarians. These seminaries usually numbered between 15 and 50 students, and they were associated with the local Jesuit educational institution.

The German College served as the model, then, for a number of other national colleges in Rome, including the Greek College (1577), the English College (1578), the Hungarian College (which merged with the German College in 1580), and the Maronite College (1584). Later came the Scottish College (1600), the Irish College (1628), and in 1627 the College for the newly erected Congregation for the Propagation of the Faith (*Urbanum*) which prepared priests for service in missionary areas. Meanwhile, older religious orders established institutions in Rome.

The Dominicans' *Angelicum* was founded in 1577, and the Franciscan College of St Bonaventure came into existence in 1587. So Rome became a centre of clerical education in the latter part of the sixteenth century, a position it has held up to the present day.

A principal concern of the Fathers at Trent was to make provision for the education and formation of the diocesan clergy. Indeed, during the Middle Ages there existed no system or effective norms for clerical education. Increasingly clerics attended a university while residing at one of its colleges, but the majority of diocesan clergy prepared for their office through attendance at cathedral schools and a form of apprenticeship at a cathedral or with a pastor. Trent's decree of 15 July 1563 stipulated that each diocese was to have its own seminary for the education of its clergy. The bishop was to be in control of the institution. The seminarians were to be at least 12 years of age and able to read and write, and bishops were to make special efforts to recruit them from among the poor. They were to live a common life by themselves in a building of their own, and they were to bear the clerical tonsure and wear clerical dress. Daily Mass and regular confession and Holy Communion were to be features of their life. Instruction was to take place in the seminary itself with its own faculty, so, implicitly, not in the university. The decree foresaw as the chief subjects for study the humanities, Scripture, and the liturgy, with a special emphasis on preparation for the hearing of confessions. Nothing was said about speculative or scholastic theology. With its intent to separate seminarians from the dangerous world around them, the decree fostered a clerical awareness as a group set apart. It did not, we should note, prescribe that all future priests had to pass through the seminary.

Trent's decree eventually had far-reaching effects on the church, but implementation took decades and even centuries, and its history is often obscure. Many seminaries were not strictly Tridentine in character, in that the students followed courses at a university or Jesuit college since the seminary did not have its own faculty. The intent to have a seminary in each diocese was excessively ambitious, since many dioceses possessed neither the financial nor the human resources to support a decent faculty. Some seminaries failed, and others were small, designedly or not, with 15 to 20 students. Opposition to the seminaries frequently came from those who were expected to pay for them, for the most part members of chapters and other holders of benefices whose income was to be taxed. Many bishops and other clerics had studied at university colleges and considered these adequate to the task. Nor did they want to compete with these university colleges or with the colleges established by the Jesuits and other religious orders. Then, of course, simple inertia hindered the foundation of seminaries.

Tridentine seminaries caught on gradually in Italy and in Spain. Charles Borromeo established one in Milan as early as 1564, and Pius IV did the same for Rome the next year, but there the seminarians went to class at the Jesuits' Roman College. The year 1566 saw the establishment of a seminary for the diocese of Novara, just to the west of Milan and the largest diocese in Italy territorially after Milan, and two subordinate seminaries came into existence there in 1573 and 1581. The mainstays of the curriculum were the *Roman Catechism*, liturgy, homiletics, and cases of conscience. Neither theology nor Scripture was a part of the curriculum at Novara and, it seems, in many Italian seminaries, probably because these were considered unnecessary in many parishes, especially in mountainous Alpine areas. The seminaries in Novara existed alongside grammar schools and colleges, including one founded by the Barnabites and especially the Cannobian School established by a legacy in 1603 and taken over by the Jesuits in 1624, who would conduct it until their suppression in 1773. Many seminarians studied there in addition to or instead of at the seminary, in what may have been a pattern for Italy. Early on, seminaries came into existence in a number of other Italian dioceses, for example in Rieti in 1564, in Imola and Ravenna in 1567, in Rimini and Bologna in 1568, in Velletri in 1570. By one account there were 198 seminaries in Italy by 1700, many of them small and some probably only grammar schools for prospective ordinands.

Twenty diocesan seminaries were founded in Spain before 1600, including those at Granada (1564), Burgos (1565), and Barcelona (1593). Eight more followed in the course of the seventeenth century, and by the end of the next century there was a total of 45. They seem to have been, generally, of mediocre quality. The seminary founded at Cuenca in 1584, amounted in 1624 to 24 young men between 12 and 18, who then continued their education at the nearby University of Alcalá. So they followed a developing pattern in Cuenca that resulted in the near-doubling of the number of priests with university degrees to 45 per cent in the generation after Trent. Spanish reformers often preferred university degrees for the clergy.

Germany saw only slow growth in the number of Tridentine seminaries. One was founded at Eichstätt in 1565, but it failed, as did all diocesan seminaries that appeared in Germany prior to 1600. For a time the Bavarian dukes favoured the university college, one of which they founded at the University of Ingolstadt in 1576, the *Albertinum*. But the model generally followed in Germany was that of the seminary closely attached to, or a part of, a Jesuit college. The *Albertinum* was incorporated into the Jesuit college at Ingolstadt in 1599, where the seminarians could then take advantage of the courses at the university. The college at Munich added sufficient courses in philosophy and theology to prepare students for the ministry. A similar situation prevailed at Mainz, where the college evolved into an academy. The papacy, as we have seen, came to the assistance of clerical education in Germany not only with the German College but with further papal seminaries which were associated with Jesuit institutions. Only in the seventeenth century did successful diocesan seminaries appear: at Passau (1638), Regensburg (1654), and Freising (1691). The shortage of diocesan priests, and of seminaries, was particularly acute in the Habsburg territories.

France was the country where the Tridentine seminaries enjoyed the most extensive influence, though here too the initial movement was slow and the situation to be dealt with discouraging. An archdeacon of Bourges remarked in 1643 that 'there are priests who do not understand a word of Latin'. At roughly the same time, visitors in the diocese of Autun characterized pastors as 'absolutely inept', 'ignorant, without any instruction', 'of mediocre capacity and knowledge'. The Cardinal of Lorraine saw to the establishment of a seminary at Rheims in 1567, but its success was limited. A flurry of foundations followed the Edict of Melun in 1581, whereby the French clergy accepted the Tridentine decrees, and there were 16 by 1620. Nearly all of these were residences where as few as 10 students lived as they took courses at the local Jesuit college.

Only near the mid-point of the seventeenth century did the seminaries begin to flourish in France, where 40 came into existence between 1642 and 1660. Cardinal Richelieu and Vincent de Paul both championed the new seminaries. In his *Political Testament* Richelieu insisted on the importance of the formation of priests for genuine church reform in France, and he supported the new societies of common life, the Oratorians, the Sulpicians, the Eudists, and especially the Lazarists who were founded with a view to assisting in the education of priests. Vincent was convinced that the provisions of Trent stipulated that the seminaries take students when they were still too young. His practice was to wait until they were closer to ordination and then to provide them with a more intense priestly, spiritual formation. Initially, this was provided in a retreat that lasted from two to 12 weeks, usually at a religious house such as Vincent's headquarters at St Lazare outside Paris. Eventually, this evolved into a course of one, two, and then five years, with an interruption to serve for a year in a parish, for example, as a schoolteacher. Students were not accepted until they had completed the course in humanities. The study of Scripture dominated the curriculum, followed by courses in moral theology, liturgy and chant, as well as homiletics. Only at the end of the century was systematic theology introduced, usually either of the Jansenist or the Molinist variety. By the mid-eighteenth century there were 153 seminaries, sometimes more than one in a diocese. The Jesuits were in charge of 32, but they came on the scene late, having assumed the responsibility for 22 after 1682 at the urgent request of Louis XIV, who was anxious to counter the influence of Jansenism in the Oratorian seminaries.

A practice that Vincent de Paul fostered, that contributed to clerical reform, was the monthly conference in which priests from five to 10 parishes came together to discuss a pastoral or theological issue. This was a form of continuing education. A schedule was drawn up for the year, and participants were expected to come prepared for the discussion. Complementary to these were similar conferences for the whole diocese. The first was held at Beauvais in 1646, and the practice took hold in the greater part of the French dioceses, serving not only to keep the priests alive intellectually, but also to create a common bond among them. Bishops encouraged priests to acquire their own libraries. Prominent in these were extracts from the works of Charles Borromeo, who exercised a great influence on the formation of French priests. More significant still was the theology of priesthood of the 'French School' elaborated by Cardinal Bérulle. According to this 'there were two types of persons, those who receive and those who communicate the spirit, the light, and the grace of Jesus. The first are all the faithful, the second are the priests.' This exalted view of the priestly vocation undoubtedly contributed to the common *esprit* increasingly evident among the French diocesan clergy that was not found elsewhere. Yet it also probably helped to set pastor off more clearly from parishioners, as did the soutane he now faithfully wore and his more reserved deportment. Of course, this attitude did not take root everywhere, probably much less in mountainous areas, but it clearly influenced the performance of the French clergy.

Certainly, by the early seventeenth century the quality of the diocesan clergy improved, but this was probably due to factors other than the seminaries, especially to the Jesuit colleges. But the seminaries clearly had an impact on the clergy's substantial improvement by the early eighteenth century. This becomes evident when we look at three criteria: residence, virtue, and pastoral performance meaning regular celebration of the liturgy, administration of the sacraments, and preaching. This improvement applies principally to pastors of parishes with their assistants – that is, those with the care of souls. Other diocesan clergy were the canons in cathedral and collegiate churches, who in some areas were necessarily of the nobility, and the many priests who served as chaplains to various institutions such as schools or hospitals, or perhaps as schoolmasters or tutors and did not have direct care of souls. Some had little more clerical obligations than to say Mass regularly at a chapel for a deceased person. It was among these priests without care of souls where most problems were to be found, at least in Italy, where there was a plethora of clergy. In the northern Italian diocese of Imola, in the second half of the eighteenth century, there were roughly 250 priests engaged in parishes compared to over 600 without direct care of souls, and this apart from members of religious orders.

A frequent obstacle to the appointment of effective pastors was the rights of patronage held by rulers, nobility, monasteries, and cathedral chapters, all of which Trent had recognized if for no other reason than that the council realized the futility of attempting to dismantle the system. This greatly limited the freedom of bishops, who in some cases directly controlled only a minority of parish appointments in their dioceses. In some instances, and this was the case often enough in the Austrian lands well into the seventeenth century, aristocrats with the right of patronage refused to name any pastor, thus retaining parish revenues for themselves. On the other hand, in some places a committee of parish leaders advertised an opening and then interviewed applicants before presenting a list to the patron, who then normally would accept their choice, not wanting to impose a priest whom he knew would be unwelcome in the parish. In village parishes in the diocese of Speyer, for example, candidates were invited to give a trial sermon and were then ranked accordingly. Yet the bishop normally retained even in the case of patrons the right to veto appointments. In the course of the seventeenth century educational requirements were laid out and examinations were instituted, for example, in the archdiocese of Cologne, which a candidate needed to satisfy before installation in a parish.

There were obviously differences in performance among geographical regions, with the pastors in France eventually acquiring the highest grades. Cities and towns were the centres of reform. They were clearly better served by the parish clergy than were rural areas whither improvement came only slowly, but did come. Increasingly, rural pastors came from the towns and cities and faced the challenge of accommodating to village life. They were now better educated and more conscious of their clerical status after a period of relative segregation during their formation.

To generalize about the state of the parish clergy in Italy and Spain in the later sixteenth and seventeenth centuries is risky, once one moves beyond an overall widespread improvement. Regional differences were evident. In both peninsulas the influence of the religious orders predominated. Throughout the seventeenth century the clerical population expanded in both areas, peaking in Italy in the early eighteenth century. The clergy of Novara grew in both numbers and education during the period. Most pastors there, rural as well as urban, knew how to properly administer the sacraments and teach catechism, and the content of their libraries showed that they could capably and intelligently undertake the care of souls even though their knowledge of theology and scripture was not extensive. Urban pastors presumably did better, and the same was true of other north Italian dioceses including Milan. The situation to the south of Rome is not so clear. In the Spanish diocese of Cuenca, 90 per cent of pastors were resident by 1595, and within a generation the degree of learning among the younger parish clergy changed dramatically for the better, with many more pastors in possession of a degree in theology. Improvement in conduct kept pace, with the younger clergy more likely to be faithful to their commitment to celibacy. But progress elsewhere in Spain, and especially in the dioceses of Aragon, seems to have come about much more slowly.

A study of 65 questionnaires employed by episcopal visitors in west and south German dioceses, 26 for the sixteenth century and 39 for the seventeenth, help inform us about the rate of reform in this area. The questions tip us off to the changing concerns of the visitors, and what they did and did not consider problems. Shortly after 1600 there was a point where their interest shifted from the elimination of abuses to the encouragement of positive developments, and from the pastor himself to his associates like the sacristan and schoolteacher, to the community, and to the material conditions of the church and parish property. Residence is never mentioned, so that presumably it was not a serious issue. After 1600 regular services were held on Sundays and feast days, but questions remained about other sacraments until about 1630. Concubinage ceased to be a major issue after 1600; queries about other forms of misconduct, such as not wearing ecclesiastical clothing, drunkenness, carousing, gambling, and hunting, decline after the turn of the century and then virtually disappear after 1628. The visitors seemed to presume the orthodoxy and adequate theological knowledge of the pastors after 1612, and to turn more to inquiries about the frequency of their own confession and their practice of meditation or mental prayer.

A similar pattern appears in the visitation reports for the roughly 20 parishes in the *Landkapitel* of Mergentheim in the diocese of Würzburg from 1583 to 1631, when the Swedish invaders of the Thirty Years War arrived. By 1600 concubinage nearly ended, and parishioners were much less tolerant of it than early in the century. Drunkenness was mentioned only once, and brawling four times. Nor was orthodoxy an issue at any point. From the start of the period Mass was celebrated regularly on Sundays and feast days, but after 1600 the visitors began to inquire about Mass on the minimum of two weekdays. Some pastors failed here, but by 1620 the situation was in order, and in some parishes there was daily Mass. One can see the change in the pastors' own regularity in approaching confession: in 1607 most confessed two or three times a year; in 1613, bi-monthly; and by 1631 monthly, when many had a regular confessor from among the local religious. On the other hand improvement was not found everywhere. There were frequent reports of pastoral negligence, absenteeism, and misconduct on the part of priests other than pastors of parishes.

A less favourable picture emerges from a study of roughly 300 parishes of the archbishopric of Trier located in present-day western Germany and Luxembourg, an area, to be sure, ravaged by war during much of the early modern era. Here parish committees exercised considerable power alongside the pastor, and visitors interviewed them as well as the pastor. A recurring theme was the constant disputes between the two, which often ended in court. There were no complaints about residence, and basic demands for liturgy and the sacraments were met, but barely. There was no obligatory examination for appointment to a pastorate until 1700.

In the Habsburg lands of Austria and Bohemia there was a dearth of diocesan priests throughout the seventeenth century, and this was only remedied by the reforms of the eighteenth century. The bulk of the pastoral work fell to the religious orders, the Capuchins, the Carmelites, and the Jesuits, as well as members of the monastic orders who served in parishes which their houses had incorporated. Dioceses were too large, and parishes were too few, there being only three, for example, in Vienna, a city in which many religious orders were well established in 1700. In 1635 there were only 257 resident pastors for 636 Moravian parishes, and many of these were religious. The situation changed little before 1700. Twenty per cent of the parishes in Bohemia still lacked priests at that time.

The greatest improvement in the quality of parish priests took place in France, even though the movement in this direction started late. The seminaries, the clergy conferences, and retreats eventually had their effect. Bishops, often enough under pressure from complaining laity, were more ready to discipline pastors living unworthily. In 1670 a pastor of the diocese of Paris who publicly flaunted his relationship with his housekeeper was temporarily removed from his parish and ordered to spend time in the seminary, meanwhile supporting a replacement out of his own pocket. Whereas absenteeism had been widespread in the diocese of La Rochelle around 1600, no more than seven cases turned up in visitations between 1648 and 1667. Inventories of pastors' libraries show a rising level of theological knowledge and, as we have seen, by the end of the seventeenth century catechetical instruction was normal in most French parishes. Generally speaking, the pastor now lived in modest comfort, and he wore the proper ecclesiastical dress, the cassock, which set him off from the laity. The 'bon curé' became a familiar figure of the Old Regime in France.

7

EVANGELIZATION BEYOND EUROPE

The sixteenth-century expansion of Europe into Africa, Asia, and the hitherto unknown Americas introduced a period of European domination of the world that ended in the twentieth century. Inaugurating the era was the arrival of Columbus on the Bahamian island of San Salvador in 1492 and the disembarkment of the Portuguese Vasco da Gama in the Indian port of Calicut six years later. Both voyages followed decades-long European efforts to reach the lands beyond the Muslim Middle East and North Africa and the riches believed to lie there. The earth-encircling voyage of Ferdinand Magellan in the service of Spain from 1519 to 1522 showed that all the oceans of the world were interconnected, but only the advance into Mexico and then Peru alerted Europeans to the extent and significance of the Americas. For Europeans there gradually came into existence a much more extensive world than they had ever conceived. It was for this emerging world that Francisco de Vitoria in the 1530s sought to formulate the principles of an international law.

With European expansion came, for better and for worse, the most ambitious campaign of Christian evangelization since the days of the early church. By 1550 perhaps 10 million people had been baptized as Catholic Christians in the Americas alone. Many Catholics saw in this rich harvest God's providential compensation for the losses to the Protestants in Europe and to the Turks in the East. Extraordinary heroism marked the era but so did misunderstanding and exploitation of newly known peoples. For over a century missionary efforts proceeded under the aegis of the *Patronato* and the *Padroado* accorded the two

147

Iberian powers by the papacy. Their hands were often heavy ones, and their colonists' greed, cruelty, and lust frequently stood in the way of effective missionary activity. Yet there existed little alternative to cooperation with the Iberian monarchies.

In Rome towards the end of the sixteenth century there emerged a new missionary universalism, finding expression, for example, in the *Universal Relations* which Giovanni Botero began to publish in 1591. It looked to a programme of world-wide evangelization, comprising not only the peoples across the seas but also the Protestants in Europe, the Eastern Orthodox, and the Turks and other Muslims. The upshot was the foundation in Rome in 1622, following initiatives dating back to the 1560s, of the papal Congregation for the Propagation of the Faith or Propaganda Fide to oversee the whole Catholic missionary effort.

This was a period of fateful cultural encounters between Europeans on the one hand and both primitive and highly advanced societies on the other. These non-European societies posed explicit challenges to the church about accommodation and adaptation just as the changing culture and society of Europe itself offered implicit ones. Were Native American Indians to be considered full human beings with all the attendant rights or were they rather the 'natural slaves' of Aristotle as some maintained? What about Africans and Asians? Were pagan religions to be uprooted and a new beginning attempted or were the religious and human values of these societies to be interpreted as building blocks towards the construction of indigenous Christian cultures? What was to be the role, if any, of force or pressure in bringing peoples to hear and to accept the Gospel? These were issues Catholics had to face. Division of opinion over them was not uncommon, and it was sometimes combined with rivalry among religious orders or between seculars and regulars.

In his *On Securing the Salvation of the Indies* of 1588 the Jesuit José de Acosta drew on missionary experience up to his time and helped to formulate future policy. His analysis is helpful for understanding the mentality of enlightened missionaries. Acosta distinguished three levels of barbarians, by which he meant non-Christians. The first were those whose degree of civilization was virtually the same as the Europeans. These were the Chinese, the Japanese, and many peoples of the Indian subcontinent. They could be expected to accept Christianity on the basis of rational persuasion enlightened by the grace of God. To attempt to use force in their cases would only be counterproductive. In the second category were those peoples who did not possess writing, yet manifested sophisticated political organization and a degree of magnificence in their religious worship but commingled with severe deviations from the law of nature, such as human sacrifice. Such were for Acosta the Aztecs and the Incas. For them to appreciate and come to the knowledge of the Gospel, a Christian government was required. But they were to be permitted as much freedom and autonomy as possible within this framework. To the third level were assigned many nomadic and semi-nomadic American Indian peoples as well as indigenous groups of the Moluccas and South Seas. According to Acosta, they were savages, sometimes scarcely human, who needed to be treated as children in order to be elevated to a level of humanity capable of receiving the Gospel. Force would need to be employed in their case, but in a gentle manner respectful of their fundamental human rights, so as not to alienate them. Usually they would have to be weaned from their nomadic ways and placed in an urban setting before they could be effectively evangelized. So Acosta advocated the organization of Christian Indians into settlements usually called 'reductions'.

Columbus's early reports from the Indies to Ferdinand and Isabella advertised a likely new harvest of Christians among the simple people he found there. But he himself subjugated natives in his desire to locate and extract the precious metals he pursued. A proper missionary effort began with the arrival of a group of Franciscans in 1500, and as the Spaniards seized the islands of the Antilles, the first dioceses in the Americas were established at Santo Domingo and Concepción de la Vega on Hispaniola in 1508 and at San Juan in Puerto Rico in 1511. Forced labour, violence, uprooting, and especially European diseases generated a drastic and tragic depopulation among the natives of the Caribbean islands. Meanwhile a team of Dominicans had arrived. One of them, Antonio de Montesino, was in 1511 the first to protest publicly against the Spanish treatment of the natives. The result was the Laws of Burgos the following year, which aimed to ease the burden on the Indians. Furthermore, it was determined that to satisfy the demands of justice, henceforth before the Spaniards proceeded against a people, they were to read to them, in Spanish to be sure, the provisions of the Requirement, a legal document that started with the origin of the world and ended with the bulls of Alexander VI bestowing the islands on the Spaniards. If the Indians surrendered to the Spaniards and allowed the

Gospel to be preached, then all would go well with them. If they did not do so, then the Spaniards would proceed vigorously and subject them by force. Opponent of these procedures and champion of the Indians' cause was Bartolomé de Las Casas, who in 1502 landed as an 18-year-old in Hispaniola. Slaves were imported from Africa as more durable labour than the Indians, and by 1517 they made up two-thirds of Hispaniola's population. Las Casas initially supported this measure as a way of relieving the Indians, but he later profoundly repented of it.

Soon conquistadores crossed over to the mainland, first to Panama and Nicaragua and then to Mexico, where Hernando Cortés led the expedition that in 1521 conquered the Empire of the Aztecs. Their capital was at Tenochtitlan, located on a marshy island in Lake Texcoco in the central valley of Mexico and connected to the mainland by three causeways. With its population of from 200,000 to 300,000 or more, its system of dikes and canals, and its magnificent temples, it exhibited an urban life hitherto unknown to the Spaniards in America. Yet the Aztecs were essentially an agricultural people who did not possess a domestic animal strong enough to pull a plough. They ruled and administered an empire of perhaps 12 million that extended over most of central and south Mexico and comprised a number of peoples, some of whom were restive under Aztec domination and resented subjugation by them. Aztec religion was polytheistic, and human sacrifice was practised on a large scale, drawing victims from the subject peoples.

Ruthless, debauched, greedy, yet a man of Christian convictions who genuinely sought the conversion of the Indians, Cortés was a complex personality. Landing with his company of several hundred at Ulúa on Good Friday, 1519, Cortés had the Mercederian friar Bartolomé de Olmedo who accompanied him explain the principal points of Christian doctrine, in a foreign language, to the amazed natives. Olmedo cautioned the conquistador to moderation as Cortés ordered the destruction of pagan idols. Moving inland and assembling allies from among dissident peoples, he reached Tenochtitlan where he was amicably received by Montezuma, the Aztec Emperor, a gesture Cortés reciprocated by taking him into custody. A rising of the Aztecs expelled the Spaniards and cost Montezuma his life, but Cortés soon returned, and after a siege of two and one-half months, and with the assistance of his native allies, took Tenochtitlan. The Aztec capital was razed, and Mexico City gradually took form over its ruins. The Spaniards quickly extended their conquest over the surrounding area, and in October 1522 Cortés was named governor and captain-general of New Spain.

Systematic evangelization of the Aztecs began with the arrival of 12 Franciscans in 1524, whose number suggested a parallel with the 12 Apostles. Shortly after their arrival, the 12 organized a series of conversations with the Aztec elite, in which they laid out, presumably through interpreters, the fundamentals of Christian doctrine. 'Fear not, we are men as you', they began, perhaps intending to counter a widespread Aztec notion that the Spaniards were divinities long anticipated to arrive from the East. 'We are only messengers sent to you by a great lord called the Holy Father, who is the spiritual head of the world, and who is filled with pain and sadness at the state of your souls', they continued. 'He has sent us to search out and to save your souls. This is why we have come. We do not seek gold, silver, or precious stones; we seek only your health.' A clinching argument was that the powerful God of the Spaniards had given them victory over the Aztecs whose deities could not protect them. After instruction numerous baptisms took place.

The Dominicans arrived in Mexico in 1526, and the Augustinians in 1533, and these three mendicant orders, known as friars, undertook the evangelization of the Americas. The Franciscan Juan de Zumárraga was named first Bishop of Mexico City in 1530. Starting with Adrian VI, the papacy, because of the shortage of secular priests, granted the friars the privilege of preaching and administering the sacraments independ-ently of the bishops. This situation led to friction and conflict over privileges and eventually power that was to characterize the church in Latin America for a long time. Generally speaking, most settlers origin-ally formed towns, thus transferring to New Spain the municipal culture of the homeland.

The early missionaries envisioned an Indian church, if only implicitly. The friars in New Spain concentrated their activity first on the more settled areas of the central Mexican plateau and its extensions. Here mass conversions were the rule, frequently overtaxing the missionaries' resources. The missionaries encouraged the formation of separate villages or towns for the Christian Indians that combined traditional Indian and Spanish ways of life. From 1536 to 1618, Spanish legislation prohibited Spaniards other than missionaries from spending more than two successive days in an Indian village. The purpose was to protect the Indians from the Spaniards and to allow more easily for their instruction and christianization. Some credit the policy with the maintenance of Indian culture and property to the extent that they were preserved. It was probably a necessity later when dealing with nomadic or semi-nomadic tribes, but its initial disadvantage was that it isolated the Christian Indians excessively from other groups. More importantly, since the friars generally controlled these towns in a paternalist fashion, often from a fortified convent, the system hindered the growth of responsibility and self-direction of the Indian communities.

The missionaries generally aimed to uproot pagan Indian religion, yet they made determined efforts otherwise to maintain an Indian identity, and even to build on aspects of Indian religious behaviour. Bishop Zumárraga reported in a letter of 1532 that he had destroyed 500 temples and 20,000 idols. On the other hand, places sacred in pre-Colombian times became the sites of Christian churches or shrines. Liturgical pomp, processions, and festivals had all been features of pre-Colombian religion, and these were widely employed by the mendicants. They also built on the tradition of theatre in pre-Colombian religion. Plays with biblical themes, such as a representation of the Last Judgment performed in the 1530s with 800 indigenous participants, were sometimes integrated into the liturgy. Fear of hell was a regular theme.

The friars' linguistic achievement was stupendous. A crucial decision to be made was whether to make use of the Indian languages to express theological concepts or to employ Latin or the European vernacular. The danger of the first option was that indigenous associations distorted concepts and led to syncretism; that of the latter was to introduce terms foreign to the native tradition and likely to render the religion foreign. The missionaries in New Spain opted decisively for the latter. To designate God, for example, they never used the term *teotl*, which was taken from Nahuatl, the principal language of the Aztec Empire. Despite the policy of the crown to the contrary, the friars discouraged the Indians' learning Spanish, to protect them from Spanish influence. Over 120 languages were spoken in Mexico when the Spaniards arrived, in 22 of which the Franciscans produced books or manuscripts within a century of their arrival. The policy of the missionaries, in general, was to promote the use of one language over an extended territory. In New Spain this was Nahuatl. Since it was only to a small degree a written language, the missionaries had to develop an alphabet, with the use of Latin letters. Eventually there poured from the presses Nahuatl catechisms, prayer books, and song books.

Missionaries in Mexico made use of catechetical instruction and of schools just as did their brethren in Europe. Pre-baptismal instruction was minimal, since there remained the opportunity for further instruction in the villages and towns after baptism. Usually knowledge of the Our Father, the Creed, the Ten Commandments, and the Six Commandments of the church were required, along with some knowledge of the sacraments. Polygamy, which was practised only by rulers, was an issue for a time. The crown encouraged initial indulgence in the matter, and the problem died out with time. Youth was a focus of attention, as was the case in Europe. The Franciscan Pedro de Gante founded the first school in America in 1523, at Texcoco, even before the arrival of the 12, and he was to remain an apostle of schools until his death in 1572. The school of San Francisco in Mexico City was his creation, and he directed it for nearly 40 years. At one point it numbered almost 1000 students. These were primary schools for native boys rather than colleges, where besides religion, reading, writing, arithmetic, and singing were the main subjects. Sons of the elite often boarded, and received a more thorough instruction. Pedro de Gante was also instrumental in the foundation of a large number of technical schools for the training of native craftsmen. For a time there was experimentation with schools for girls, and pious women were brought over from Spain to conduct them, but they did not work out, and once there was time for Christian families to emerge among the Indians, it was thought better to leave the girls within the family until they were married.

Hospitals as well as schools were founded by the missionaries, of particular need because of the frequent epidemics. In 1583 the Archbishop of Mexico City claimed that all the Indian 'head towns' had hospitals. These were built and supported by the Indians themselves, and they also often served as hostels for travellers and 'food pantries'. Confraternities were popular, expressing as they did the Indians' sense of community, and often they were associated with hospitals. As in Spain, there were confraternities of the Blessed Sacrament and the Rosary, and flagellant confraternities attracted the Indians.

The schools for the Indians produced a lay colonial elite: catechists, cantors, sacristans, musicians, but no priests. This was a failure with far-reaching consequences for the church in Mexico, understandable as it may have been in the circumstances. Bishop Zumárraga and his fellow Franciscans founded the College of Santa Cruz at Santiago Tlatelolco outside Mexico City, which opened in 1536 with 60 students. One goal envisioned for it was the preparation of future priests. Latin and philosophy were taught, and at the upper levels Latin was the language of instruction. But the school flourished for only a generation or so, then declined rapidly due to opponents who were angry at the alleged uppitiness of Indian Latinists and fearful of heresy. The issue of a native clergy remained controversial, and in 1555 the first provincial council held in Mexico City prohibited the ordination of Indians, mestizos, and blacks. Nor were male Indians allowed into the religious orders at this time. These were fateful decisions for the future of the church in Mexico. If the College at Santiago Tlatelolco had educated only one Indian bishop, the history of the Mexican church might have turned out much differently.

To what extent did the Indians of New Spain assimilate Christianity? That remains a debated issue even today. Once the Spaniards were in control, it was very difficult for them to resist Christianity openly. Some on the fringes of the area under discussion did, as is evident from the serious rebellion in New Galicia in 1541. Most opposition was expressed through passive resistance, dissimulation, flight into more remote areas. Elements of paganism and superstition did survive; of this there is no question. Sometimes idols were buried next to crosses, so that while seeming to venerate the latter, some Indians intended to worship the former. Even contemporaries had reservations about the depth of the Indians' conversion, which was one reason for the prohibition of ordination. Yet there were also instances of Indian heroism in their new faith. Were the Indians less Christian than folks in remote areas of Europe? The issue is one that will perhaps never be fully resolved. What must be avoided are one-sided arguments.

In the 1530s, Francisco Pizarro reduced the Inca Empire in Peru. There he seized the Inca leader Atahualpa, and despite the Inca's surrender of his gold and acceptance of baptism, Pizarro had him executed, an atrocity that incensed Vitoria and other theologians when the news reached them. As the Spanish government extended its control, reining in the freewheeling conquistadores, it established civil and ecclesiastical administrations, often building upon native structures already in place. Lima was founded in 1535 as seat of the viceroyalty of Peru, and in 1546 it became an archbishopric. Meanwhile, in 1545 the Spaniards discovered the vast deposits of silver at Potosí high in the Andes in today's Bolivia, and the following year they became aware of the rich mineral resources at Zacatecas in central New Spain. Both mines greatly raised the demand for cheap Indian labour.

Protests from the friars in the Americas about enslavement and ill-treatment of the Indians rose in volume from the initial sermon of Montesino in 1511 onward. Yet even with good will, it was difficult for the government in Spain to enforce laws and regulations on its frontier in far-away America. Until his death in 1566 Las Casas stood out as the most vocal critic of Spanish behaviour and advocate of the Indians, but he was by no means alone. His work on behalf of the Indians began in 1514, opposing their enslavement as well as the forced labour integral to the *encomienda* or plantation system that was instituted in much of Spanish America. His attempt to establish a model settlement of Indians in New Granada, separated from the Spaniards, in 1520–1 failed, but he persistently travelled throughout Spanish America, to Peru and Guatemala and then back to Spain – he made seven Atlantic crossings – to lobby on behalf of the Indians. From 1544 to 1547 he served as bishop of Chiapa, where his attempt at peaceful evangelization failed, and in 1547 he returned to Spain permanently to devote himself entirely to the Indians' cause at court. His agitation was supported to a greater or less degree by other Dominicans and Franciscans, though some opposed him too.

The year 1530 saw the prohibition by the Spanish Crown of any further enslavement of Indians, but pressure from the colonists forced its reversal four years later. This unleashed a campaign of the friars on behalf of the Indians. It was supported by the Franciscan Bishop of Mexico City, Zumárraga, and the Dominican Bishop of Tlaxcala, who to be sure were opposed by the Dominican provincial Domingo de Betanzos, who could not accept the full rationality of the Indians. Prompted then by Dominicans in Rome, Paul III issued in June 1537 the bull *Sublimis Deus*, condemning as stemming from Satan the view 'that the Indians of the West and South, and other people of whom we have recent knowledge should be treated as dumb brutes created for our service, pretending that they are incapable of receiving the Catholic faith', and asserting 'that the Indians are truly men and that they are not only capable of understanding the Catholic faith but, according to our information, they exceedingly desire to receive it'.[1] He went on to declare that neither the Indians nor other peoples who might be discovered were to have their liberty or property taken from them, even though they were not Christians. Nor were they to be in any way enslaved.

Charles V was not happy with this alleged intervention in Spanish affairs, and in 1538 he determined that the future publication of any papal document in Spain would require a royal *placet*, thus extending the *Patronato*. The New Laws of 1542, then, prohibited further use of the *encomienda*, with marginal exceptions, and they stipulated the abolition of existing enslavement. Their measures did not go far enough for

Las Casas, who wanted immediate freedom for the Indians and restitution of the property that had been seized from them.

Finally, on 16 April 1550, in an unprecedented action for an imperial power, Charles V suspended all further licences for conquest or discovery in the Americas until the morality of Spanish procedures was clarified. This measure was probably also prompted by the assessment that now that the more heavily populated territory of the Americas had been brought under effective control, a new method was necessary to extend the Spanish reach into the lands of a more nomadic and primitive population.

At the instigation of Charles V, there now took place the famous debate over the morality of Spanish policy in America, held at Valladolid in two sessions in 1550 and 1551 before a panel of 14 theologians and governmental councillors. Las Casas argued on behalf of the Indians against Juan Ginés de Sepúlveda, a humanist and Aristotelian who applied to the Indians Aristotle's position that some men were by nature slaves suited only to serve others. At issue was not Charles's fundamental title to America, which Vitoria and others defended, as we saw earlier, but subsequent Spanish policy towards the Indians. Two questions predominated: could Spain continue to wage a just war against the Indians and, if so, how was this to be done?

For Sepúlveda four reasons justified Spanish war on the Indians: their grave sins against nature such as cannibalism and human sacrifice and their idolatries; the propagation of the faith which would be made easier by their prior subjection; the protection of the weak among the Indians; and, most significantly, the inferiority of their natures. This last point Sepúlveda stressed, calling the Indians *homunculi* or 'little men' and contrasting their scarce vestiges of humanity, science, and letters, with the achievements of the Spaniards. The task of the superior Spaniards, he contended in what would become a standard argument for imperial powers, was to evangelize and gradually civilize them. For this their subjugation was first necessary. Nearly as in the Requirement, the barbarian Indians were first to be informed of the many religious and civilizing advantages the Spaniards intended to bring them, and then they were to be given the opportunity voluntarily to submit to Spanish overlordship. Should they refuse to do so, and this Sepúlveda expected normally to be the case, then the Spaniards could justly make war on them, confiscate their property, and as was generally the case then in just war, enslave them. If they submitted, they would fall under a milder Spanish tutelage.

Drawing heavily on his *Apologetic History*, a massive 870 folio pages of largely anthropological data, Las Casas countered his opponent's claim that the Indians were not fully rational beings. The organization of the Indian empires matched the political skills of the European nations, and the temples of Yucatan compared favourably with the Egyptian pyramids. Indeed, in some respects, like their marriage customs and their manner of rearing children, they outdid the legendary Greeks and Romans. They were as human as any other people, Las Casas contended, his argument implicitly asserting that no people is inferior in its fundamental humanity. For Las Casas, evangelization ought to go forward as he and his fellow Dominicans had hoped to proceed in Chiapa, peacefully. Preachers should simply be dispatched to the Indians to announce the Christian message. In dangerous areas where the Indians were unfriendly, he foresaw the construction of fortresses to protect the evangelists, and then the gradual conversion of the people by persuasion and good example. This was, indeed, similar to the method later employed by the Spaniards in California and the American southwest. There was to be no war against the Indians.

Neither side won a clear victory in the debate. The judges as a group could come to no conclusion, and writings continued to appear on both sides of the issue. Las Casas persevered in his cause until his death, and the Basic Law of 1573, which regulated the Spanish advance into new lands until the end of the colonial period, incorporated many of his principles. Henceforth the word 'pacification' was to be used, not 'conquest'. The Spaniards were to lay out for the Indians the many benefits, temporal and spiritual, that the Spaniards intended to bestow on them, including peace and a secure legal system, better communications, and especially the saving grace and faith of Christ. Indian vices were to be dealt with patiently. Should the natives still prove recalcitrant, refusing to submit to the Spaniards and to allow the preaching of the Gospel, then the Spaniards might resort to the moderate application of force, a provision to which Las Casas never would have agreed. There was to be no Indian slavery.

The debate at Valladolid did not deal directly with the controversial institution of the *encomienda*, which dated in America from the days of Columbus and was intended to satisfy the Spaniards' insatiable need for tribute and labour on land and later in the mines. In America, even humble settlers from Spain considered themselves *hidalgos*, and they did not plan to dirty their hands with manual labour. The *encomendero* was granted the privilege of tribute and labour from the Indians in exchange for his protection of them and his provision of the means of their Christian instruction. Not all the missionaries opposed this arrangement, provided the colonists carried out their part of the bargain faithfully, but Las Casas did, arguing that it limited the Indians' freedom and interfered with their way of life. The New Laws of 1542 foresaw the beginning of the end of the institution, but the colonists effectively stood in the way of their implementation, even murdering a viceroy in Peru in 1546 who attempted to carry them out. Further initiatives were suggested at least to modify the institution, but those that were legislated were nearly impossible to enforce at such a distance.

The 1550s saw the appointment of new officials who were to work with Indian leaders, to see that the necessary labourers were available, especially for the mines, which were becoming of crucial importance for financing the wars of Philip II in defence of the faith. The hope was that eventually the Indians would become free, salaried workers, and to a degree this happened. By this time the Spaniards had adopted for the mines of Potosí a preconquest form of forced labour, the *mita*, by which a contingent of some 13,500 Indians was provided for the mines at Potosí every seven years. Even more punishing was the *mita* at Huancavelica near present-day Ayacucho. Spanish officials, religious, and even bishops reported that the precious metals extracted at Potosí were 'tainted with the blood of the Indians'. In 1575 a group of Dominicans protested that the system violated both divine and natural law and hindered the evangelization of the Indians. But the viceroy Francisco de Toledo outmanoeuvred them, and secured the approval of the archbishop of Lima and many other religious, who later claimed that they had been deceived in the matter. The issue of the mines was only resolved with their exhaustion in the mid-seventeenth century. But forced Indian labour persisted in Spanish America in various forms, and for it the church must bear partial responsibility, despite the persistent efforts of some churchmen in the spirit of Las Casas.

By the 1570s the church in America was becoming more and more a Spanish colonial church. In 1568 the crown determined that the *Patronato* was to be fully exploited to the exclusion of all outside influence even on parish appointments, and that the church was to be firmly Spanish. A provincial council at Lima that same year prohibited the ordination of Indians, as had the earlier council at Mexico City, though several years later another council modified the prohibition slightly. The Indians were pushed to the margins socially, even though their population of from eight to nine million, according to surveys undertaken by Philip II, vastly outnumbered the 120,000 Spaniards and Creoles (those of Spanish blood born in America), and the 230,000 mestizos, mulattos, and blacks. Many churchmen continued to labour paternistically for their welfare, like the saintly Toribio de Mogrovejo, Archbishop of Lima from 1581 to 1606 and beloved of the Indians, but the advocacy of their rights or protests against the system in the spirit of Las Casas greatly diminished. The Crown became less sympathetic to protests and now suppressed books like those of Las Casas that questioned the manner of the *Conquista*. Only in the later eighteenth century were Indians ordained to the priesthood in significant numbers.

The Jesuits first arrived in Spanish America in the late 1560s, where within 50 years they established colleges for the Creoles in all the major cities, as well as colleges for the sons of Indian leaders, grammar schools for Indian children, and confraternities for various groups including black slaves. To finance these ventures they acquired from benefactors an enormous amount of landed wealth. They brought with them a renewed missionary spirit. Jesuits and Franciscans were henceforth to lead the further missionary activity into the outlying areas among Indian peoples that would continue for two centuries. Often this effort was combined with Spanish pacification, and if not characterized completely by the spirit of Las Casas, it bore a much different stamp than the *Conquista*. To become famous were the Jesuit Reductions, especially among the primitive Guarani Indians in parts of present-day Paraguay, Argentina, and Brazil, which were inspired by earlier Franciscan models. Started in 1609, to protect the Indians from Spanish and Portuguese marauders and slavers and to facilitate christianization, they ended with the expulsion of the Society of Jesus from Spanish America in 1767 when they numbered more than 80,000 Indians organized into more than 30 Reductions or towns.

Spain did not formally take possession of the Philippine Islands until 1569, though Magellan had claimed them for the crown in 1521. Communications were difficult, since the journey had to be made via New Spain. The Augustinians began to evangelize there in 1564, and other orders followed. Royal instructions called for peaceful pacification of the islands, and this was more or less what happened. Those on Luçon and Cebu welcomed Christianity as a block to Islam; Mindanao with its large Muslim population was not pacified until the nineteenth century. The city of Manila was founded in 1571, became a bishopric in 1581, and an archbishopric in 1595. By 1591 there had been 650,000 baptisms, and in the following century natives were ordained to the priesthood. Spain looked to China and Japan from the Philippines. The islands were to become the Spanish Catholic country of the Far East.

The Portuguese had begun pushing down the west coast of Africa in the late thirteenth century. In 1434 they passed beyond the forbidding Cape Bojador for the first time. Nine years later at Arguin they picked up their first cargo of African slaves, transporting 230 of them back to the port of Lagos in the southwestern Portuguese province of Algarve. This was the start of the early modern intercontinental slave trade. Not that black Africans had not been enslaved before. For centuries Muslim Arabs had brought them across the Sahara Desert into the Middle East and up into North Africa, from where some had been sold to European masters. But this was the first direct contact between Europeans and black Africans and a decided escalation of the trade in slaves. The taking of slaves was justified by their infidelity, whether they were Muslims or pagans, and by the salvation made possible for them by their Christian masters. Portugal, with its population of less than one million, needed labour. Before long the province of Algarve was 10 per cent black, and as the two races mingled, there developed a racial mix that anticipated colonial Brazil.

Portuguese ventures down the African coast in search of a route to the East Indies proceeded with the establishment of factories, that is, a combination of fortress and trading post, along the way. Bartholomew Diaz reached the Cape of Good Hope at the tip of Africa in 1487, and Vasco da Gama in 1498 became the first European to reach India by sailing around Africa. In 1500 Pedro Alvares Cabral, while heading for the Indies, was blown off course and found himself landing in what was to become Brazil, which he claimed for Portugal. Soon the Portuguese laid claim to a commercial empire that stretched from the Cape of Good Hope to Malacca near present-day Singapore. It was based on control of the sea and was organized around factories at strategic ports. For a number of reasons the Portuguese did not attempt to colonize, as did the Spaniards in America. They often established themselves in areas already populous and sometimes highly developed or with a climate uncongenial to Europeans, and they simply did not have the population to supply settlers. Goa on the west coast of India was made the capital of the empire in the east in 1510, and in 1539 it became the seat of a diocese with jurisdiction from the Cape of Good Hope to the Far East. In his effort to make it a fully Christian city the Portuguese governor, Afonso de Albuquerque, massacred 6000 Muslims by his own account. The city did become a Christian stronghold, but there remained Muslims as well as Hindus, which Christians encountered here for the first time. In 1513 the Portuguese reached China, and in 1542 Japan, but both these civilizations were able to determine their own terms for contact with Europeans.

At first the Portuguese paid little attention to Brazil, where they did colonize. In 1532 the crown assigned a number of hereditary grants to *donatarios* with virtual sovereign authority, who freely enslaved Indians and brought black slaves from Africa to work the anticipated plantations. But this system did not work out, and a more centralized government was established at Bahia in 1549 under a governor-general. Brazil long remained a frontier society, with only four cities in 1620 in contrast to the urban character of the heart of Spanish America. The fact that Brazil possessed neither a printing press nor a university during the whole colonial period made it much more dependent on the home country for clerics and civil officials than Spanish America. Portuguese America in 1620 numbered roughly 200,000 people: Portuguese, Indians, mixed, Africans and mulattos, whereas Spanish subjects in America exceeded 10 million. Nor was there in Brazil a legal status halfway between slave and free as there was in Spanish America with the Indians subject to *encomenderos*.

The Jesuits came to Brazil with the governor-general in 1549, and they were to be the dominant religious order in Portuguese America. By the time they arrived the slave trade had disrupted the way of life of the semi-nomadic Indians in the hinterlands of the Portuguese settlements, the Tupis to the north and the Guaranis to the south. One argument used to justify slavery in the areas was the cannibalism of the Tupis. The exploitation of the Indian men as labour and women as concubines in this frontier society horrified the early Jesuits. As early as in 1551 the Jesuit Manuel da Nóbrega founded a Reduction for the Tupis near present-day São Paulo; indeed, he is reckoned today as the founder of the city. By 1570 40,000 Indians lived in 14 villages where the Jesuits exercised a severe discipline while christianizing them. But these collapsed within 15 years, because of epidemics, the concentration of Indians in larger settlements than those to which they were accustomed, and the continued depredations of the slavers. Eventually both the Indians and the Jesuits pushed further and further into the interior, where Portuguese and Spanish Jesuits established the aforementioned Reductions in territory that overlapped the two colonial empires.

Africa always remained of secondary interest to the Portuguese after the East Indies and Brazil, a situation that obtained also for missionary activity. It was important chiefly for the slave trade necessary to support the burgeoning plantation economy in Brazil. As early as in 1491 the king of the Congo, perhaps the largest homogeneous political unit in Africa, converted to Christianity, and for a time there was hope for the development of a Christian kingdom there, especially under Afonso I who ruled from 1506 to 1543. Some African clergy were ordained, a step that was never taken in Brazil, but no native bishop was ever installed despite repeated requests by the king. Though nominally independent, in reality the kingdom was a Portuguese dependency and subject to the *Padroado*. In 1608 a Congolese envoy was dispatched to Rome with another request for a non-Portuguese bishop. He died in Rome; but his mission does seem to have confirmed the growing sentiment in Rome for what became the Propaganda. The Jesuits maintained a college in the Congo capital from 1625 to 1675, but by that time the kingdom was long in decline, partly because the Portuguese assigned priority to Angola, their colony to the south. It was of more value for the slave trade, even though the Congolese also participated in the trade.

The pope and many Spanish churchmen spoke out against the enslavement of American Indians, and it was prohibited in Spanish America after 1542. This was not the case with black Africans. The Portuguese initiated the traffic in African slaves; the French, the Dutch, and the English all took part. The Spaniards never did, although Spanish America was a prime market for slaves, receiving at least 1,500,000. Altogether, it is estimated that 10 million Africans were transported to the Americas as slaves from the late fifteenth to the early nineteenth century. Of this total the largest number, 3.6 million, were taken to Brazil. In contrast, only about 400,000 were sold in British North America.

Early Fathers of the Church, as well as medieval Scholastics, condemned slavery as opposed to both the law of nature and the Gospel.

But neither church nor civil law prohibited it, and indeed, slavery has been a feature of many civilizations high and low. Slaves were a part of the Mediterranean tradition by 1500, when there were about 100,000 Muslim and African slaves in Spain, in addition to those in Portugal. What actually drove the intercontinental slave trade was the powerful demand for labour in America. Another justification given for it was that the slaves had been legitimately purchased from their own rulers, as was often the case in fact. Missionaries argued that at least the African slaves were snatched from their idolatry, baptized, and so prepared for salvation. In some cases conscientious missionaries attempted to catechize the Africans before they departed for America, so that they could be baptized lest they die as a result of the terrible rigours of the journey.

There were Catholic voices that protested against the African slave trade, but they were few and they were not loud. Bartolomé de Albornoz, a Franciscan moralist at the University of Mexico City, in his *The Art of Contracts* (1571) denounced the trade, and in particular the argument that at least the souls of the Africans were saved. 'But I do not believe', he wrote, 'that it can be demonstrated that according to the law of Christ the liberty of the soul can be purchased by the servitude of the body.' Two Jesuits, Alonso de Sandoval and the sainted Peter Claver, laboured heroically for decades on behalf of the blacks at Cartagena on the northern coast of South America, the point of arrival for slaves coming to Spanish America. Sandoval, in his *On Securing the Salvation of the Ethiopians* (1627), argued eloquently the case for the full rationality and other human qualities of the Africans, but neither he nor Claver protested the system itself. The Portuguese Jesuits in Angola and especially in Brazil, where they owned extensive lands, benefited from slave labour. The rector of the Jesuit college in Loanda in Angola wrote Sandoval urging him to set aside his scruples regarding the slave trade which, he wrote, many moralists including those on the royal council in Lisbon had approved. The great seventeenth-century Jesuit preacher, António Vieira, who has been called the Portuguese Las Casas for his efforts to end the enslavement of Indians, like many others who ministered to the African slaves, sympathized greatly with their lot, but he too fell short of advocating abolition.

Missionary activity in Goa among both the Portuguese and the Indians properly began with the arrival of Franciscans in 1518. They also evangelized the humble pearl-fishing Paravas on the Fishery Coast to the south. On 6 May 1542 there landed in Goa, that 'Babylon of the East', Francis Xavier, one of the initial six companions of Ignatius Loyola and perhaps the greatest Christian missionary since Saint Paul. To him more than to any other individual was due the establishment of the church in India, the Malay Archipelago, and Japan, and his frequently reprinted letters stirred up interest in the Asian missionary venture throughout Catholic Europe. King John III of Portugal had requested diligent, zealous priests from Ignatius for work in his Asian dominions. Xavier departed from Rome with one companion on two days notice when the Jesuit who had been slated for the appointment fell sick. The title of nuncio apostolic was given him by Paul III, and his first task was to care for the Portuguese and native Christians and then to survey the outlook for missionary activity in the East. At least three of the nearly 11 years between his departure from Lisbon and his death he spent on the high seas. He did not come equipped with knowledge of the religions and cultures of the East, and initially showed little interest in them. Most of his evangelizing activity was with primitive peoples, until he came to Japan. He had minimal contact with the Indian literati. Most of his first three years in the East were devoted to instructing the poor Paravas. Accompanied by three seminarians, he travelled tirelessly from village to village, his evident goodness and force of conviction overcoming difficulties of communication. The primitive Macuans on the southwestern coast called for baptism, and there in late 1544, after brief instructions, he baptized 10,000, anticipating that the schools he foresaw, coupled with Portuguese pressure, would keep them constant.

Opportunities then attracted him to the Malay Archipelago, where he evangelized first among the mixed population of the Portuguese emporium at Malacca and then moved on to found missions among the Malays and the savage headhunters of the Molucca Islands. Returning to Goa in 1548, where more Jesuits had arrived to reinforce him, Xavier began to develop the College of Holy Faith into a centre for the education of native priests and catechists for the huge diocese of Goa. The college had been founded prior to his arrival but was then entrusted to the Jesuits. He recognized the need for an indigenous clergy, but he hesitated to receive natives into the Society of Jesus.

Xavier's vision soon fixed on a land only reached by Europeans five years previously, Japan. Conversations in Malacca with a Japanese, Anjiro, convinced him that, unlike the pearl fishers in India or the

headhunters of the Moluccas, this people was cultured and sophisticated. A Portuguese ship with Francis, the newly baptized Anjiro, and
several companions on board sailed into the Japanese port of
Kagoshima on 15 August 1549. His enthusiasm for the Japanese, 'the
best people yet discovered', came through in his first letter from Japan,
which was printed 30 times before the end of the century. Language
was a barrier. With the help of Anjiro, Xavier drew up a simple catechism in Japanese, which he then memorized and used as the basis of
his first preaching. Like the friars in Mexico, he faced the problem of
how to translate 'God'. He first used the Japanese term *Dainichi*. After
realizing that it carried unacceptable connotations, he turned to the
Latin *Deus* in its place. This was a hint of the coming Rites Controversy.
Initially, Francis planned to secure an audience with the emperor, but
after a long journey to the capital of Miyako, he failed to secure a hearing but also learned that the emperor had become a mere shadow of
what he had formerly been. Real power now rested with regional figures, the daimyos. In addition, whereas his evangelical poverty had
endeared him to the poor pearl fishers of India and to the Malays, it
repelled the Japanese, especially the elite whose support he needed.
They admired display. So the flexible Francis approached the daimyo
of Yamaguchi accompanied by an entourage, outfitted in suitably fine
robes, and bearing an assortment of gifts. The result was permission to
preach, the use of a vacant Buddhist temple, and within two months a
harvest of nearly 500 converts. In late 1551 the daimyo of Bungo welcomed him. Then, having received his first mail since arriving in
Japan, he determined to return to India to attend to issues of the
broader Asian mission. Left to the care of his companions were about
2000 Christians in five communities.

Meanwhile, Francis recognized that the way to the conversion of
Japan lay through China; the Japanese looked to the Chinese for wisdom. An elaborate plan to secure access to China as a member of a
Portuguese embassy fell through. Xavier died of a fever on 3 December
1552 on the island of Sancian off the coast of China, waiting for
another ship promised him for the voyage to Canton and into China. It
never came.

Goa remained the centre of the Christian enterprise in the East. An
archbishopric in 1558, it was made primatial see of the East in 1600,

with six suffragan dioceses. The Portuguese Inquisition opened an office in 1561. Five provincial councils convened there from 1567 to 1606, and catechisms in various Indian languages were published, the first in Tamil in 1554. Divisions among the missionaries, and within the orders, emerged over the approach to the Asian peoples. A forceful advocate of accommodation to the higher Asian cultures was the Italian Jesuit Alessandro Valignano, who arrived in Goa in 1574 as the formal representative of the Jesuit superior general. He was to have a profound influence on the Jesuit missions for the 32 years he remained in the East.

Christianity made slow progress on the Indian subcontinent, and this mostly among the marginalized of Indian society. The Nestorian Christians of the Malabar coast, who traced their origins back to the Apostle Thomas, were united with Rome in 1599 and received their own bishopric, but only after tortuous negotiations and political unrest. Another schism took place in 1653, but nine years later about two-thirds of this community of 100,000 returned to union with Rome. Cochin to the south of Goa emerged as a centre of evangelization towards the interior and towards Ceylon.

The Italian Jesuit Robert de Nobili was responsible for an innovative, accommodationist initiative in south India. The Jesuits had laboured for years at Madura with scarcely any success, partly because they required converts to assume a Portuguese style of life. Inspired by the example of Matteo Ricci in China, de Nobili recognized the need to approach Indian culture from the inside if one was ever to attract upper-caste Hindu brahmins to Christianity and, in their wake, many of the lower castes. His plan called for him to appear as the nobleman he was, equal to an Indian rajah, and as an ascetic holy man living a life of austerity in the Hindu style. He learned Tamil easily, and then, in order to read the sacred books of the Vedas, he mastered Sanskrit, the first European to do so. He avoided contact with pariahs, which Brahmins thought polluted them. Slowly inquirers appeared at the door of his bare hut, and with them he pursued a ministry of conversation and dialogue, familiar as he was now with their traditions and appreciative of the Indian penchant for speculative thought. By 1609 there were 60 Brahmin converts whom de Nobili allowed to wear the signs of their caste, considering these to be free of superstition. He began to envision Hindu converts ordained to the priesthood, and Sanskrit accepted as a liturgical language. There were problems, he realized, with the Hindu caste system, which he analyzed carefully in a manuscript of 1613. Later he foresaw Jesuits who as pandarams and ascetics of the Sudra class might have contact with the pariahs or outcastes, so bridging the caste system.

But opposition of fellow Jesuits and ecclesiastical authorities in Goa coalesced against him, and he and his few Jesuit colleagues were accused of reversion to paganism. Many hearings and appeals followed, but Pope Gregory XV put the stamp of approval on his procedure in 1622. Though only a handful of Jesuits followed de Nobili in his chosen role, he had opened doors and shown that one could be both Christian and Indian. It is estimated that at his death in 1656 close to 40,000 converts had been baptized as a result of his influence. Yet the caste system would long be an issue for Christians in India, and many of de Nobili's practices were voided by a papal legate in 1704.

In Japan the church continued to grow after the departure of Xavier. It faced the familiar problem of finding a suitable language to express the doctrines of the faith. A new catechism of 1558 suppressed a number of Japanese or Buddhist terms which appeared ambivalent, and replaced them with Portuguese or Latin words. The Buddhist term for hell, for example, was replaced by *inferno*. Catechumens were put through an intense course of instruction of at least 20 days before baptism. Once the first daimyo was converted in 1563, others followed, and their subjects came in their wakes. Some mass conversions took place, and by 1570 there were between 20,000 and 30,000 Christians under the care of 30 Jesuits assisted by Japanese laymen and laywomen. Valignano in his visit to Japan from 1579 to 1582 helped overcome a dispute among the Jesuits over accommodation, and he encouraged their study of the language. The foundation of two seminaries prepared the way for a native Japanese clergy, thus further establishing the church. Valignano arranged for a Japanese embassy composed of four young Christian nobles to the pope and the King of Spain. They remained in Europe for eight years, causing a sensation. When they returned they brought with them a printing press to print theological and devotional works in Japanese. The island of Kyushu contained 130,000 Christians by 1582.

But trouble was on the horizon. In the 1580s a general, Toyotomi Hideyoshi, regent of the nominal emperor, came to acquire increasing power with a view to re-establishing a central authority. Initially favourable to Christianity, his suspicious nature soon induced him to be wary of it as an instrument of foreign influence. Spanish missionaries from the Philippines, Jesuits and later Franciscans, began to appear in Japan after the union of the Spanish and Portuguese crowns in 1580. They proved to be more aggressive and less accommodationist, thus fostering Hideyoshi's fears. In 1587 he decreed the expulsion of all missionaries, but the decree was not enforced, and 65,000 more Japanese entered the church in the next decade. Then enforcement came, triggered by the remark reported of a Spanish ship's pilot that Spain used missionaries to prepare the way for conquest. Thirty Christians were put to death at Nagasaki on 5 February 1597, six Spanish Franciscans, three Japanese Jesuits, and 17 Japanese laymen. Hideyoshi did not press the persecution further for fear of losing the trade with the Portuguese.

Missionaries continued their work, Spanish Dominicans and Augustinians now as well as Jesuits and Franciscans. The year 1601 saw the ordination of the first Japanese priests, and eventually there were 50 of them, 32 Jesuits, nine diocesans, three Dominicans, and one Franciscan and one Augustinian. Twenty-one of them died as martyrs. A civil war followed Hideyoshi's death in 1598, from which Tokugawa Ieyasu emerged as the victor and founder of a military dynasty that lasted into the nineteenth century. Seeing a danger to his policy of centralization in the Christians, whom he feared might call on outside assistance, and increasingly able to play off Dutch and English traders against the Portuguese and Spanish, he renewed the persecution which then slowly intensified. A decree of banishment of all Christians was issued in 1614. The anti-Christian, isolationist policy continued to escalate after the death of Ieyasu in 1616. Many apostatized, over 4000 were martyred by 1630. In 1637 peasants of the thoroughly christianized area around Nagasaki rose in the Sbimabara Uprising. This was suppressed the following year with Dutch assistance. Thirty thousand Christians lost their lives in the ensuing slaughter. Christianity would now exist in Japan only underground, until the nineteenth century.

The most famous of the disputes over missionary accommodation to a new civilization played itself out in the vast, mysterious Chinese Empire, and has become known as the Chinese Rites Controversy. The issues were contested not only in ecclesiastical circles but among the scholars and savants of Europe, who for over a century engaged in an acrimonious polemical literature. The outcome was to have a major impact on the future practice of missionaries.

Francis Xavier died in 1552 with his eyes fixed on China. Subsequent missionaries shared his vision, and merchants looked in the same direction for markets. In 1557 the Portuguese were allowed to establish a factory at Macao located on a peninsula south of Canton, and this became the base from which both missionaries and merchants aimed to enter the empire. The Italian Jesuit Michele Ruggieri, on the basis of brief experience in India, insisted that a ready knowledge of the language and an adaptation to Chinese ways were essential for successful work in China. He first visited Canton in 1580 with a company of Portuguese merchants, where his careful observance of the formalities impressed the Chinese. But his approach found little favour with his fellow Jesuits until Valignano, during a stop in Macao, threw his full support behind him. Soon Ruggieri was invited to establish a Jesuit house at Chaoching outside Canton, but he was forced to leave after a change of governors and an imprudent attempt of Spanish Franciscans from the Philippines to settle in the area. He returned to Chaoching in late 1582 with another Jesuit selected for the mission by Valignano, Matteo Ricci.

Ricci was the real founder of the Chinese mission. Born in 1552 in Macerata, Italy, he always remained mindful of his family. Writing many years later from China, he urged them to 'continue to write [to me] and even in more detail, because it is impossible for me to forget'. After three years of study at the German College in Rome, he entered the Jesuits in 1571, bringing with him a humanist formation that would help him bridge the gap to the Chinese civilization. He arrived in Goa in 1578, where he was ordained a priest in 1580. Valignano sent him to Macao early in 1582 and there he plunged into the study of Chinese. When they opened the house in Chaoching, he and Ruggieri set out to create a Sino-Christian synthesis and so gradually to establish the church in Chinese society. They were not interested in mass baptisms, which also might threaten the authorities and lead to persecution, as indeed happened in Japan, and they pursued contact with the prestigious scholar-official or mandarin class. With the help of Chinese friends, Ricci translated a Latin catechism into Chinese. Ruggieri soon returned to Italy exhausted, but Ricci persevered, perfecting his Chinese. Despite hostility on the part of the common people, who mistrusted foreigners, Ricci gradually drew mandarins into conversation by making use of Western science to stimulate the interest of his interlocutors. He was extremely well versed in mathematics, astronomy, and cartography, later drawing up his famous Map of the World which placed China right at the centre. By 1586 there were 40 converts.

Ricci persisted. Under pressure he was forced from Chaoching in 1589, but he was able to secure a residence in Shaochou further into the interior and closer to the capital, Beijing, which was now his goal. Three years later he made his final visit to Macao and saw Valignano for the last time. Now he and his new colleague, Lazzaro Cattaneo, realizing that Buddhist monks did not enjoy such high repute, shed the Buddhist garb they had worn until then and dressed as scholars, mandarins as it were from the west. The Confucian classics were now Ricci's object of study; his intent was to point up analogies between Confucian positions and those of the Master of Heaven, the Christian God. In 1595 he completed his *Treatise on Friendship*, which drew largely on Cicero's famous essay and was to become a Chinese classic. Humane values resonated in the East. The next year he finished his *True Account of God*, which was based on his conversations with Chinese scholars and was also to find a place among the classics.

That year there followed a move to Nanchang and later to Nanking, where he held nearly continual open house for interested Chinese. With three fellow Jesuits he was permitted finally to travel to Beijing to present gifts to the Ming emperor, and then to open a house in the capital. He hoped to secure official toleration for Christians, but when on the scene he decided to be satisfied with the tacit toleration they enjoyed. Scholars had to come to Beijing for examinations for imperial service, and they and others now flocked to him for conversation, leaving 20 calling cards on an ordinary day and as many as 100 on a holiday. When he died in 1610, Ricci left behind four Jesuit residences in China, with about 2000 Christians, a small number compared with the 300,000 in Japan at the time. He received a special burial monument in Beijing, which the Chinese Communist government restored in the 1970s, thus recognizing his role in Chinese history.

Strictly speaking, the Rites Controversy revolved around three main issues; on the first two Ricci as superior of the mission took a clear position in a directive of 1603. But there were divisions over other practices too. The first had to do with the ceremonial honours paid to Confucius periodically by members of the mandarin class and required of them at the time of their final examinations. The second was associated with the traditional veneration of ancestors through prostrations (the kotow), the burning of incense, and the offering of food before their graves or commemorative plaques. The third was the familiar terminological issue, especially the use of the Chinese terms for Lord of Heaven and Supreme Lord or Ruler Above to denote the Christian God. Ricci decided, on the basis of his study of the Confucian classics, that the first two rites were neither idolatrous nor superstitous, but were in fact at least in origin civic observances and so permitted to Christians. The Jesuits generally followed him in this. He did not take a clear stand on the terminological question, and the Jesuits on the mission were themselves divided over it.

In the years immediately after Ricci's death, some Jesuits found Ricci's method excessively accommodationist, and impatient of results, they began to preach more directly among ordinary people. Groups of Chinese intellectuals rejected Ricci's interpretation of Confucius, and the issue became involved in Chinese politics with a party of reform among the mandarins favouring the Jesuits. The result by 1617 was an imperial edict expelling the Jesuits, but it was strictly implemented only in Nanking. Soon the situation grew more favourable, but the edict was not revoked. Meanwhile, Rome allowed the Jesuits in China to wear a headpiece during Mass in the Chinese style and to celebrate the liturgy in Chinese, though the Jesuits never took advantage of the latter concession. The real successor of Ricci as leader of the mission from 1630 until his death in 1666 was Johann Adam Schall von Bell, a native of Cologne, who resided at court largely by virtue of his part in imperial calendar reform. The determination of the calendar of rites and ceremonies was an imperial prerogative and a symbol of the emperor's power. The participation of Schall brought him enormous prestige, and he was able to steer the Jesuits successfully through the tumultuous politics of the Manchu defeat of the Mings and the establishment of the new dynasty in 1644. The Jesuits now operated on two fronts, at court and among the people.

Meanwhile Spanish Dominican and Franciscan missionaries entered China from the Philippines in 1633. They opposed the accommodationist method of Ricci, and the result was confusion among the Christians and provocation of Chinese officials. Eventually, on the basis of complaints sent to Rome, Pope Innocent X in 1645 forbade many Jesuit practices, but upon Jesuits' further explanation of their position, Alexander VII in 1656 reversed his predecessor. His decree lulled the Jesuits in China into a false security, so that they were not prepared for the papal condemnation of the rites by Clement XI in 1715 and its reaffirmation in 1745 by Benedict XIV. This destroyed Ricci's accommodationist attempt to penetrate Chinese culture and society, and made Christianity appear hostile to the Chinese way of life.

Throughout the tumult of the establishment of the Manchus, Christianity continued to grow; in 1663 there were about 114,000 Christians in China with not more than 25 missionaries. Persecution burst upon the church the following year, and nearly all the missionaries were imprisoned in Canton. As early as 1644 there had come into existence a series of Ordinances for Christian congregations without a priest, and these often served as guidelines throughout the coming decades. Missionaries now realized the need for a native clergy, and the first priest was ordained in 1664, but the next three not until 1688. In the course of the next century nearly 100 Chinese were sent to Naples for preparation for the priesthood. One Jesuit who was not imprisoned in 1664 was the Belgian Ferdinand Verbiest. He remained at court as imperial mathematician and finally in 1671 secured the release of those imprisoned in Canton. Then in 1688, in response to Verbiest's appeal for help, the first French missionaries arrived in China. They gave the mission new impetus, and were to serve as the chief propagators of Chinese culture in Europe during the eighteenth century. Apart from the rites themselves, all missionaries agreed on the need to adapt to Chinese ways. A decree of toleration was issued by the emperor in 1692, but in 1723 a series of local persecutions began, and ended in the general anti-Christian persecution of 1784–5. The chief reason for this hostility seems to have been the fear that both Christians and Muslims were potential allies of foreign invaders. Jesuits remained in the service of the emperor in Beijing, but their influence on policy was nil. The suppression of the Jesuits was a further blow to the mission, but by this time missionaries sent by the Propaganda played a major role in China.

The papal Congregation for the Propagation of the Faith came into existence in 1622 under Pope Gregory XV, with the purpose of overseeing all the church's far-flung missionary activity. It was a product of the new Roman universalism and, of course, it extended Rome's reach. Most importantly, the foundation of the Propaganda was an attempt to separate the church's mission from the state's sphere of activity and so to assert the primacy of the spiritual. In this sense it fostered a form of secularization and it pointed towards the future. By the 1560s the disadvantages to the church of the Iberian *Patronato* and *Padroado* were becoming manifest. Yet Philip II rejected the attempts of Pius V in 1568 and Gregory XIII in 1572 to intervene in the church in Spanish America. Unfortunately, the Propaganda was never able to function significantly in either Spanish or Portuguese America, due to the opposition of the respective monarchs.

The Propaganda promoted major initiatives, especially in Asia. It encouraged the establishment of indigenous churches, and it fostered an approach that started with the formation of local congregations and moved upwards, in place of the medieval model usually employed by the Jesuits that aimed first at the conversion of the ruler or ruling class and in its wake the remainder of the people. The general thrust of the Propaganda's policy was towards accommodation to non-European cultures, better preparation of missionaries, and especially towards the development of a native clergy. This policy was greatly influenced by Francesco Ingoli, the far-seeing secretary of the Congregation, a diocesan priest, who held office from its foundation until 1649. He realized clearly that a native clergy, regular as well as secular, was essential to the establishment of the church in a society or culture, and he saw in the reluctance to ordain natives to the priesthood a desire on the part of colonial powers to retain control over the church. Especially in times of persecution, a native clergy was required that could not be readily expelled or be easily identified with foreign interests. For Ingoli the Jesuits were too tied to the interests of the Iberian powers and often intolerant of other orders as, for example, in their persistence in retaining complete control over the university in Prague or insisting on a missionary monopoly in certain areas.

A particular goal of the Congregation was to end or at least modify the rivalry among the religious orders and the ill-will between religious and secular clergy that often characterized the church's missionary effort. Propaganda introduced more religious orders into the missions, the Capuchins especially in the Middle East and Germany, the Discalced Carmelites in the Middle East and Persia, and the Lazarists of Vincent de Paul in North Africa and Madagascar. The Paris Foreign Mission Society, which was founded in 1659 and recognized by Rome five years later, received the support of Propaganda for its work especially in the Far East. The Propaganda rejected the Portuguese claim by virtue of the *Padroado* to the appointment of bishops in the East in areas not actually under Portuguese control, such as China and Japan. Propaganda favoured there, instead of bishops, the appointment of vicars apostolic who were granted jurisdiction as direct representatives of the pope. In some places jurisdictional confusion reigned, and conflicts ensued, with the Jesuits as the most prominent missionary order often on the side of the *Padroado*.

One early success of the Propaganda was in Indochina, where the first vicars apostolic were dispatched. There in Tonkin Jesuits expelled from Japan and led by Alexander de Rhodes founded a lively Christian community. Well-trained lay catechists made up its backbone but there were few priests and no bishops. After unsuccessfully seeking priests in Italy to serve in Indochina, de Rhodes travelled to Paris, where he contacted the community of priests that would soon become the Paris Foreign Mission Society. In 1658 two members of this group were named vicars apostolic. Since the Portuguese refused to transport them, they travelled by the hard overland route through Syria, Persia, and India to Indochina. Hampered by a local war, they then settled in Ajuthia, the capital of Siam, which became the centre of their activity in East Asia and soon the site of a seminary for native priests. This marked the advance of the Propaganda into areas claimed by the *Padroado*, and it set off conflicts that spilled over into India and especially into China. Persecutions in Indochina and China in the late seventeenth and eighteenth centuries indicated the need to create native clergy and to concentrate on building up local congregations and parishes. When the European missionaries returned after the persecution in China from 1664 to 1670, they recognized the achievement of the Chinese Dominican priest Lo Wen-tsao in sustaining the local congregations, and he as a bishop in 1688 ordained an early group of Chinese diocesan priests.

The church's missionary activity in the early modern period testified to its vitality. In its reach it was becoming a universal church, yet despite creative initiatives, it remained overwhelmingly European in character. The efforts, especially on the part of Propaganda, to escape from the tutelage of the absolute monarchies had met with only partial success.

8

THE CHRISTIAN IN THE WORLD

An Academic Speech: Are Contemporary Politicians to be Considered among the Number of Christians? – so read the title of an oration by the English Catholic theologian Thomas Stapleton, which was published post-humously in Munich in 1608. It pointed to an old issue that seemed to engross and even torture leading figures of the sixteenth and seven-teenth centuries after Machiavelli brought it to the surface anew in 1513. He contended in the *Prince* that

> there is such a difference between how men live and how they ought to live that he who abandons what is done for what ought to be done learns his destruction rather than his preservation, because any man who under all conditions insists on making it his business to be good will surely be destroyed among so many who are not good. Hence a prince, in order to hold his position, must acquire the power to be not good, and understand when to use it and when not to use it, in accord with necessity.[1]

In other words, a ruler or man of politics could not adhere consistently to moral principles, at least as understood in a traditional Christian sense, and be successful, that is, maintain and increase the power of his state.

The same issue was taken up by the Spanish diplomat Juan de Vera y Figueroa in *The Ambassador*, a dialogue first published in 1620 which became a classic guidebook for diplomats. What should an ambassador do when the prince he represented was clearly in the wrong? To this query the interlocutor responded that 'in giving a satisfactory answer to this question, the greatest difficulty of this material will have been

175

solved', involving as it did, 'what is an ordinary thing in government, the clash of the useful with the good'. The ensuing discussion introduced a distinction between a good man in an absolute sense and a good man in a relative sense. He who sought absolute goodness ought to retire to a life of contemplation in the country, and certainly not pursue activity in the world of affairs.

Could a full Christian life be lived by a person active in the world, not only by the politician but also by the courtier, the businessman, or married person? One of the foremost achievements of the Catholic Reform, as well as the Reformation, was the assertion of the validity of the worldly or lay vocation as a Christian way of life. This affirmation, and even more so the attempt to demonstrate how to live it out in practical life, constituted a principal effort, if an implicit one, to accommodate to the changing world of the sixteenth century, and especially to the increasing number of educated lay people. But there were dissenters who shared the view of Machiavelli, and indeed, the tension sensed between the demands of the good and the useful characterized the era.

The issue of the role of the Christian in the world came to the fore in another, though less direct, way. In this case it was a matter of the relationship among disciplines. To what extent did or should Christian theology rooted in the Biblical revelation control developments in the emerging sciences or in other realms of thought? In this regard there would in the long run continue to take place a gradual secularization, understood as the assumption of relative autonomy by various disciplines. This process, which originated far back in the Middle Ages, was at work, for example, in Vitoria's elaboration of an international law based on the law of nature rather than on revelation. But the process continued to meet with resistance, as we shall see in the Galileo Affair, where church authority came to the aid of dubious theological claims over science.

Prominent voices sided with Machiavelli on the incompatibility of political success with Christian morality. A powerful current of thought within the Christian tradition called for great reserve towards the active life in a sinful world. Spiritual writers popular in the sixteenth century, such as Thomas à Kempis, whose *Imitation of Christ* was probably the most widely read book after the Bible, warned about participation in its affairs. Machiavelli's friend, the historian and diplomat Francesco Guicciardini, agreed that at least in present circumstances one could not govern states according to Christian laws. Towards the end of the century Montaigne expressed a distaste for politics because of the conflicts between its demands and those of morality.

But this was not the view prevalent in early modern Catholicism. It rather reaffirmed the position of pre-Machiavellian Renaissance humanism that the active life, and especially participation in politics, was a noble Christian calling. Then the renewed Thomism of the sixteenth century stamped its imprint on the Catholic Reform, and with it an optimistic vision of human nature and of a widespread harmony between nature and its completion in grace. A powerful, pessimistic Augustinian countercurrent persisted, particularly among French Jansenists, which stressed man's and the world's sinfulness, but it did not predominate. Francisco Vitoria brought with him to Spain in 1522 the revived Thomism whose spirit he had breathed in at Paris. Cajetan represented it in Rome. Both of them defended the rights based in natural law of the peoples across the seas. Ignatius Loyola and his early companions were influenced by the lectures they attended as students in Paris on Aquinas's *Compendium of Theology*. By the time they came to Rome, Aquinas was in vogue there. For them humanist education fitted well with the study of Aristotle and Aquinas. Not surprisingly, Aquinas was the author recommended by the Jesuit *Constitutions* for the study of theology. Later the Jesuit schools, and especially the theatre, exalted the active life in the world and aimed to exhibit the harmony between it and the Christian virtues.

The *Spiritual Exercises* of Ignatius Loyola implied a world-affirming spirituality. Especially at the beginning in the Principle and Foundation, and at the end in the Contemplation to Obtain Divine Love, creation or the sum total of God's creatures were considered to be gifts of God meant to lead men and women back to God. This creation remained fundamentally good even after original sin and mankind's subsequent misuse of God's creatures. Secondly, as we saw earlier, one goal of the *Exercises* was to enable the exercitant to discern God's will and to embrace that will with his own personal choice. This choice usually concerned life decisions involving vocation, that is, for religious life, the priesthood, or married life, or perhaps the choice of career. For one already fixed in a vocation or career, the decision involved the way in which God was calling him to live within this framework. The point for our purposes is that an individual could do God's will or follow Christ in any state of life or in any career. In other words, for Ignatius one could live a full Christian life in the world as well as in the convent or monastery. So Ignatius helped point the way to a lay spirituality.

Still more important in this development was Francis de Sales, the gentle yet firm Bishop of Geneva whose *Introduction to a Devout Life* has endured as a Christian classic up to the present day. His contribution as an outstanding personality of the Catholic Reform has been generally undervalued. Francis was born at the family chateau of Sales near Thorens in Savoy in 1567. After eight years of study at the Jesuit college of Clermont in Paris, he moved to Padua, where he received his doctorate in civil law in 1591, all the while pursuing on the side private study of theology with a view to the priesthood. While he was at Clermont, and perhaps again in Padua, severe interior temptations, especially to despair of his own salvation, afflicted the young man. So later, as a master spiritual director, he was able to sympathize with the trials of others. To the initial chagrin of his father who anticipated a career in law for his eldest son, Francis was ordained a priest on 18 December 1593. He then assumed a position as provost in the chapter of the cathedral of the Bishop of Geneva, whose seat had moved to the town of Annecy in Savoy after the Reformation. The next year saw Francis undertake with his cousin Louis the evangelization of the peasants of the Chablais. This rough mountainous, heavily Calvinist area had recently been returned to the suzerainty of the Duke of Savoy. During the next four years, as he won back to Catholicism most of the area's 50 parishes, he demonstrated that the most fruitful way to win over heretics was not through pressure and force, nor even debate and controversy, but through charity and example. Three times he travelled to Geneva itself, where he conversed amicably with Calvin's formidable successor, Theodore Beza.

After he was named coadjutor Bishop of Geneva in 1597, ecclesiastical and political affairs took Francis to Rome and then in 1602, for nearly nine months, to Paris. There his preaching and his conversation won over people, court, and Henry IV, who attempted to attach him to the hierarchy of France. While in Paris he frequented the circle of *dévots* around Barbe Acarie, daughter and wife of magistrates, *'la belle Acarie'* as she was called, who would end her life as Marie de l'Incarnation in the newly opened Carmelite convent of the Teresian Reform. Consecration as Bishop of Geneva followed in late 1602 and then 20 years of constant labour – visitations of his 450 parishes, preaching, voluminous correspondence, journeys of ecclesiastical and diplomatic import. They included another extended stay in Paris in 1618–19 where the principal goal was to negotiate the marriage of the Duke of Savoy's son, Victor Amadeus, with the sister of Louis XIII. While preaching the Lenten sermons at Dijon in 1604 Francis first encountered the 32-year-old Jane Frances de Chantal, recently widowed with five children. Their meeting was to flower into one of the great friendships of religious history, its record preserved in their correspondence, and it resulted in 1610 in the foundation of the Order of the Visitation at Annecy. Francis died at Lyons in December 1622.

Although much of Francis's correspondence was devoted to the spiritual direction of men, he was especially impressed by the aspirations for a more profound Christian life of women that he encountered on his journeys. One of these was Louise de Chastel, the 20-year-old wife of Claude de Charmoisy, ambassador of the Duke of Savoy to the Republic of Bern and a distant relative of Francis. Her experience at court in Paris had not prepared her for life in rural Savoy. Francis recognized in this young woman a call from God to a deep religious life, or as he would put it, a life of 'devotion'. In Lent 1607 Louise, in Annecy for a legal matter, asked Francis to serve as her spiritual director, and he in turn wrote to Jane Frances de Chantal, 'I have just found in our sacred nets a fish that I had desired for four years. ... She is a lady as good as gold, infinitely fit to serve her Lord; if she perseveres she will do so with fruit.' Further legal business summoned Louise to Chambery. Before she departed, Francis wrote out for her a set of instructions to guide her in the life of the spirit, and he entrusted her to the care of the rector of the Jesuit college in Chambery. After reading these instructions, the rector immediately wrote Francis encouraging him to publish them. Francis recognized an opportunity to reach a wide audience, and so, after some further work, published the *Introduction to a Devout Life* in 1609.

Francis addressed the *Introduction* to a fictional 'Philothea', that is, a soul loving or in love with God, male or female or in other words, as he elaborated, to those aspiring to devotion. 'Charity is spiritual fire and when it bursts into flames, it is called devotion. Hence devotion adds nothing to the fire of charity except the flame that makes charity prompt, active, and diligent not only to observe God's commandments but also to fulfill his heavenly counsels and inspirations.' After remarking that most spiritual writers wrote for folks removed from the world, or at least desirous of retirement from it, Francis stated that

> my purpose is to instruct those who live in town, within families, or at court, and by their state of life are obliged to live an ordinary life

as to outward appearances. Frequently, on the pretext of some supposed impossibility, they will not even think of undertaking a devout
life. ... [God] commands Christians ... to bring forth the fruits of
devotion, each according to his position and vocation. Devotion must
be exercised in different ways by the gentleman, the worker, the servant, the prince, the widow, the young girl, and the married woman.
Not only is this true, but the practice of devotion must also be
adapted to the strength, activities, and duties of each particular person. I ask you, Philothea, is it fitting for a bishop to want to live a
solitary life like a Carthusian? Or for married men to want to own no
more property than a Capuchin, for a skilled workman to spend the
whole day in church like a religious, for a religious to be subject to
every sort of call in his neighbor's service, as a bishop is? Would not
such devotion be laughable, confused, impossible to carry out? Still
this is a very common fault, and therefore the world, which does not
distinguish between real devotion and the indiscretion of those who
merely think themselves devout, murmurs at devotion itself and
blames it, even though devotion cannot prevent such disorders. No,
Philothea, true devotion does no harm whatsoever, but instead per-
fects all things. When it goes contrary to a man's lawful vocation, it is
undoubtedly false ... every vocation becomes more agreeable when
united with devotion. Care of one's family is rendered more peace-
able, love of husband and wife more sincere, service to one's prince
more faithful, and every type of employment more pleasant and
agreeable.

Later, when discussing proper dress, Francis remarked, typically, 'For
my part, I would have devout people, whether men or women, always
the best dressed in a group but the least pompous and affected.'[2]

So Francis instructed Philothea about the life of the Christian in the
world. His descriptive, psychological method appealed to the individual's experience and was reminiscent of Montaigne's *Essays*, which the
author knew well.

By Francis's death in 1622, at least 40 editions of the *Introduction to a
Devout Life* had appeared, and it had been translated into the major
European languages. Protestants read it too, often in an edition purged
of peculiarly Catholic features such as Eucharistic piety. Francis spoke
to the heart of a European religious elite that crossed class lines. A second major work, the *Treatise on the Love of God*, followed from his pen in
1616, written in French and addressed to a lay elite more advanced

in the spiritual life than Philothea. In the first four books Francis presented his philosophy of human nature as an apology for the faith that was directed against the unbelief of a growing group of libertines. He argued that Christian faith was the explanation and aspiration of the human soul, and he displayed his mastery of human psychology as he treated comprehensively the gradual unfolding of the Christian life in prayer and love. Both his major works placed him in an affective, experiential tradition. This tradition would wither later in the century as rationalism became dominant in Catholic theology partly as a result of the confrontation with the new philosophy of Descartes, who died in 1650.

Others before and after Francis wrote in the same sense as the *Introduction*, but none as effectively as he, gifted as he was with a clear, luminous style that left its mark on the writing of French. The Spanish Jesuit Luis de la Puente published in four volumes between 1612 and 1615 his *Perfection in All the States of Christian Life*. The first dealt with the Christian life in general, and the three subsequent volumes took up the three states or 'republics': the secular state, that is, family life as well as governmental and other types of service; the religious state; and the ecclesiastical state, that is, of those in orders.

At exactly the same time, in 1613, *On the States of Life*, by the Jesuit Joannes Busaeus (or Buys), came off the press in Mainz. He took the term 'state of life' in a broad sense. His treatment of the soldier followed his treatment of the physician and preceded that of the monk, and he devoted sections to married people, children, the aged, and a whole book to peasants. The French Jesuit Nicholas Caussin's *The Holy Court* first appeared at Paris in late 1624, and it was published in increasingly expanded two- and three-volume editions, and in translations in the major European languages throughout the seventeenth century. This work certainly was one reason for his later appointment and controversial tenure as confessor to Louis XIII from 1637 to 1640. His audience, as the title indicates, was the court. Even in that ambience the Christian life could be lived, Caussin contended, echoing Francis de Sales, and from the court examples would emanate to 'sanctify the world'.

But to return to Machiavelli's challenge, most Christians were unwilling to accept that he excluded them in practice from political life. First published in 1531/2, *The Prince* and the *Discourses* were placed on the Index of Paul IV in 1559 and on that of the Council of Trent in 1564. Many authors took up their pens to argue against his position, usually on philosophical or theological grounds. Obviously, he touched a raw nerve in the Christian body. Then in the same year, 1589, there appeared two books, one in the south of Europe and the other in the north, which launched a narrower Antimachiavellian tradition. They were the two most widely read political works of the first half of the seventeenth century: the *Reason of State* of the Italian priest and councillor to several princes, Giovanni Botero, and the *Six Books of Politics or Teaching on the State* of the Flemish humanist scholar, Justus Lipsius. This tradition attempted, first, to meet Machiavelli on his own terms, that is, to demonstrate that his agenda for the development of a powerful state would in fact only bring it to ruin. Secondly, it sought to develop a detailed, practical programme that showed how a ruler operating with solid Christian principles could maintain and develop a powerful state and so be successful politically.

Contemporaries read the Antimachiavellians because they addressed a problem keenly experienced during the period: tension between the demands of the good and the useful made by life in the world and especially by life in the world of politics. Two types of arguments characterized Antimachiavellian efforts to reconcile the good and the useful: providentialist and intrinsic or immanent pragmatism. The first required faith, the second did not. Providentialist pragmatism argued that God bestowed victory and success in this world, at least in most cases, on princes and peoples that served him faithfully and uprightly, either through a direct, miraculous intervention in the course of events, or more likely, through skilful guidance of natural or secondary causes. Intrinsic pragmatism argued from the nature of the act itself, apart from any divine intervention. Moral action by its very nature was useful, immoral action was counterproductive. The lie was a standard example; it was always in the long run unprofitable since it undermined confidence and trust in its perpetrator. Moral action was reasonable, immoral action was unreasonable. Machiavelli was unreasonable as well as immoral and irreligious. In other words, violation of the law of nature, which was based on reason, inevitably brought its own retribution on individuals and states.

Antimachiavellian concern with practice fostered casuistry, that is, the careful analysis of individual moral actions and the application of general principles to them. It became increasingly characteristic of both

Catholic and Protestant moral thought. What precisely was immoral action? To be sure, an outright lie was wrong, but was it deceit to mask one's intentions or to leave certain things unsaid? The problems casuistry tried to deal with arose out of a complex society where changing circumstances presented new situations for which answers were not ready at hand.

The term 'reason of state' had been used in Italy prior to the publication of Botero's *Reason of State*, but his book made it popular. Born in Piedmont in 1544, Botero joined the Jesuits in 1560 in Rome, but then left the Society in 1580. Charles Borromeo took him into his service and made him his secretary in 1582. After Borromeo's death in 1584, Botero accompanied the young Federico Borromeo, Charles's cousin, to Rome, where he served as his tutor and councillor from 1586 until 1595 when Federico returned to Milan as archbishop. While in Rome Botero enjoyed contact with its intellectual and ecclesiastical elite, and papal secretary and former emissary to Germany, Minuccio Minucci recommended Botero's volume to the court of Munich in 1591. In contrast to many subsequent authors, Botero defined reason of state in an eminently positive sense as 'knowledge of the means suitable to create, preserve, and expand' a powerful state. The term *reason* carried a particular implication for him. He argued that the ruler who sought a powerful state did best to seek the well-being of his subjects in a fashion that was moral and so reasonable. Machiavelli's programme was unreasonable. As a contemporary admirer wrote, 'Botero is marvelous. He has so accommodated morality, justice, and obligation with the advantage of the prince so as to merit in this respect immortal praise.' By reconciling the demands of the good and the useful into an excessively facile harmony, Botero eliminated the tension and overstated his case. He had his critics as well as his admirers.

For Botero three features of a powerful government were the support of the people, in other words, its reputation; unity of religion; and most importantly, economic development. Reputation was a composite of love and fear of the ruler that existed in the subjects; it was for Botero 'the foundation of every government of a state'. Reputation was produced by the ruler's *virtù*, a combination of traditional virtue and the political virtuosity exalted by Machiavelli. His discussion led Botero into the popular topic of the relationship between appearance and reality. He contended that piety, for example, which was essential to a ruler's reputation, could not be counterfeited over a long period of time, as Machiavelli affirmed it could. Botero distinguished three forms of reputation: natural reputation, which corresponded to reality; artificial reputation, which resulted from conscious exaggeration of reality; and adventitious reputation, which also exaggerated reality but not as a result of a conscious effort to do so but rather as a stroke of luck. Neither of the last two endured, Botero argued. But this did not mean that a prince could not or should not polish his image. He should hide his weaknesses and assign unpopular tasks to others. A prince's image was like a painting. Just as a painter might exceed the limits of truth as long as he remained within the limits of verisimilitude, so might the prince in developing his image. In this manner Botero drew on contemporary art theory. But appearance was never enough; enduring reputation had to be founded in reality.

Botero saw religion from the perspective of providentialist and intrinsic pragmatism, in that it was valuable because of the divine aid it won for the state and for the virtues it engendered in the subjects. Like Machiavelli, he pointed to the importance attached to religion by the Romans, and he so underlined its utility that he approached reducing it to a mere tool of government himself. Though at first he appeared opposed to the increasing intervention in ecclesiastical matters by rulers, Botero granted them a major role in church affairs, thus fostering the state control of religion that characterized the Counter Reformation. The prince should see to it that the people enjoyed the services of good pastors and preachers, look to the material needs of the clergy, provide suitable places of worship, and promote church programmes with funds and with his authority.

Botero was an early mercantilist – that is, he advocated government's active promotion of economic development, as did other Antimachiavellians. Their mercantilism weighs against the argument that Counter Reformation Catholicism was responsible for the economic decline of Italy and Spain in the seventeenth century. The explanation for this lay elsewhere, for example, in the long wars of the period and in an aristocratic ethic that had little to do with religion. Botero was most creative in laying out a programme of economic growth. Expansion of the state was for him economic and demographic growth rather than territorial gain. The connection between the wealth of subjects and government revenue was clear to him. The prince who fostered the wealth of his subjects increased his own power since it provided his tax base. Regular taxation should be the prince's main source of revenue, Botero contended, as opposed to *ad-hoc* grants. His programme included agriculture but stressed industry and foreign trade.

People were the most productive resource. The wealthiest areas of Europe were Italy, the Netherlands, and France, he asserted, none of which was rich in natural resources but all of which possessed skilled workers and businessmen. Botero criticized Spain's failure to develop industry and its social attitudes which disdained manual work and business activity.

A shortcoming of Botero's economic programme was his virtual prohibition of usury, which meant at the time the taking of any interest on a loan, not just exorbitant interest. In this respect he lagged behind many contemporary moralists. The church's condemnation of usury dated from the early Middle Ages when in an agricultural society the moneylender was considered an exploiter of the poor and a parasite on society who pocketed money without any real labour. This prohibition remained on the books in the sixteenth century, and was reiterated by Sixtus V in 1586. Botero cited 'divine precepts' as one reason for his hostility to usury.

But since the beginnings of a commercial economy in the Italian city-states in the thirteenth century, and especially in the fifteenth and sixteenth centuries, moral theologians increasingly questioned the prohibition of usury and narrowed its application. This was an exemplary case of the use of casuistry to adapt to the changing nature of the economy, and especially to the new role of money as capital for investment. One justification for the taking of interest that became popular in the fifteenth century was 'loss of gain' (*lucrum cessans*), that is, if a merchant instead of investing money elsewhere, for example, in goods to be sold, made a loan, he could charge interest as compensation for his loss. The papacy itself, along with many Italian states, fostered *monti di pietà*, with the purpose of making money available to the poor. The *monti* involved two forms of loans. Investors, at interest, placed money in a fund from which it was then lent to the poor, initially at no interest, until it became obvious that the fund could not be maintained without some charge on the loan to the poor too. The sixteenth century saw widespread approval of the triple or 'German' contract. Through an elaborate contractual apparatus that avoided an outright loan, it in effect permitted a 5 per cent interest charge. The Belgian Jesuit Leonard Lessius, in his *On Justice and Law* of 1605, after a thorough analysis of the Antwerp market, greatly expanded the application of *lucrum cessans*. By this time moralists generally tended to allow credit operations so long as the interest rate was not excessive and the poor were not exploited. But some rigorists remained.

The Antimachiavellian Lipsius straddled the confessions for a time before definitively returning to his early Catholicism and to a chair at the University of Louvain in 1590/1. In his extensive treatment of deceit under the heading of 'mixed prudence', Lipsius the casuist appeared as he attempted, unsuccessfully, to bridge the gap between the good and the useful. His introductory words were reminiscent of Machiavelli. 'Among what kind of people do we live? the clever, the malicious. They seem to be made up of fraud, fallacies, and lies.' This was the world of politics. Citing Plutarch, he made use of a figure employed by Machiavelli. 'When one does not succeed wearing the skin of a lion, it is necessary to play the fox.' But this did not constitute a complete departure from the good, he added quickly; it mixed the useful with the good. Just as wine did not cease to be wine if a little water was poured in, so prudence did not cease to be prudence if just a drop of deceit were added. Deceit was then broken down into slight, medium, and serious. The first, which amounted to hesitation in trusting others and an ability to conceal one's thoughts, he recommended. The second, bribery and lying, he tolerated. The third, perfidy and injustice, he condemned outright. Lying caused him the most trouble, and he was obviously uneasy about it. Rarely did he cite Scripture, but here he adduced a number of texts to show that to lie was to violate divine law. The dilemma he saw. 'I will scarcely extricate you or myself from this if not through what the Bishop suggested.' Then he cited Augustine in a passage taken over by Aquinas. 'There are some types of lies in which there is not great guilt but which are nevertheless not without guilt.' In this class he put 'little briberies' and 'white lies' used by a good and legitimate prince against evil persons for the sake of the common good. Otherwise such medium deception was a sin and a great sin, 'no matter how the old hands at court may laugh at me'.

'If any prince has come to ruin, it was not because he was good but because he did not know how to be good.' So read another rejoinder to Machiavelli written by the Spanish cleric, writer and long-time diplomat Diego Saavedra Fajardo. His *The Idea of a Politico-Christian Prince Represented in One Hundred Emblems* appeared in its definitive form at Milan in 1643, and it became in the third quarter of the seventeenth century a popular book read across confessional lines. As the title indicates, Saavedra's purpose too was to reconcile Christianity and successful politics. Yet his use of emblems, the body of which were essays reminiscent of Montaigne, permitted him to allow for a certain ambiguity or ambivalence as he attempted to harmonize the good and the useful. He explicitly rejected Lipsius's mixed prudence, but in reality the two authors were not distant in their application of casuistry to deceit. Like Botero, Saavedra called for a policy of economic development that 'represented a true reason of state' as an alternative to the 'politics of these times' which 'took for granted malice and deceit at every turn'. He encouraged a piety that emphasized a work ethic that would benefit the temporal welfare. Spain lagged behind economically not because of a lack of resources but because of an unwillingness to work. Noble status was the goal of everyone, and too many entered religious life. An excessive number of feast days kept peasants and craftsmen from work, and they wasted time on pilgrimages and other practices that bordered on superstition. Like Botero and other Antimachiavellians, Saavedra in his effort to exhibit the harmony between the good and the useful tended to instrumentalize religion for the benefit of the state. He praised the regulations issued by Venice to curb donations to the church, which provoked an interdict of 1605 and a bitter contest with the papacy.

The Christian's relationship to the world made up the main issue in the prolonged, painful dispute in France between the Jansenists and the Jesuits, in which the genius Blaise Pascal stood out as a brilliant if one-sided polemicist with his *Provincial Letters* of 1656/7. In this instance the point was not so much directly whether the Christian could live in the world – many Jansenist figures did so, though they tended to withdraw to their retreat at the former female Cistercian convent of Port Royal outside Paris – but the value of human activity *vis-à-vis* divine action and the need of the church to adapt its moral teaching to a changing world. Significantly, Jansenists sided against the Jesuits in the Chinese Rites Controversy. They generally denied the value of the virtues found among the pagans across the seas because these virtues were not explicitly Christian. Politics surely influenced the dispute. Richelieu, his successor as first minister Cardinal Jules Mazarin, and Louis XIV all considered the Jansenists politically dangerous. Hence their general support for the Jesuits. Jean Duvergier de Hauranne, the Abbé de Saint-Cyran, who with Cornelius Jansen stood at the origins of the movement, spent the last five years of his life in prison because Richelieu considered him a threatening figure of the *dévot* party. Furthermore, in the rivalry between the seculars and the regulars, which colours much of the whole tale, Saint-Cyran vigorously took the side of the secular clergy, especially in his *Petrus Aurelius* of 1633 attacking the Jesuits.

The Protestant Reformation brought to the fore the relationship of God's grace and man's free will in the work of justification. Luther, and Calvin more so, argued that original sin so impaired man's free will that only those whom God predestined were saved, without any meaningful participation of their own free will. Trent condemned this position, as we have seen, while asserting the divine initiative in the process of salvation and preserving a role for man's free will. But this was not the end of the matter on the Catholic side. Jesuits led by Luis de Molina, and Dominicans led by Domingo Báñez, argued over the more precise contributions of grace and free will until Pope Paul V silenced both parties in 1607. Meanwhile, the Louvain theologian Michael Baius, drawing upon his reading of St Augustine, continued to hold positions similar to those of the Reformers, many of which were condemned by Rome in 1567 and again in 1579. A leading opponent of Baius at Louvain was the young Robert Bellarmine.

The Flemish Jansen, who was to continue the tradition of Baius at Louvain, came to Paris as a 19-year-old student in 1604. There he became friends with the student Saint-Cyran, and the two of them spent nearly five years together in study of the church Fathers at Bayonne, Saint-Cyran's home town, from 1612 to 1617. Jansen returned to a professorate at Louvain in 1617, where he found himself often at odds with the Jesuits. In 1628 he began work on *Augustinus* – for which he is said to have read all the works of St Augustine through 10 times, and the works on grace 30 times – which was finally published in 1640, two years after his death. The volume exhibited a profound theological pessimism with its emphasis on the effects of original sin on human nature and its assertion of a divine determinism that seemed to exclude man's free will in the work of salvation. Only action by the *parlement* of Paris prevented the Sorbonne from condemning propositions from the *Augustinus* in 1649, and Pope Innocent X in 1653 did condemn five propositions drawn from the book after the case was brought to Rome. The Jansenist party opposed this condemnation. It was now led by Antoine Arnauld, son of a *parlementaire* family with a long history of resistance to Jesuit influence in France, and it was centred at the former convent of Port Royal outside Paris. The Cistercian community there, of which Angélique Arnauld, sister of Antoine, was abbess and which Saint-Cyran had served as spiritual director, had moved into the

city in 1626, to remain there until 1648. In an effort to evade the con-
demnations, some Jansenists admitted that the five propositions were
heretical but denied that they could be found in *Augustinus*. Neither
church nor governmental authorities would accept this qualification,
and further pressure was placed upon the Jansenists and especially the
community of Port Royal to accept the condemnation. Arnauld was
expelled from the Sorbonne in February 1655. At this point Pascal
intervened with his *Provincial Letters*, and the affair caught the interest
of the general public. By the publication of the fifth provincial letter
6000 copies were being printed clandestinely.

Saint-Cyran, Arnauld, and their followers had long questioned contemporary, especially Jesuit, moral teaching. They considered it to be
excessively accommodating or laxist. This moral teaching had greatly
expanded following the Council of Trent's insistence that in the sacrament of penance mortal sins be confessed according to genus and
species, and the council's determination that priests be better equipped
to hear confessions. Theologians developed courses of 'cases of conscience' to prepare priests for the confessional, and for these courses
they wrote tomes of *Instructions in Moral Theology*, applying moral principles to cases the confessor might expect to encounter – that is,
instructing him in casuistry. Sometimes the tomes' authors in their
desire for completeness described cases of unusual complexity or of a
highly speculative nature that bordered on the inane. The result was
a moral theology that focused on the approval or disapproval of individual acts and on minimal obligations under the law, rather than on
the fundamental moral attitude or posture of the individual involved
or on the more desirable course of action in a situation. This was a dis-
tortion to which the Jansenists rightly called attention. Yet a main function of the casuists was a crucial one, the application of traditional
principles to a changing society regarding, for example, the freedom of
a girl to choose a marriage partner, attendance at the theatre, or the
taking of interest on a loan. Jansenists insisted on the norms of the
early church Fathers, whereas many Jesuits argued that new situations
required flexibility. The issue was an old one for the church.

Blaise Pascal was an outstanding scientist and mathematician, a master of lucid French, and a Jansenist associate. Born in 1623 to the family of a magistrate, he lived as a youth for a time in Paris until his father
was appointed intendant of Normandy in Rouen in 1639. Precocious as
he was, early on he took part in experiments that led to the invention
of the barometer, and later he made significant contributions to the

infinitesimal calculus and the theory of probabilities. By the time his father died in 1651 – his mother had died when he was four – the family had returned to Paris where Blaise pursued his scientific work and engaged in the lively social life of the capital. His sister Jacqueline, to whom he was very close, entered the convent of Port Royal over his opposition. He himself then underwent a profound religious conversion on the night of 23 November 1654, a remembrance of which he carried in a locket around his neck for the rest of his life. From then on he was a frequent visitor to Port Royal, though he never became a full-fledged member of the Jansenist circle there.

Pascal's partisan, scintillating *Provincial Letters* appeared, anonymously, between 23 January 1656 and 24 March 1657; only in 1659 did the person of the author become known. The first 10 were addressed to a correspondent in the country or a 'provincial', the next six to the Jesuits themselves, and the final two to Francis Annat, the leading Jesuit at court. The three letters at the start dealt with the issue of grace, free will, and the five propositions, and the last two returned to this topic. The others attacked and ridiculed the moral teaching of the Jesuits, which in fact was taught by many others too. The strategy was to bring into disrepute the moral doctrine by citing some admittedly far-fetched conclusions reached by some Jesuit moralists and so to impugn by association the Jesuit teaching on grace. One Jesuit, designated correctly as lax, was termed 'the lamb of God' because he took away the sins of the world, that is, he made it so difficult to fulfil the conditions necessary for serious sin. Later in the 1660s and 1670s the papacy did condemn as laxist a number of positions criticized by the *Provincial Letters*. Fundamental to Pascal's thrust was the charge that the Jesuits acted 'as if the faith, and tradition, its ally, were not always one and the same at all times and in all places; as if it were the part of the rule to bend in conformity to the subject which it was meant to regulate'.[3] He accused the Jesuits of inventing ways to circumvent the prohibition on usury which, in fact, was outdated.

Jesuit authors responded to the *Provincial Letters*. They accused Pascal of assigning to the whole Society of Jesus positions advocated by one or two of its members, or attributing only to the Society positions held equally by other moralists, of failing to make necessary distinctions, and of lifting citations out of context. But they could not match the polemical skills of Pascal. Nor did they ever put the issue of the need to accommodate to changing times as clearly as they might have, though they did allude to a Jansenist theological antiquarianism.

The Jansenist controversy continued to agitate France through the reign of Louis XIV and beyond, but after the 1650s it became increasingly more a political contest than a theological dispute. The French government tended to see in Jansenist resistance to ecclesiastical and monarchical authority a danger to the crown. Port Royal was virtually closed down for a time, until a tacit compromise was reached in 1669. Shortly before his death in 1715 Louis XIV secured from Rome another condemnation of Jansenism in the bull *Unigenitus Dei Filius*. By that time Port Royal had been permanently shuttered.

The Jansenist position on grace, undercutting human free will as it did, made God appear arbitrary, violated a certain sense of justice, and ran counter to human experience. By doing so it helped open Christianity to attack by the Enlightenment. The *Provincial Letters* had been a resounding success, and they remain a classic of French literature, but Pascal himself feared subsequently that they might not only damage the Jesuits but end up alienating people from Christianity itself, with their mockery of casuistry and a humanist position on grace. Many of the sisters at Port Royal thought that Pascal violated Christian charity in the *Provincial Letters*. Pascal also was concerned about the impact of the rationalist Descartes. So he determined to undertake an apology for Christianity that would lead not to the God of the philosophers and even to a type of deism, as did many contemporary Catholic apologists, but to the God revealed in Jesus Christ. As he wrote in lapidary fashion: 'Two extremes: to exclude reason, to admit reason only.'[4] He advanced a basic argument, similar to the psychological approach of Francis de Sales, that Christianity best corresponded to human experience. Man's high ideals proceeded from his state before original sin, and his wretchedness from the fall. The affective tradition also remained alive in Pascal, awakened by his profound experience of God's love at the time of his conversion. As he put it, 'The heart has its reasons which reason does not know.'[5] Yet he died in 1662 before he could complete his project. What remained were his *Penseés* or *Thoughts*, consisting of the notes he had gathered. Scholars have attempted to organize these fragments, many of them brilliant insights, in the manner they thought Pascal intended, but there has been little consensus. Unfortunately, no followers emerged to continue his, and to a degree Francis de Sales's, style of argument, so that as the Enlightenment came on, mainline Catholic theology turned excessively rationalist in its approach and not rooted also in experience or affectivity.

The Galileo Affair marked a failure of church authority to respond adequately to the challenge of the emerging new science, and up to the present day it has cast a long shadow on the relationship between religion and science. Hence the current determination of Pope John Paul II to put the affair behind the church once and for all. Galileo's condemnation represented a victory for excessive claims of theology to control the new science. The claims were supported by church authorities who were put on the defensive by the Protestant Reformation and who feared laymen dabbling in the interpretation of Scripture. Galileo enjoyed considerable support within the church. Personal dislikes and differences of temperament also influenced the course of events, and Galileo himself must bear some responsibility for the outcome. He did always consider himself a faithful son of the church. Some have argued convincingly that part of his intent was to put the church on the side of the new science or at least to prevent the church from condemning it.

Galileo appeared on the European stage in 1610 when three models of the universe were in competition: the old Aristotelian model, the Copernican, and the model of Tycho Brahe which attempted a compromise between the two. It was the time of what later historians called the Scientific Revolution. By this was meant, first, the destruction of the Greek vision of the universe, which dated from Aristotle and was modified by Ptolemy in the early Christian era, and second, its replacement by a vision of the world knowable by science that was reduced to bodies or particles in motion in abstract space governed by universal laws expressed mathematically and verifiable by observation or experiment. So the mechanistic vision of the universe came to birth. The revolution took place initially in astronomy and in physics, and it stretched from the publication of Copernicus's *On the Revolution of the Heavenly Spheres* in 1543 to the appearance of Newton's *Mathematical Principles of Natural Philosophy* in 1687, which represented the victory of the new model of the universe.

In the Aristotelian system the earth was at the centre of the universe, and at its outermost boundaries was the sphere on which the stars were located. Within this sphere were a series of concentric spheres on which sat the planets as well as the moon and the sun. All the spheres encircled the earth once every 24 hours, thus accounting for our day and night. The first sphere above the earth was that of the moon. All the heavenly bodies above the sphere of the moon were composed of a type of unchangeable matter which was essentially different from the matter in the space beneath the moon. The system had shortcomings, which astronomers throughout the centuries noticed and attempted to remedy by closer observation, but it was a brilliant synthesis that corresponded to normal sense experience and to the intuition that the heavens were the place of stability and perfection.

Copernicus like many others realized the weaknesses in the prevailing system of the heavens. He argued that we would be able to predict the movements of the heavenly bodies more accurately if we placed the sun and not the earth at the centre of the universe, and postulated that the earth turned once daily on its axis and encircled the sun once annually. His theory violated common sense; we do not feel the earth moving or turning. It also was based on a highly sophisticated mathematics which was intelligible only to initiates. Long fearful of the reaction it might provoke, Copernicus agreed only on his deathbed to publish his work. Lucas Osiander, the individual who assumed responsibility for seeing it through the press, was aware that Luther and probably many others did not welcome the system because of its divergence from the traditional vision of the world. So in an unsigned preface to *On the Revolution of the Heavenly Spheres* when it appeared in 1543 he asserted that Copernicus was only putting forth a hypothesis. That was to be a fateful statement.

Instant fame came to Galileo in 1610 when he published *The Starry Messenger* reporting his discoveries in the heavens that were made with the help of the telescope he had developed and then turned skywards. At the time he held a modest position in the academic world as professor of mathematics at the University of Padua. Born at Pisa in 1564 to a father who was both a composer and a theoretician of music, the young Galileo studied at the University of Pisa after a brief stay in the novitiate of the Vallombrosan Order. In 1589 he became a professor of mathematics at that university, but after quarrels with Aristotelian philosophers he moved to Padua in 1591. Many of the ideas with which he would revolutionize physics in his *Discourses on the Two New Sciences* of 1638 were first worked through during these early years. Meanwhile, the system of Copernicus found few adherents. One was the German Protestant Johannes Kepler, who became court astronomer to Emperor Rudolph II in Prague in 1601. Galileo wrote to him in 1597 that he had been for some time himself a Copernican. The Danish astronomer Tycho Brahe, Kepler's predecessor in Prague, elaborated a system of his own that took over features of Copernicanism but kept the earth at the centre of the universe. In his *Starry Messenger* Galileo announced that he had located four planets that revolved around Jupiter, indicating that not all the heavenly bodies circled the earth. This and other lesser discoveries told against the prevailing Aristotelian system. Later in 1610 Galileo moved back to Tuscany as Philosopher and Mathematician to the Grand Duke, and in 1611 he journeyed to Rome as a celebrity where the Jesuits of the Roman College, led by the now elderly Christopher Clavius, feted him, and Pope Paul V assured him of his good will.

Galileo now set aside his other researches and pursued with zeal the cause of Copernicanism. He had uncovered weaknesses in Aristotle's system, and the professional Aristotelians were the first to attack him, one professor at Pisa allegedly refusing to gaze through the telescope. Galileo's *Letters on Sunspots* of 1613 reported the changes he observed on the face of the sun showing that it was not composed of unchangeable matter. This publication also involved him in a bitter dispute with the Jesuit Christopher Scheiner over priority of discovery of the sunspots. Then the Aristotelian philosopher Ludovico delle Colombe raised the dispute to a new, theological level by asserting that Galileo's Copernicanism went against Scripture. Others followed suit, arguing that Scripture passages, such as '[God] fixed the earth upon its foundation, not to be moved forever' (Psalms 103, 5), demonstrated that the earth remained stationary. When his disciple, the Benedictine Benedetto Castelli, reported that Scriptural arguments against Copernicanism had come up in conversation at a dinner party at the Grand Ducal court, Galileo hastened to write up his views on the subject in his 'Letter to Castelli'. This in turn was handed over to the Inquisition in Rome. The discussion shifted to the possibility of reconciling Copernicanism with Scripture.

Galileo and Cardinal Bellarmine now became the two chief protagonists. The two shared the conviction that there could be no ultimate conflict between faith and reason or, more appropriately in this case, between Scripture interpreted correctly and scientific findings demonstrated to be true. But Bellarmine made inappropriate claims for Scripture, and this was the root of the whole problem. He insisted on maintaining a literal interpretation of Scripture unless Galileo demonstrated, in a strict sense of the term, the truth of Copernicanism. This Galileo realized he was unable to do at the time. Bellarmine laid out his position in a letter of 12 April 1615 to the Carmelite Paolo Antonio Foscarini, who had published a book attempting to reconcile Copernicanism with the Scripture. The Council of Trent, according to Bellarmine, declared that Scripture was not to be interpreted against the general sense of the early Fathers of the Church. But the Fathers clearly understood the passages about the movement of the sun and the immobility of the earth in a literal sense. The fact that this was not a matter of faith or morals was not to the point, according to Bellarmine. By virtue of their authorship by the Holy Spirit, the Scriptures could not err in any respect. Should Galileo demonstrate the truth of Copernicanism, Bellarmine conceded that the Church would have to reconsider the interpretation of the passages in question. Meanwhile Galileo was free to advocate Copernicanism as a hypothesis. Bellarmine was aware of the preface to *On the Revolutions of the Heavenly Spheres*, but not of its composition by Osiander. Some scholars have read into Bellarmine's position a sophisticated understanding of scientific methodology. He was merely telling Galileo to treat as a hypothesis, they argue, what Galileo realized himself he had not yet proven. But this is to misunderstand the contemporary meaning of hypothesis. It did not designate then, as it does today, a scientific theory about reality not yet proven but anticipated to be proven. In the early seventeenth century hypothesis meant for astronomers a calculating device that enabled accurate prediction of the movements in the heavens; it was not a statement about reality, not even a provisional one.

Galileo's response to Bellarmine's letter to Foscarini was found in his 'Letter to the Grand Duchess Christina', a reworking of his letter to Castelli. It manifested a solid grasp of principles of Biblical interpretation. Even if they had all agreed on the issue, he wrote, and there was no evidence that they had, the Fathers of the Church never intended to take a formal position on the movement of the earth since it had never been an explicit issue for them. More importantly, the issue was not one of faith and morals where the Bible could not err, but a scientific issue. It was a matter for scientists, not Scripture scholars or theologians, to decide. Apparently citing Cardinal Baronius from a conversation long ago in Venice, Galileo noted that the Bible was not about the heavens but about the way to get to heaven. Nor was it written for scientists; rather it used the everyday language of ordinary people who spoke of the sun rising or setting without intending to make a scientific statement. Many Biblical passages obviously could not be taken literally, as when they attributed to God hands or feet, or feelings of anger. Galileo realized from his reading of Copernicus that, despite the preface, the Polish astronomer intended his theory to apply to reality. But with a degree of inconsistency, he did admit that in scientific issues where the evidence available spoke more or less equally for each side, the Scriptures might be introduced as a factor. Why did he assert this?

Probably because he thought the evidence in support of Copernicanism placed it outside this category of issues and because he reckoned, too optimistically as it turned out, that if he could only get the theologians to investigate the issue seriously, he could convince them of the truth of Copernicanism and so of the need to depart from the traditional interpretation of Scripture.

Against the advice of many of his friends, and of the Florentine ambassador in Rome who sensed political traps, Galileo once again took the road to the Eternal City. His purpose seems to have been to vindicate himself, to prevent the church from condemning Copernicanism, the disastrous results of which he foresaw, and perhaps to win the church's formal support for the new vision of the heavens. He had many supporters in Rome. Once again Roman society feted and lionized Galileo. The Holy Office declared that its inspection of the 'Letter to Castelli' turned up no grounds for prosecuting him, and he himself wrote in early February that gossip about his alleged heresy no longer circulated. But his enemies had not been inactive. Galileo then overreached himself when, through the mediation of a friendly cardinal, he attempted to present to Pope Paul V a new argument for the Copernican system. This was the proof from the operation of the ocean's tides which he later featured in his *Dialogue on the Two World Systems*, but which proved to be inconclusive.

Fearing now that the matter was getting out of hand, the pope asked the Inquisition to look into it once again, and it then turned to its theological consultors for an opinion. Their judgment was the decisive moment in the Galileo Affair. Following the lead of Bellarmine, they designated the assertion that the sun was the centre of the world and completely immobile to be 'formally heretical inasmuch as it expressly contradicts the doctrine of Holy Scripture in many passages'. That the earth rotated on its axis and encircled the sun was declared to be 'at least erroneous in the faith'.[6] The Holy Office then acted on this judgment and deputed Bellarmine to communicate the results to Galileo in a private audience. Exactly what took place in this audience remains controversial up to the present day, and is important for the legal aspects of the trial. At the least, Galileo was admonished to relinquish his Copernicanism and to teach it no longer. He accepted this judgment, though with good reason he thought that he could still hold it 'hypothetically'. Subsequently, the Congregation of the Index condemned Foscarini's book as well as any attempt to reconcile Copernicanism with Scripture, and it condemned, for the first time, Copernicus's *On the*

Revolutions of the Heavenly Spheres, until it was corrected. There was no mention of Galileo by name. He remained in Rome for another three months. Before returning to Florence he obtained a testimonial from Bellarmine that he had not been forced to abjure his opinion nor to undertake any penance. As a good Catholic, he did not want to live under the suspicion of heresy.

Galileo now lay low, disappointed that he had not carried the day for Copernicanism. His efforts were directed to propagating it more indirectly. Following the comet of 1618, he became involved in an academic battle with the Jesuit Orazio Grassi over its explanation. His *Assayer* of 1623 was a brilliant polemic that ridiculed his opponent in a manner that was bound to stir resentment. Personal antipathies played a part in the denouement of the Galileo affair. The election of his friend Maffeo Barberini as Pope Urban VIII in 1623 delighted Galileo, who sensed a new opening. The following year he once again visited Rome, where the pope lavished praises on him in six long audiences. But Urban did not rescind the measures of 1616. In Galileo's mind there was uncertainty about exactly how far he might venture in the new circumstances. He now began work on his *Dialogue on the Two Great World Systems*, the Aristotelian and the Copernican, but bad health long slowed his progress. Finally, it was completed in 1630, and after considerable lobbying, Galileo secured permission for its publication. Coming off the presses in February 1632, it generated an uproar, and in August the Inquisition ordered a halt to its sale or further publication.

In October Galileo was ordered to report to the Inquisition in Rome, and his excuses of poor health were disregarded. He arrived in February 1633. There he learned that the charges against him were violation of the admonition of the Holy Office delivered by Bellarmine and of the decree of the Index Congregation of 1616. Bellarmine, who might have been able to help him now, was long dead. Galileo at first argued that he had not defended Copernicanism in the *Dialogue*, but this was manifestly not the case despite the disclaimer that he had inserted in the preface of the book. Friendly officials in Rome then worked out with him the equivalent of a plea bargain, wherein Galileo would admit fault in carrying the case for Copernicanism in the *Dialogue* beyond what was allowed, and would then receive a mild penance. If the case had ended at this point, it would probably never had had the historical impact it was to have. But enemies of Galileo now got to Pope Urban. They convinced the pope, who already felt Galileo had taken advantage of his good will, that the scientist had acted maliciously in publishing the *Dialogue*, and had mocked the pope in the character of Simplicio, the slow-witted Aristotelian. The result was that the plea bargain was set aside, and Galileo as highly suspect of heresy was forced to abjure publicly. The picture of a humiliated Galileo on his knees before the court reading his abjuration is the image of the Galileo Affair that has stuck in the public consciousness. Three of the 10 cardinals who made up the Congregation of the Inquisition, including the pope's own nephew, Francesco Barberini, refused to sign the sentence.

Galileo remained under a mild form of house arrest for the rest of his life. But even as his sight failed him, he completed his *Discourses on the Two New Sciences*, which brought to a conclusion the researches of his earlier years and earned him a revered place in the history of science. He died in 1642.

So church authority and a conservative Catholic mainstream enabled a flawed theology to triumph over science in perhaps the best-known failure at adaptation of the Counter Reformation church. Whether or to what degree the condemnation of Galileo significantly inhibited Catholics from the practice of science is controversial. Many prominent Catholic scientists came to the fore subsequently, such as Pascal himself, the anti-Aristotelian Capuchin Valeriano Magni (1586–1661), Castelli's student, Giovanni Alfonso Borelli (1608–70) who made significant discoveries about the mechanical basis of physical processes, and the Jesuit Giovanni Battista Riccioli (1598–1671), who created an improved map of the moon in 1651. The Jesuits introduced more mathematics and physics into their colleges. Yet for the most part, Catholic scientists tended to focus on the experimental and to steer clear of broadly speculative or theoretical elements in their investigations, thus avoiding clashes with church authority. The exception was Descartes and many Cartesians who then did fall victim to authority. So Catholic scientists generally remained outside the mainline of the new scientific thought and wedded under constraint to a theoretical Aristotelianism. Only in the following century did the Galileo Affair become a symbol of alleged Catholic obscurantism and in the nineteenth century a symbol of conflict between religion and science.

A course of events analogous to the Galileo Affair, but with a different outcome, took place at the imperial court in Vienna during the deliberations over the Peace of Prague in the winter of 1634/5, just after the sentence of Galileo. There the issue was the acceptability of concessions made to the Protestants in terms of toleration and surrender of ecclesiastical property which were called for by the draft of the peace. Involved in the deliberations was a group of 24 theologians who were summoned to court to assess the issue and submit their individual opinions. They met under the chairmanship of Cardinal Franz von Dietrichstein, Bishop of Olomouc, through February and early March 1635. The parties were the same that had existed at Catholic courts through most of the Thirty Years War, the moderates and the militants. At the head of the moderates among the theologians was the Spanish Capuchin Diego de Quiroga, who had come to Vienna in 1631 as the confessor of the Infanta Maria Anna, wife of the future Emperor Ferdinand III. The Jesuit Lamormaini continued as the champion of the militants, but his influence on policy was flagging.

The moderates argued in a fashion similar to Galileo. The function of theology and the theologians was to determine certain principles but then to allow the men of politics to apply the principles to the concrete situation. One could make concessions to the Protestants if compelled by necessity – that is, if the alternative was the prolongation of a war that the government could no longer support and that was barbarizing the population to the ruin of all religion. That was a theological position. But the emperor and his councillors had to decide whether a state of necessity existed. So the moderates left a certain autonomy to politics, just as Galileo argued that theology's role was not to decide among the systems of the world but to leave that to the scientists to determine on the basis of scientific evidence.

The militants, for their part, contended that the theologians were not to remain in the realm of principle, but were also to take part in the determination of whether a state of necessity really existed or not. So theology dictated specific policy. The chief reason for the militants' position was their belief that the war was, for Ferdinand, not merely a religious but a holy war. They believed that God had entrusted to Ferdinand, and to the Catholic princes in Germany, the mission of rolling back Protestantism at least to its condition in 1555, and that he promised them divine assistance in this enterprise. To the militants this assistance had been made clear by the many unexpected victories God had granted the Catholics in the course of the war. To turn back from this enterprise was to display lack of confidence in God, to sully the honour of the House of Habsburg, and to sin. So the militant position was based on an alleged divine revelation, not derived directly from Scripture to be sure, but explicitly described as similar to the mission given to the Hebrew kings of the Old Testament to conquer the Promised Land. The militants were similar to the opponents of Galileo, who located in the Scriptures a prohibition of Copernicanism at least until science was able to demonstrate its truth.

In Vienna the moderates won the day. Neither in Vienna nor in Rome was the contest between theology and politics or science. Rather it was between two forms of theology. The theology of Galileo's opponents and of the militants interjected itself or divine revelation directly into the determination of scientific issues or the formation of policy. Galileo's and the moderate theology left to science or to politics a proper relative autonomy which amounted to a healthy form of secularization. The fact that each side won one battle shows that the issue was very much alive in the mid-seventeenth century with its implications for the Christian in the world, especially the Christian scientist or politician. But despite the outcome of the Galileo Affair, momentum was gathering on the side of greater independence from theology, a movement to be welcomed as long as theology itself remained vigorous in its own sphere. As we have seen, it was becoming excessively rationalist and divorced from experience.

9

CONCLUSION

This book has proposed that early modern Catholicism, that is, Catholicism from roughly 1450 to 1700, is best characterized by Catholics' response to the five major changes of the long sixteenth century. So I have written about how this response reshaped Catholicism during the early modern era rather than about the 'Counter Reformation' or 'Catholic Reform'. These terms are not adequately comprehensive to denote the full reality of early modern Catholicism, but I have employed them nevertheless because they designate a substantial part of it and because they have a long tradition behind them. The period fits the pattern of Christianity's recurring accommodation to contemporary society and culture, a phenomenon that is extremely evident in our own day. The rise of the Protestant churches in the sixteenth century illustrates this process too; they represented rival attempts to meet the challenges of the time. Whether one considers Catholicism to be the agent or the subject of this adaptation, and it was both, the church was anything but monolithic with its different directions and various spiritualities. Such diversity of approach, despite the controversy it generated, was ultimately a sign of health.

Two desires figured prominently in the active refashioning of Catholicism, and one or the other undergirded most movements for change. Not surprisingly, they also very much influenced the course of the Protestant Reformation. The first was the desire to live Christianity to the full in the world. It was found chiefly among an elite, usually urban, women as well as men, and it generated dynamism and creativity. Highlights of the response were Ignatian and Salesian spirituality, which were based on a world-affirming Thomism and fostered an individual piety, elementary schools and especially colleges and universities which prepared students for life in the world, confraternities which sought to sanctify worldly activities, and casuistry which aimed to help the serious Christian find his way in an increasingly complex world. The new orders and congregations promoted greater activity in the world for their male and especially for their female members.

The second desire was the widespread one for order, which was so much a feature of the later sixteenth and the seventeenth centuries. After the changes and upheavals of the early decades of the sixteenth century, and in light of the wars that followed, people wanted religious, political, and social order. This pursuit of order encouraged consolidation or confessionalism within the church, greater centralization, and close bonds with the state. To the yearning for order amidst apparent chaos corresponded the need for discipline, self-discipline as well as social discipline, which has recently been recognized as a feature of the age. With it overlapped the trend towards rationalization and systematization, which is commonly attributed to the period. These two desires were often in tension with each other, but both pointed the way towards the future and in this sense contributed to the coming of the modern world.

How was the refashioned and reformed Catholicism of 1700 different from that of 1450?

The Catholic Church no longer encompassed all Latin Christianity. It now shared Europe, unwillingly, with other, Protestant Christian churches. Lost to it were England and Scotland, Scandinavia, more than half of Germany, large sections of the Netherlands and Switzerland, and areas in Central Europe. Within these territories it maintained the allegiance of Catholic minorities who often struggled under adverse circumstances.

By 1700 Catholic doctrine had long been clarified with respect to most Protestant positions. This was a great achievement of the Council of Trent which contributed to order and to a sense of Catholic identity. It was a main feature of confessionalism with parallels in the Protestant confessions. Gradually it was communicated to the faithful in many ways, but especially through catechetical instruction and education. Popular devotions with medieval roots emphasized uniquely Catholic beliefs and practices which Trent had reaffirmed: Corpus Christi, veneration of Mary and the saints, prayer for the souls in purgatory, processions, pilgrimages, celebration of feast days. They were instrumental in the maintenance of popular Catholic consciousness well into the eighteenth century and beyond.

The structure of the church became both more papal and, to a degree, more clearly defined or rationalized. Trent and its aftermath represented a victory for the papacy over the bishops as a group and over local episcopal authority, even though the council issued no document on this question. Conciliarism was dead; there would not be another ecumenical council until 1870, well after the French Revolution, and it declared papal infallibility. Indeed, it is hard to see how an ecumenical council could have been convened in the seventeenth or eighteenth centuries given the state churches and the rivalry among the states; it was difficult enough to conduct a papal election. The papacy also triumphed over the college of cardinals. Just as in most contemporary states the prince secured the upper hand over representative bodies and moved towards a more centralized government with a bureaucracy, so did the pope in the church. It would be easy to exaggerate this. Recent scholarship has emphasized the limits to early modern absolutism even to the point of dismissing the term itself. So I have generally avoided the term 'absolutism', but the trend in this direction is evident. The claim to the exclusive right to interpret the council and reorganization of the congregations, plus many other measures, strengthened papal government at the centre, and further utilization of nuncios lengthened its reach for a time. No metropolitan archbishop or provincial council consolidated a strong position *vis-à-vis* Rome, as Borromeo may have envisioned happening. The new presence of the Jesuits and the Capuchins, and the continued activity of the centralized mendicant orders, also bolstered the position of the papacy within the church.

Bishops under the provisions of Trent strengthened their hand within their dioceses in many ways; ordination and education of priests were made their responsibility, the pastoral activity of exempt religious orders was placed more fully under their control, and their powers of visitation of religious institutions augmented. Further down the line, the importance of the parish as the basic unit of ecclesiastical organization was affirmed, and the responsibility of the pastor emphasized. He was primarily responsible for the instruction of the faithful and the administration of the sacraments in his parish. He was the official representative of the church at marriages, and he kept the records of baptisms and marriages. Yet the churches of the many religious orders and the confraternities frequently associated with them remained central to

Catholic religious life, especially in the cities, and they offered Catholics an alternative to the parish that was not available to Protestants.

To meet the needs of the time, new religious orders and congregations, male and female, made their appearance, founded from below by charismatic individuals such as Angela Merici and Ignatius Loyola, Vincent de Paul and Louise de Marillac. Their emergence represented the most creative response to the changing world. The Jesuits developed a spirituality that combined a life of prayer with active ministry in a new way, and this spirituality in turn influenced many subsequent religious congregations, especially those of women. A new form of community life for priests took shape with the Oratorians, Lazarists, and Sulpicians, who were particularly vigorous in France and contributed greatly to the formation of priests there. Two non-clerical male congregations, the Hospitallers of St John of God and the Christian Brothers of de la Salle, took up two newly prominent ministries, care of the sick and education.

First in Italy, but above all in France, the Netherlands, and the Rhineland, despite considerable official opposition, women's congregations broke through to new forms of organized ministry in the world. The Ursulines stood out for their work in education, numbering as many as 10,000 to 12,000 in France alone in 1700, but there were many other groups including Vincent's Daughters of Charity for whom ministry to the sick and the poor came first. Many of these women's groups were local or regional in character. They offered women new opportunities for religious growth in the world, and they greatly enhanced the church's ministry to women.

The new religious orders and congregations and their older mendicant colleagues carried much of the pastoral mission and evangelizing activities of the church in Europe and overseas. Their churches and confraternities remained vigorous in the towns and cities, and they provided the faithful with a variety of spiritualities. Conflicts over jurisdiction between regulars and seculars continued to be a feature of church life.

Catholicism was much more universal and international in 1700 than in 1450, having just concluded a period of unparalleled missionary expansion. A new catholicity was a part of its identity; the missionary Francis Xavier was popularly venerated throughout Catholic Europe. Contemporaries saw the gains made across the seas as compensation for the losses to the Protestants in Europe. Bernini's magnificent colonnade enclosing St Peter's Square in Rome, which was completed in 1666, reached out to embrace symbolically a more diverse crowd of peoples than would have been the case 200 years earlier. The church was firmly established in Central and Latin America, and in the Philippines. It also reached coastal areas of sub-Saharan Africa and territories of the Indian subcontinent, Ceylon, the East Indies, and into Indochina and China itself. A church in Japan had been founded, flourished briefly, suffered intense persecution, and then was forced into an underground existence. But one can hardly call a failure a venture which produced so many faithful ready to suffer for their beliefs and able to endure for two centuries without contact with the outside world. In 1700 the outcome of the Chinese Rites Controversy was still in doubt; by mid-century the decision had been taken against the accommodationist position. At the end of the century Chinese Catholics too showed great courage confronting vigorous persecution.

The foundation of the Propaganda in 1622 represented a general effort to assert the influence of Rome in the missionary field and in particular against the *Patronato* and the *Padroado*. This failed in the Americas, but it did have some success in Asia in areas not effectively under Portuguese control and in the Middle East and North Africa. The emergence of the Propaganda was a step in the direction of separation of church and state, in that the church attempted to reclaim for itself a role which out of necessity it had abdicated to the colonial powers.

Yet despite heroic efforts, one cannot speak of an indigenous church in the lands across the seas. Missionaries and colonists faced enormous challenges as they encountered new and unknown cultures. Particularly in the area of language, so obviously essential for communication, did the missionaries produce feats of accommodation. There was a genuine effort on the part of the mendicants and Las Casas to create a native Indian church in the Americas, which the Jesuits took up later on in their Reductions. In comparison with other colonial powers, the Spanish government aimed to respect the rights of the Indians and did succeed, for the most part, in preventing their enslavement, if not their employment as forced labour. Yet Spanish policy from the 1570s onwards dictated that the church in the Americas would be dominated by the Creoles and that the Indians would be pushed to the margins. Critical in this regard was the decision not to ordain native Indians to the priesthood. In Asia innovative and courageous attempts – one thinks especially of Ricci and de Nobili – were made to combine elements of indigenous culture with Christianity. Whether they went too far in their accommodation still remains controversial. In any event, they were condemned by Rome but only after long hesitation.

By 1700 the Catholic Church occupied a much-weakened position with regard to the various European states: France, Spain, Portugal, the Italian and German states along with the Habsburg Monarchy. An analogous situation obtained in the Papal States themselves, where governmental officials, usually clergy, exercised authority over ecclesiastics. The *Staatskirchentum* or state churches of the eighteenth century were in place, with Gallican France and then Spain in the forefront. This was the most negative legacy of the period; perhaps it was unavoidable. Responsible for the situation were many factors: the frequent concern of rulers for the welfare of the church, especially when churchmen were slow to take up reform; the dynamic of government towards greater control; papal policy favouring concordats with the states and neglectful of local bishops, in the earlier years often with the intent of disarming conciliarism; and the dependence of the church on the support of the state in the struggle against Protestantism, in the foreign missions, and in its efforts at reform. From the Spanish Inquisition to the reformation commissions of the Habsburg Monarchy, government enforced orthodoxy and frequently oversaw the performance of religious duties such as the annual reception of Holy Communion. This close association of the church with monarchical government grew more pronounced in the course of the eighteenth century, and would come crashing down in the wake of the French Revolution. Only gradually would the idea of separation of church and state assert itself and in many ways free the church from the state's embrace.

With respect to their position in international relations, the Renaissance popes functioned chiefly as rulers of an Italian state that played a modest role in European politics beyond Italy. Their prestige as international political figures rose in the second half of the sixteenth century, during which Pius V took the lead in organizing the victorious Holy League against the Turks, and Clement VIII helped mediate the Peace of Vervins in 1598. Scholastic philosophers elaborated an indirect power of the pope in temporal affairs for the new world of sovereign states. But papal international stature declined during the Thirty Years War and especially after the Treaty of Westphalia in 1648, and by 1700 the papacy's role on the international stage diminished to a modest one once again.

The religious wars came to an end by 1700 and international toleration among Christian states was in place. Religion would no longer be a significant cause of European wars. The contest with Islam continued but its religious character lessened. Only gradually did Catholic and Protestant states extend legal toleration to dissenting minorities; the Peace of Westphalia required it to a limited degree in the states of the Empire. Louis XIV's Revocation of the Edict of Nantes in 1685 definitely set back the trend towards toleration, bringing France more or less into line with England. Dissidents or heretics were often tolerated in practice long before they were tolerated in law. Official toleration would only become the rule in the nineteenth and even the twentieth centuries.

The sixteenth century saw the unleashing of a prolonged effort to christianize the people of Europe by both Catholics and Protestants. Bishops, members of religious orders, diocesan clergy all took part in the Catholic endeavour along with lay confreres. The initiatives of the new religious orders and the reform measures taken at Trent aimed at a pastoral renewal which supported this evangelization.

Two prominent methods of evangelization were the traditional one of preaching and the newly emphasized catechetical instruction. Trent stressed both, expecting, perhaps unrealistically, the pastor to both preach and conduct Sunday school each week, a goal towards which slow progress was made. Preaching was systematized in the internal missions that the religious clergy staged in the towns and countryside of Catholic Europe. As time went on, catechetical instruction became a feature of missions. The early modern period was surely for Catholics, as for Protestants, the age of the catechism. Perhaps no image would be more typical of it than the parish priest or Ursuline sister instructing young people gathered about them, the Ursuline still within the convent walls.

Systematic schooling or education was the most prominent, innovative pastoral response of early modern Catholicism to a changing Europe. Protestants moved in the same direction, but without the assistance of the religious orders. Both Catholics and Protestants assumed the Renaissance optimism about education and, in their Latin schools, about the effectiveness of the humanist curriculum for moral as well as intellectual formation. Students were to be formed who would live as Christians in the world. No doubt religious instruction and the discipline of religious practice was the priority. But in the age of print, reading was an increasingly valuable asset, and a tool of religious instruction too, so that it had to be learned along with catechism. Next in the elementary schools came writing then, especially with the Piarists, arithmetic. For the boys the Piarists and Christian Brothers added training in a trade, and for the girls the Ursulines promoted domestic skills. At the level of the college or Latin secondary school, the Jesuit *Plan of Studies* provided a system which was taken over in part by other educators. The colleges, then, Jesuit and others, helped to prepare the clergy and civil servants needed by contemporary society, and they also catered to the ambition of middle-class parents for the advancement of their sons. Eventually, aristocrats too found education necessary or at least fashionable.

The large-scale involvement of members of religious orders, and especially Jesuits, in the colleges inevitably led them to interest in secular subjects, classical literature, science, and the arts. The correspondence of Jesuits on scientific matters has led some recent scholars to call the Society of Jesus the first scientific society. Theatre, ballet, and music evolved in an analogous fashion from instruments of catechetical instruction to often high levels of public performance. So the church entered the world more extensively through education, demonstrating anew the harmony between faith and secular activity.

Universities, of course, were a creation of the Middle Ages. But they proliferated in the early modern era as they took on more and more the confessional function of preparing clergy and civil servants for large states and small territories alike. Even more than in the colleges, participation in universities required the broadening of the interests of religious in different areas of learning. Many Catholics, and the Jesuits in particular, in contrast to the Piarists, were reluctant finally to part company with Aristotle in science. In the Galileo Affair church authority guided by Bellarmine erroneously asserted a right of theology to intervene directly in a scientific question and upheld, at least indirectly, Aristotelianism in science. So it missed an opportunity at adaptation and instead initiated a division between Catholicism and the new science, even though many Catholics remained active in areas of science. Later the Galileo Affair was to become a symbol of an alleged incompatibility between religion and science.

The Council of Trent called into life a new form of educational institution, the diocesan seminary. Seminaries were slow in developing. Many were associated initially with colleges, academies, or universities. Yet by the early eighteenth century they had clearly helped to improve the level of the diocesan clergy. This was the case especially in France, where they were often conducted by the societies of common life and where they contributed to a new *esprit* among the diocesan clergy. On the negative side they may have isolated the clergy further from the people and fostered a style of clericalism. Rome itself became a centre of clerical education during the early modern period, and especially with the foundation of the Roman College, for a time it stood out as a hub of intellectual activity.

Catholic piety tended to become more individual and personal during the early modern period, at least among the religious elite. This development correlated with the Renaissance sense for individuality. Well before the Reformation a growing interest in meditation and mental prayer was evident, and it was helped along by the availability of printed books of devotion. More regular confession gave the individual penitent more frequent access to the priest, and the confessional box itself made the sacrament more private. Casuistry developed further as a response to questions raised by a changing society, and one of its purposes was to apply moral principles to individual circumstances. Priest and penitent discussed such matters in the confessional. Marriage became more a matter of individual choice and commitment, less an affair of family or parental decisions. The Ignatian *Exercises* proposed a method by which the individual through prayer and careful attention to his own interior movements could hope to discover the particular plan or will of God in his case.

All these developments pointed towards a more individual piety. Yet it does not seem that much was lost in the way of communal piety when compared with the later Middle Ages. The Sunday liturgy remained the centre of village life; perhaps it was now celebrated with more decorum and with a few more people receiving Holy Communion. Many traditional medieval devotions such as the Corpus Christi procession were revived, which were major events for communities large and small and expressive of their Catholic identity. Membership in confraternities does not seem to have declined but rather, at least in rural parishes, to have increased; this would indicate a sense of community. Devotion to and concern for the souls in purgatory fostered community between the living and the dead in the Communion of Saints.

Catholic piety in the early modern period manifested a new activist bent, especially in its emphasis on educational and charitable work. The renewed emphasis on these works – it was certainly not something completely new since it dates from the earliest years of Christianity – appeared first in Italy in the later fifteenth century. One result was the activist character of the new orders and congregations. Perhaps even more important were the many confraternities, such as the Marian Congregations or the Confraternity of Christian Doctrine, that involved lay people in organized charity and education. Often they were associated with religious orders. These confraternities sometimes functioned as schools for leadership and organization among lay people.

More significant still for Catholic piety in the early modern period was the conviction that Christianity could be lived to the full in the world. This was evident in the new religious orders and congregations. But its significance was greatest for the layman, especially for the lay elite. One need not retreat from the world in order to be a follower of Christ. This issue was most explicit in the debate over Machiavelli, who brought it to the fore with his assertion that the sincere Christian could not succeed in politics. It was precisely this affirmation that horrified many Christians and that accounts for his infamous reputation. Fortunately, a healthy Thomism, Ignatian and Salesian spirituality, and a host of writers argued that a Christian life was possible not only in politics but in business, at court, and in many other worldly careers or vocations, and they attempted to show how this could be done. An enormous casuist literature sought to guide Christians in making the moral decisions called for by changing situations. Confraternities often supported laymen in their efforts to live in the secular world. Catholicism as well as Protestantism insisted upon the value of the worldly vocation. So even in a time of increasing clerical self-consciousness, the lay vocation received substantial new support. Thus many genuine Christians released their energies into the world with positive results beyond measurement. This was a major achievement of early modern Catholicism.

Yet accommodation to the world was sometimes excessive. Casuists occasionally went too far in establishing a harmony between the good and the useful, and so they marginalized the element of the cross in the Christian life. The Jansenists had a point in this regard. Antimachiavellian writers too easily aligned the interest of the church with the state and so promoted the dangerously close alliance of church and government.

Did the religious knowledge and practice of Catholics grow during this period? Were they a more disciplined people? The general answer would have to be affirmative, especially if we are realistic about expectations. But the degree of growth both intensively and extensively is much more difficult to determine, and certainly open to dispute. There were wide variations geographically and differences between cities and towns, and rural areas, as we have seen all along. Urban areas obviously profited most from the church's educational efforts. Religious knowledge and practice seem to have been highest by 1700 in France, north and central Italy, the Spanish Netherlands, and western and perhaps southern Germany. Spain and the Habsburg lands lagged behind. This assessment mirrors more or less the level of education and the performance of parish priests as the effort at clerical reform gradually showed results. By the early eighteenth century the parish clergy of France stood out. Significantly also, the regions where women's congregations sprouted up to advance the church's ministry generally produced the most successful christianization. Does this mean that in any place all abuses were ended or all superstition was uprooted? Hardly. But there was undeniable improvement.

As the eighteenth century progressed, Catholicism would confront more profound challenges, especially from the more intense *Staatskirchentum* and then from the Enlightenment and in the French Revolution. But that is another story.

NOTES

1 Introduction

1. This term designates first of all the act of 'confessing' or professing a particular faith; secondly, it indicates the content of that which is confessed or professed, as in the Augsburg Confession; finally then it comes to mean the group that confesses this particular content, the church or 'confession'.

2 The New Religious Orders

1. The terms 'order' and 'congregation' in this period were not always clear. An order usually meant solemn vows, varying degrees of exemption from the local bishop, acceptance of one of the major rules (Benedictine, Augustinian, Franciscan), and for women cloister. A congregation indicated simple vows and usually subordination to local diocesan authority. A confraternity usually designated an association of lay people, sometimes including clerics, organized under a set of rules, to foster their common religious life and usually to undertake some common apostolic work. In some cases confraternities evolved into congregations, as was the case with many of the third orders, and congregations evolved into orders.
2. There is no effort here to list all the new orders and congregations that appeared in the sixteenth and seventeenth centuries.
3. An English translation of *Regimini Militantis Ecclesiae*, the papal bull of 27 September 1540 establishing the Society of Jesus, is found in John Olin, *The Catholic Reformation: Savonarola to Ignatius Loyola: Reform in the Church, 1495–1540* (New York: Harper and Row, 1969), pp. 203–8.

3 The Council of Trent and the Papacy

1. *The Complete Works of Montaigne: Essays, Travel Journal, Letters,* trans. Donald M. Frame (Stanford, CA: Stanford University Press, 1957), p. 940.

6 Education

1. *Ibid.,* p. 957.

7 Evangelization beyond Europe

1. The Latin original, along with an English translation of *Sublimis Deus*, is found in Francis Augustus MacNutt, *Bartholomew de Las Casas: His Life, Apostolate, and Writings* (Cleveland, OH: A. H. Clark, 1909), pp. 426–31.

8 The Christian in the World

1. *Machiavelli: The Chief Works and Others*, trans. Allan Gilbert (Durham, NC: Duke University Press, 1965), vol. 1, pp. 57–8.
2. Francis de Sales, *Introduction to the Devout Life*, trans. and ed. John K. Ryan (New York: Doubleday Image Books, 1989), pp. 34, 41, 43–4, 193.
3. Blaise Pascal, *The Provincial Letters, Pensées, Scientific Treatises* (Chicago, IL: Encyclopedia Britannica, 1952), p. 29. Translator of the *Provincial Letters* is Thomas M'Crie.
4. *Pensées*, no. 253, *ibid.*, p. 220. Translator is W. F. Trotter.
5. *Ibid.*, no. 277, p. 222.
6. Cited in Jerome J. Langford, *Galileo, Science, and the Church*, 3rd edn (Ann Arbor, MI: University of Michigan Press, 1992), p. 89.

SELECT BIBLIOGRAPHY

The following summary is not meant to be a comprehensive bibliography, nor does it comprise all the sources consulted in the writing of this book. It does indicate the principal sources and is intended to serve as a guide for further reading. English-language works are featured.

General and Chapter 1

Two valuable multi-volume surveys are Jean-Marie Mayeur, Charles and Luce Pietri, André Vauchez, and Marc Venard (eds), *Histoire du Christianisme des origines à nos jours*, vol. 7: *De la réforme à la Réformation (1450–1530)*; vol. 8: *Le temps des confessions (1530–1620)*; and vol. 9: *L'âge de raison (1620/30–1750)* (Paris, 1992–7), and Hubert Jedin and John Dolan (eds), *The History of the Church*, vol. 5: *Reformation and Counter-Reformation*, and vol. 6: *The Church in the Age of Absolutism and Enlightenment* (New York, 1980/1; German original, 1967/70). The former incorporates recent scholarship, the latter is traditional in its approach. Helpful bibliographical essays are found in John W. O'Malley (ed.), *Catholicism in Early Modern Europe* (St Louis, 1988), to be complemented for Italy by William V. Hudon, 'Religion and Society in Early Modern Italy – Old Questions, New Insights', *American Historical Review*, 101 (1996): 783–804. Hubert Jedin's pathbreaking *Katholische Reform oder Gegenreformation?* (Lucerne, 1946) surveys the older literature on the terminology of Counter Reformation and Catholic Reform. H. Outram Evennett, *The Spirit of the Counter-Reformation*, ed. John Bossy (Cambridge, 1968) has greatly influenced the approach of this book. Two contrasting, stimulating interpretative surveys are Jean Delumeau, *Catholicism between Luther and Voltaire: A New View of the Counter-Reformation* (London/Philadelphia, 1977; French original, 1971), and John Bossy, *Christianity in the West, 1400–1700* (New York, 1985). John O'Malley's position is best articulated in his 'Was Ignatius Loyola a Church Reformer? How to Look at Early Modern Catholicism', *Catholic Historical Review*, 77 (1991): 177–93. The most complete general treatment of confessionalism and confessionalization in English is R. Po-Chia Hsia, *Social Discipline in the Reformation: Central Europe, 1550–1750* (London, 1989), but see also Wolfgang Reinhard, 'Reformation, Counter-Reformation, and the Early Modern State: A Reassessment', *Catholic Historical Review*, 75 (1989): 383–404, and the more recent publication by Wolfgang Reinhard and Heinz Schilling (eds), *Die katholische Konfessionalisierung*,

Reformationsgeschichtliche Studien und Texte, 135 (Münster, 1995), which contains a number of fine contributions. A solid recent survey is R. Po-Chia Hsia, *The World of Catholic Renewal, 1540–1770* (Cambridge, 1998); significantly, it starts and ends later than this book, and it adopts a different interpretative framework.

Theodore K. Rabb's *The Struggle for Stability in Early Modern Europe* (New York, 1975) remains an outstanding intrepretative essay that elaborates the changes of the first decades of the sixteenth century and shows how they were assimilated into a new European synthesis by the late seventeenth century. Eugene F. Rice, Jr, with Anthony Grafton, *The Foundations of Early Modern Europe, 1460–1559*, 2nd edn (New York, 1994), is a concise, well-written survey. An up-to-date general reference work is Thomas Brady, Jr, Heiko A. Oberman, and James D. Tracy (eds), *Handbook of European History, 1400–1600: Late Middle Ages, Renaissance, and Reformation*, 2 vols (Leiden, 1994; reprinted Grand Rapids, 1996), which, despite the title, does occasionally reach into the seventeenth century.

R. N. Swanson, *Religion and Devotion in Europe, c. 1215–c. 1515* (Cambridge, 1995) provides a judicious, sympathetic survey of its topic up to the eve of the Reformation. Larissa Taylor, *Soldiers of Christ: Preaching in Late Medieval and Reformation France* (New York, 1992), compares preaching before and after the Reformation. For the Spanish Inquisition, see Chapter 3.

Chapter 2

A fine series of essays with bibliography on the new religious orders of the sixteenth century is Richard L. DeMolen (ed.), *Religious Orders of the Catholic Reformation* (New York, 1994). Raymond V. Hostie, *Vie et mort des ordres religieux: Approches psychosociologiques* (Paris, 1972) locates the new male orders and congregations in the broader context of the history of religious life and provides valuable statistics. (A translation is available in a limited edition: *The Life and Death of Religious Orders* [Washington, 1983]). Dom Robert Lemoine, *L'époque moderne (1563–1789): Le monde des religieux* (Paris, 1976), looks at the orders more from a canonical perspective; John W. O'Malley, 'Priesthood, Ministry, and Religious Life: Some Historical and Historiographical Considerations', *Theological Studies*, 49 (1988): 223–57 (reprinted in *idem, Tradition and Transition: Historical Perspectives on Vatican II* (Wilmington, 1989), and Emmanuele Boaga, 'Aspetti e problemi degli ordini e congregazioni religiose nei secoli XVII e XVII', in *Problemi di storia della Chiesa nei secoli xvii–xviii* (Naples, 1982) emphasize the significance of the apostolic orientation of the new orders. A magnificent treatment of the early Jesuits that locates them firmly in their historical context is John W. O'Malley, *The First Jesuits* (Cambridge, MA, 1993). George E. Ganss (ed.), *The Constitutions of the Society of Jesus* (St Louis, 1970) is a richly annotated version of Ignatius's Constitutions. A new Penguin edition of his writings is Joseph A. Munitz and Philip Endean (eds), *St. Ignatius of Loyola: Personal Writings* (New York, 1996). For the Capuchins, Cuthbert of Brighton, *The Capuchins: A Contribution to the History of the Counter-Reformation*, 2 vols (London, 1929; reprinted Port Washington, 1971) remains the best survey.

On the new women's congregations two insightful books are Elizabeth Rapley, *The* Dévotes: *Women and Church in Seventeenth-Century France* (Montreal, 1990), and Anne Conrad, *Zwischen Kloster und Welt: Ursulinen und Jesuitinnen in der katholischen Reformbewegung des 16./17. Jahrhunderts* (Mainz, 1991). Raimondo Creytens, 'La riforma dei monasteri femminili dopo i decreti tridentini', in *Il Concilio di Trento e la riforma tridentina* (Rome, 1965), vol. 1, pp. 45–84, outlines the varying canonical status of female orders and congregations. Useful also is *Les religieuses enseignantes XVIe–XXe siècles* (Angers, 1981), a series of solid articles on various women's congregations. For Angela Merici, see Thèrese Ledochowska, *Angèle Merici et la Compagnie de Ste-Ursule à la lumières des documents*, 2 vols (Milan/Rome, 1967). A highly significant article is Craig Harline, 'Actives and Contemplatives: The Female Religious of the Low Countries before and after the Council of Trent', *Catholic Historical Review*, 81 (1995): 541–67, who, by showing the number of active female religious groups in the Low Countries in the late Middle Ages and the persistence of the contemplative tradition until the end of the Old Regime, cautions us about exaggerating either the novelty of active women religious or a decline in the attraction of the contemplative ideal in the early modern period. See also Chapter 6.

Chapter 3

The standard history of the Council of Trent remains Hubert Jedin, *Geschichte des Konzils von Trient*, 4 vols (Freiburg im Breisgau, 1958–75). Two volumes have appeared in English translation, *A History of the Council of Trent* (London, 1957/61). The decrees of Trent are found, in Latin and in English, in Norman P. Tanner (ed.), *Decrees of the Ecumenical Councils*, vol. 2 (London/Washington, 1990). Very useful still is Franz Xaver Seppelt, *Geschichte der Päpste*, vol. 5: *Das Papsttum im Kampf mit Staatsabsolutismus und Aufklärung: Von Paul III. bis zur franzöischen Revolution*, ed. Georg Schwaiger (Munich, 1959). Giuseppe Alberigo, 'L'episcopato nel cattolicesimo post-tridentino', *Cristianesimo nella storia*, 6 (1985): 71–91, looks at the role of the episcopate in the period following Trent, and John M. Headley and John B. Tomaro (eds), *San Carlo Borromeo: Catholic Reform and Ecclesiastical Politics in the Second Half of the Sixteenth Century* (Washington, 1988) is a fine collection of papers on this Archbishop of Milan during the same period. For the French bishops see the massive study of Joseph Bergin, *The Making of the French Episcopate, 1589–1661* (New Haven, CT, 1996), and for the Spanish, Helen Rawlings, 'The Secularization of Castilian Episcopal Office under the Habsburgs, 1516–1700', *Journal of Ecclesiastical History*, 38 (1987): 53–79 (and Henry Kamen and Sara Nalle under Chapter 5). Barbara Hallman, *Italian Cardinals, Reform, and the Church as Property* (Berkeley, CA, 1985) has little to say about the period after Trent.

For the papal court after Trent see three articles by Wolfgang Reinhard, 'Nepotismus. Der Funktionswandel einer papstgeschichtlichen Konstanten', *Zeitschrift für Kirchengeschichte*, 86 (1975): 145–85; 'Reformpapsttum zwischen Renaissance und Barock', in *Reformatio Ecclesiae*, Festgabe E. Iserloh (Paderborn, 1980): pp. 779–96; and 'Papal Power and Family Strategy in the Sixteenth and Seventeenth Centuries', in Ronald G. Asch and Adolf M. Burke (eds), *Princes,*

Patronage, and the Nobility: The Court at the Beginning of the Modern Age, c1450–1650 (Oxford, 1991), pp. 329–56 (and also Prodi under Chapter 4). Valuable also for Rome and the papal court from 1585 to 1689 is Torgil Magnuson, *Rome in the Age of Bernini*, 2 vols (Stockholm/Atlantic Heights, NJ, 1982/6). Peter Partner, 'Papal Financial Policy in the Renaissance and Counter-Reformation', *Past and Present*, 88 (1980): 16–62, argues for the basic continuity of papal policy and practice from the mid-fifteenth through the mid-seventeenth century.

Both the Spanish and the Roman Inquisitions have been the subject of much recent scholarship. Two fine synthetic studies are Francisco Bethencourt, *L'Inquisition à l'époque moderne: Espagne, Italie, Portugal, XVᵉ–XIXᵉ siècle* (Paris, 1995), which as its title implies is a comparative study, and Henry Kamen, *The Spanish Inquisition* (New Haven, 1998). See also Gustav Henningsen and John Tedeschi, *Inquisition in Early Modern Europe: Studies on Sources and Methods* (DeKalb, 1986), and John Tedeschi, *The Prosecution of Heresy: Collected Studies on the Inquisition in Early Modern Italy* (Binghamton, 1991), especially the article co-authored with William Monter, 'Toward a Statistical Profile of the Italian Inquisitions, Sixteenth to Eighteenth Centuries', 89–126, which offers some comparisons between the Roman and Spanish Inquisitions.

Chapter 4

An unusually stimulating volume that emphasizes the basic continuity of papal policy from the Renaissance through the Counter Reformation is Paolo Prodi, *The Papal Prince, One Body and Two Souls: the Papal Monarchy in Early Modern Europe* (Cambridge, 1987; Italian original, 1982). A summary of much of Jean Delumeau's research on Rome is his 'Political and Administrative Centralization in the Papal State in the Sixteenth Century', in Eric Cochrane (eds), *The Late Italian Renaissance, 1525–1630* (New York, 1970), pp. 287–304. There is a brief overview of the relationship between the papacy and various governments in H. E. Feine, *Kirchliche Rechtsgeschichte: die katholische Kirche*, 5th edn (Cologne, 1972). Vitoria and Suarez are discussed in Quentin Skinner, *The Foundations of Modern Political Thought*, vol. 2: *The Reformation* (Cambridge, 1978), and Pierre Mesnard, *L'essor de la philosophie politique au XVIᵉ siècle*, 3rd edn (Paris, 1969). For Vitoria see especially Anthony Pagden and Jeremy Lawrance (eds), *Francisco de Vitoria: Political Writings* (Cambridge, 1991). The best treatment of Bellarmine as a political thinker remains F. X. Arnold, *Die Staatslehre des Kardinals Bellarmin: ein Beitrag zur Rechts- und staatphilosophie des konfessionellen Zeitalters* (Munich, 1934). For Botero, see Bireley under Chapter 8.

There are three solid biographies of Philip II, each written from a different perspective: Peter Pierson, *Philip II of Spain* (London, 1975); Geoffrey Parker, *Philip II*, 3rd edn (Chicago, 1995); and, most recently, Henry Kamen, *Philip of Spain* (New Haven, 1997). Carlos Eire, *From Madrid to Purgatory: The Art and Craft of Dying in Sixteenth-Century Spain* (Cambridge, 1995), provides a fascinating study of the monarch's death. For Maximilian of Bavaria, see Dieter Albrecht's magisterial *Maximilian I. von Bayern, 1573–1651* (Munich, 1998) and Robert Bireley, *Maximilian von Bayern, Adam Contzen S. J., und die Gegenreformation in Deutschland 1624–1635* (Göttingen, 1975). Geoffrey Parker, *The Thirty Years*

War, 2nd edn (London, 1997) is the best standard account. R. J. Knecht, *Richelieu* (London, 1991), summarizes nicely most recent research on the cardinal, but see also Hermann Weber, '"Une Bonne Paix", Richelieu's Foreign Policy and the Peace of Christendom', in Joseph Bergin and Laurence Brockliss (eds), *Richelieu and His Age* (Oxford, 1992), pp. 45–69. Carl C. Eckhardt, *The Papacy and World Affairs, as Reflected in the Secularization of Politics* (Chicago, 1937), remains a useful study in English.

Chapter 5

Two perceptive books that have much to say about evangelization and popular piety in Spain are Henry Kamen, *The Phoenix and the Flame: Catalonia and the Counter-Reformation* (New Haven, 1993) and Sara T. Nalle, *God in La Mancha: Religious Reform and the People of Cuenca, 1500–1650* (Baltimore, 1992). The same is true for France of Philip T. Hoffman, *Church and Community in the Diocese of Lyon, 1500–1789* (New Haven, CT., 1984), and with a broader geographical sweep, R. Taveneaux, *Le catholicisme dans la France classique, 1610–1715*, 2 vols (Paris, 1980). There are several outstanding articles on the topic for Bavaria in Walter Brandmüller (ed.), *Handbuch der bayerischen Kirchengeschichte*, vol. 2: *Von der Glaubensspaltung bis zur Säkularisation* (Sankt Ottilien, 1993), among them Hermann Reifenberg, 'Gottesdienstliches Leben', pp. 613–39, which takes up the liturgy, a topic often overlooked in treatments of popular religion. Marc Forster, *The Counter-Reformation in the Villages: Religion and Reform in the Bishopric of Speyer, 1560–1720* (Ithaca, NY, 1992), stresses the length of time it took to develop a sense of confessional identity, and R. J. W. Evans in his masterful *The Making of the Habsburg Monarchy, 1550–1700: An Interpretation* (Oxford, 1979) has much to say about piety and religious culture. Louis Châtellier, *The Religion of the Poor: Rural Missions in Europe and the Formation of Modern Catholicism, c1500–c1800* (Cambridge, 1997; French original, 1993) analyses the development of the popular internal missions and shows their impact on later Catholicism, and John W. O'Malley, 'Saint Charles Borromeo and the *Praecipuum Episcoporum Munus*: His Place in the History of Preaching', in J. M. Headley and J. B. Tomaro (eds), *San Carlo Borromeo* (see Chapter 3), introduces several sixteenth-century Catholic writers on preaching.

Confraternities are the topic of four volumes: Christopher F. Black, *Italian Confraternities in the Sixteenth Century* (Cambridge, 1989); Nicholas Terpstra, *Lay Confraternities and Civic Religion in Renaissance Bologna* (Cambridge, 1995); Maureen Flynn, *Sacred Charity: Confraternities and Social Welfare in Spain, 1400–1700* (Ithaca, NY, 1989), which concentrates on the diocese of Zamora; and especially Louis Châtellier, *The Europe of the Devout: The Catholic Reformation and the Formation of a New Society* (Cambridge, 1989; French original, 1987), which traces the development and significance of the Jesuit Marian Congregations. A thorough study of the history and significance of processions is Sabine Felbecker, *Die Prozession: Historische und systematische Untersuchungen zu einer liturgischen Ausdruckshandlung* (Altenberge, 1995), who devotes considerable attention to the Corpus Christi procession. The Marian shrine at Altötting is discussed in Ludwig Hüttl, *Marianische Wallfahrten im süddeutsch-österreichischen*

Raum (Cologne, 1985). Robert Bireley, *Religion and Politics in the Age of the Counter-Reformation: Emperor Ferdinand II, William Lamormaini, S.J., and the Formation of Imperial Policy* (Chapel Hill, 1981), and 'Confessional Absolutism in the Habsburg Lands in the Seventeenth Century', in Charles Ingrao (ed.), *State and Society in Early Modern Austria* (West Lafayette, IN, 1994), pp. 36–53, looks at the manner and significance of the Counter Reformation programme of the Habsburg emperors.

Chapter 6

Paul F. Grendler, *Schooling in Renaissance Italy: Literacy and Learning, 1300–1600* (Baltimore, 1989), provides a clear survey of the early educational efforts of the Catholic Reform in Italy, and Miriam Turrini, ' "Riformare il mondo a vera vita christiana:" le scuole di catechismo nell'Italia del Cinquecento', *Annali dell'Istituto storico italico-germanico in Trento*, 8 (1982): 407–89, studies in detail the schools of the Confraternity of Christian Doctrine in Italy until 1600. Three books most helpful on education in France during the Old Regime are: R. Chartier, M.-M. Compère, and D. Julia, *L'éducation en France du XVIe au XVIIIe siècle* (Paris, 1976); J. de Viguerie, *L'institution des enfants. L'éducation en France, XVIe–XVIIIe siècles* (Paris, 1978); and François Lebrun, Marc Venard, and Jean Quéniar, *Histoire générale de l'enseignement et de la l'éducation en France*, vol. 2: *de Gutenberg aux Lumières* (Paris, 1981). For education in Spain, see Richard Kagan, *Students and Society in Early Modern Spain* (Baltimore, 1974).

O'Malley, *The First Jesuits* (see Chapter 2) analyses their move into education and the reasons for it. Luce Giard (ed.), *Les Jésuites à la Renaissance: Systène éducatif et production du savoir* (Paris, 1995) contains a number of stimulating contributions on Jesuit education and intellectual activity, especially Gian Paolo Brizzi, 'Les Jésuites et l'école en Italie (XVIe–XVIIIe siècles)', pp. 35–53. Miriam Turrini and Annamaria Valenti, 'L'educazione religiosa', in *Il catechismo e la grammatica*, vol. 1: *Istruzione e controllo sociale nell'area emiliana e romagnola nel '700*, ed. Gian Paolo Brizzi (Bologna, 1985) devote considerable attention to the Jesuit college of St Lucy in Bologna. For secondary and higher education in Bavaria, see the overview in Rainer A. Müller, 'Hochschulen und Gymnasien', in the *Handbuch der bayerischen Kirchengeschichte* (see Chapter 5), pp. 535–56. Jean Marie Valentin, *Le Théâtre des Jésuites dans les pays de langue allemande (1554–1680), Salut des âmes et ordres des cités*, 3 vols (Bern, 1978) is a thorough, insightful study of the Jesuit theatre in German-speaking areas; see also his 'Théâtre et spiritualité: III: Le théâtre des collèges de la fin du 15e siècle à la fin du 18e siècle', in *Dictionnaire de spiritualité*, vol. 15 (Paris, 1990), pp. 353–72.

A solid, general treatment of universities is *A History of the University in Europe*, vol. 2: *Universities in Early Modern Europe (1500–1800)*, ed. Hilde de Ridder-Symoens (Cambridge, 1996). Karl Hengst, *Jesuiten an Universitäten und Jesuitenuniversitäten* (Paderborn, 1981) surveys the Jesuits' activity in German universities until 1650 from an organizational and political perspective. Philip Caraman, *University of the Nations: the Story of the Gregorian University with its Associated Institutes, the Biblical and the Oriental* (New York, 1981), provides a brief overview of the history of the Roman College, and Peter Schmidt, *Das Collegium*

Germanicum in Rom und die Germaniker. Zur Funktion eines Ausländerseminars (1552–1914) (Tübingen, 1984), a detailed study of the German College and the influence of its alumni. Useful for seminary education in Italy are two articles by Thomas Deutscher: 'Seminaries and the Education of Novarese Parish Priests, 1593–1627', *Journal of Ecclesiastical History*, 32 (1981): 303–19, and 'The Growth of the Secular Clergy and the Development of Educational Institutions in the Diocese of Novara', *ibid.*, 40 (1989): 381–97; Peter Lang, 'Reform im Wandel: Die katholischen Visitationsinterrogatorien des 16. und 17. Jahrhunderts', in Peter Lang and E. W. Zeeden (eds), *Kirche und Visitation: Beiträge zur Erforschung des frühneizeitlichen Visitationswesen in Europa* (Stuttgart, 1984), pp. 131–90, evaluates the progress of the Catholic Reform and especially of the performance of the parish clergy in Germany on the basis of an examination of 65 questionnaires used for visitations in 17 dioceses from 1536 through 1700. Lang carries out a similar investigation for the area around Mergentheim in 'Die tridentinische Reform im Landkapitel Mergentheim bis zum Einfall der Schweden 1631', *Rottenburger Jahrbuch für Kirchengeschichte*, 1 (1982): 143–67. A solid study of the parish clergy is Alois Hahn, *Die Rezeption des tridentinischen Pfarrerideals im westtrierischen Pfarrklerus des 16. und 17. Jahrhunderts* (Luxembourg, 1974).

An adequate biography of John Baptist de La Salle is Edward Fitzpatrick, *La Salle, Patron of All Teachers* (Milwaukee, 1951). Extremely valuable for the Ursuline colleges is Philippe Annaert, *Les collèges au féminin: les Ursulines aux 17ᵉ et 18ᵉ siècles* (Namur, 1992), which summarizes a lengthy dissertation.

Chapter 7

For this chapter I have drawn heavily on the lengthy contributions by Alain Milhou and Minako Debergh to the *Histoire du christianisme* (see General and Chapter 1). An outstanding treatment of Columbus, his context, and his impact is William D. Phillips, Jr and Carla Rahn Phillips, *The Worlds of Christopher Columbus* (Cambridge, 1992). Particularly stimulating is Wolfgang Reinhard, 'Gelenkter Kulturwandel im 17. Jahrhundert. Akkulturation in den Jesuitenmission als universalhistorisches Problem', *Historische Zeitschrift*, 223 (1976): 529–90. Robert Ricard, *The Spiritual Conquest of Mexico* (Berkeley, 1966) remains a classic. Lewis Hanke, *The Spanish Struggle for Justice in the Conquest of America* (Boston, 1965), and *Aristotle and the American Indians* (Bloomington, IN, 1959) are still valuable. More recent on many of the same issues is D. A. Brading, *The First America: The Spanish Monarchy, Creole Patriots, and the Liberal state, 1492–1867* (Cambridge, 1991).

A magisterial biography is Georg Schurhammer, *Francis Xavier: His Life, His Times*, 4 vols (Rome, 1973/82). Xavier's writings are now available with an extensive commentary in M. Joseph Costelloe (ed.), *The Letters and Instructions of Francis Xavier* (St Louis, 1992). On Matteo Ricci, see Jonathan Spence, *The Memory Palace of Matteo Ricci* (New York, 1984), and for Valignano, see Josef Franz Schutte, *Valignano's Mission Principles for Japan*, 2 vols (St Louis, 1980/5; Latin original, Rome, 1951/8). A brief, balanced account of the Chinese Rites Controversy is F. A. Rouleau, 'Chinese Rites Controversy', in the *New Catholic Encyclopedia*, vol. 3 (Washington, 1967), pp. 611–17. George Dunne, *Generation of Giants: The Story of the Jesuits in China in the Last Decades of the Ming Dynasty* (Notre Dame, IN, 1962) reads very well, but may be a little one-sided. A highly valuable collection of essays on the role of the Propaganda Fide is Josef Metzler (ed.), *Sacrae Congregationis de Propaganda Fide Memoria Rerum*, vol. I, part 1: *1622–1700* (Rome, 1972).

Chapter 8

For the Antimachiavellians and the significance of the debate over Machiavelli, see Robert Bireley, *The Counter-Reformation Prince: Anti-Machiavellianism or Catholic Statecraft in Early Modern Europe* (Chapel Hill, NC, 1990), where Botero, Lipsius, and Saavedra Fajardo are also discussed. André Ravier, *Francis de Sales, Sage and Saint* (San Francisco, 1988) is a good short biography, and John K. Ryan, ed., *Introduction to the Devout Life* (New York, 1966) is a fine English edition of his classic. Fortunat Strowski, *Saint François de Sales, Introduction à l'histoire du sentiment religieux en France au dix-septième siècle*, new edn (Paris, 1928) is still useful. Some interesting articles on casuistry are found in Edmund Leites (ed.), *Conscience and Casuistry in Early Modern Europe* (Cambridge, 1988). A good introduction to the issues of Jansenism is Jean Orcibal, *Jean Duvergier de Hauranne, Abbé de Saint-Cyran, et son temps (1581–1638)* (Paris, 1947). Romano Guardini, *Pascal for Our Time* (New York, 1966) offers a penetrating interpretation of the man, and Richard Golden, 'Jesuit Refutations of Pascal's *Lettres provinciales*', in Richard Golden (ed.), *Church, State, and Society under the Bourbon Kings of France* (Lawrence, KS, 1982), pp. 83–124, sympathetically evaluates his Jesuit adversaries. There is an enormous literature on Galileo and the Galileo Affair. Three books may perhaps serve as the best introduction: Michael Sharratt, *Galileo Decisive Innovator* (Cambridge, 1994), a new biography; Maurice A. Finocchiaro, *The Galileo Affair: A Documentary History* (Berkeley, 1989), a series of pertinent documents with a fine introduction; and Jerome Langford, *Galileo, Science, and the Church*, 3rd edn (Ann Arbor, 1992). William B. Ashworth, 'Catholicism and Early Modern Science', in David C. Lindberg and Ronald L. Numbers (eds), *God and Nature: Historical Essays on the Encounter between Christianity and Science* (Berkeley, 1986), pp. 136–66, deals with the impact of the Galileo Affair on the practice of science among Catholics.

For the theological conference in Vienna in 1635, see Bireley, *Religion and Politics* (see Chapter 5).

INDEX